Apartheid's Rebels

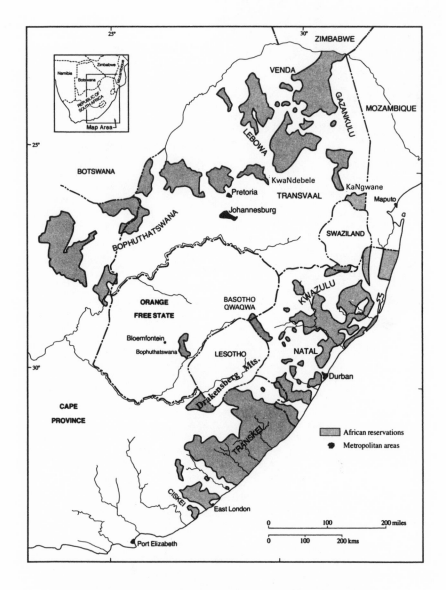

Map 1 The Black Homelands of South Africa

Apartheid's Rebels

Inside South Africa's Hidden War

Stephen M. Davis

Yale University Press
New Haven and London

The epigraph on p. xviii is from Stephen Vincent Benét, *John Brown's Body* (New York: Holt, Rinehart and Winston, 1961), p. 48.

Designed by James J. Johnson and set in Times Roman type by the Composing Room of Michigan, Inc.

Printed in the United States of America by Vail-Ballou Press, Binghamton, N.Y.

Library of Congress Cataloging-in-Publication Data

Davis, Stephen M., 1955–
    Apartheid's rebels.

    Includes index.
    1. African National Congress. 2. Government, Resistance to—South Africa. 3. South Africa—Politics and government—1978–   . I. Title.
    DT779.952.D38   1987   968.06'3   87–10680
    ISBN 0–300–03991–3 (alk. paper)
    ISBN 0–300–03992–1 (pbk. : alk. paper)

The paper in this book meets the guidelines for permanence and durability of the Committee on Production Guidelines for Book Longevity of the Council on Library Resources

10   9   8   7   6   5   4   3   2

To my parents

Contents

Preface   xi

Acknowledgments   xvii

1 Journey to Soweto   1
The ANC: Years of Nonviolence   3
Communists and Africanists   8
Sharpeville   12
Sabotage   14
Regrouping   21
Africanism Redux: The Black Consciousness Movement   24
Soweto and the ANC   26
Soweto and the PAC   31
Conclusion   33

2 Rebellion-in-Exile   36
Return to the Frontline   37
The Capital   47
The Rank and File   56
Waging Education   61
Spears and Shields   66
Paying the Bills   72
Conclusion   74

3   Linking Protest to Revolt   76
The ANC Underground   79
Seeking the United Front   85
Rivals   106
Conclusion   113

4   The "AK–47 Song"   116
Military Objectives   117
Infiltration Tactics   124
Sanctuary   131
Arming the Rebels   135
Espionage   138
War Statistics   145
Targets   147
Conclusion   155

5   The Bunker State   158
Total Strategy   159
The State   160
The Economy   164
Communication   167
Intelligence   173
Military and Police Forces   179
Conclusion   201

6   A Pyrrhic Future   203
Future Scenarios   205

Abbreviations   215

Notes   217

Index   231

Preface

"At least I can count on you to protect me if the violence comes, can't I, Cephas?" The white Johannesburg housewife, unnerved by stories of nearby riots, looked up from the newspaper at her longtime servant.

"Ma'am," he replied slowly, "you're the first one I'm going to shoot."[1]

South Africa's black rebellion lies as close as the houseboy's room off a Johannesburg kitchen and as distant as the African National Congress guerrilla headquarters in Zambia. Its course will determine not only the future of apartheid. The immense stockpiles of power, wealth, even clandestine nuclear capability, held within the country's frontiers ensure that the welfare of the region and the influence of the superpowers in Africa will depend on the outcome of South Africa's civil war.

But who are the rebels? Most press accounts barely mention an underground resistance movement. In many newspaper reports huge anti-apartheid funeral demonstrations simply appear, as if by magic. Policemen are fired upon by people who are assumed not to have guns. Armed government forces lose control over black townships even though officials describe the opposition as weak. Record numbers of bombs erupt in administrative offices, battles occur on the border, arms caches are uncovered in obscure caves. Yet the possibility that an effective insurgency may be behind these events is a notion most frequently read between the lines of news accounts rather than directly in them. The violence seems random and spontaneous rather than managed and purposeful.

Part of the reason for this mystery lies in the labyrinth of censorship laws and regulations Pretoria has constructed to suppress news of political dissent. Another part may be ascribed to the technical complexity of regular communication with guerrilla command centers in Zambia from the media hub in Johannesburg. Finally, the African National Congress's exiled leadership, distrustful of Western media, more comfortable with secrecy than public relations, and sometimes isolated from its own underground inside the country, has earned a reputation as a reluctant and irksome source of information.

The result: the war being waged behind the myriad images of protest has gone unnoticed by vast numbers of South Africans and foreigners alike. Even the most comprehensive reviews of the country's troubles have been distorted by the gap in knowledge about resistance. One respected five-hundred-page study offers just six paragraphs on the ANC guerrilla challenge. Another book contains seven long chapters on Pretoria's preparations for war and only sixteen pages on its enemy. Transfixed by the impressive tally of South African armaments, many authors have tended to pronounce the state impregnable without being able to check what sort of threat it confronts. This inadvertent inattention to the ANC means that readers hoping to assess the balance of forces fighting over apartheid can really evaluate only the government side; it has been like watching a football game with only one team on the field.

" 'Who is the ANC' is a hot question these days," observed one United States Senate staffer in 1986 as Congress prepared to vote for economic sanctions against South Africa. In debate, some senators had depicted the organization as a terrorist instrument of the Soviet Union, others as a liberal coalition comparable to the American civil rights movement. The difference often seemed to depend on which of the wildly divergent estimates of the Communist Party's strength in the ANC's leadership the speaker believed. Yet a tug-of-war over Communist numbers could provide only partial answers to questions about the rebel group's complex character. Apartheid had clearly pushed many blacks to extremes in their search for justice; but it was by no means clear that hard-core Marxists had seized control of such resistance. ANC executives demonstrated a fierce nationalism. Some were the equivalent of Christian democrats, others were socialists. Many had welcomed Soviet aid when no alternatives had appeared. A heterogeneous, often contentious and secretive federation, the African National Congress would yield little to a statistical scanning but much to a search for its soul in the history of resistance and the wrath of the townships.

Congressmen were not just confused over whether to group the ANC with Abu Nidal or Cory Aquino. They were equally baffled about whether the movement had even the slightest chance of winning its war. Those who predicted triumph summoned arguments based mostly on faith. Those certain of failure stressed reports of black disunity appearing in the censored South African press. Information closer to the truth lay out of reach, either underground in the townships or in the classified files of the security forces.

Drawing from a wide range of sources, this book seeks to sketch an investigative portrait of the shadowy ANC, and in so doing to trace a more complete picture of the war over apartheid. The South African conflict is multifaceted, ranging over such critical areas as white politics, the impact on blacks of racial oppression, the muscle of the defense forces, and Western relations with the Republic. This book does not pretend to cover all these related topics in depth, especially as many excellent texts have been written on them. While it does try to break new ground on black rebellion, this study could not have been written without reliance on the works of such distinguished scholars as Thomas Karis, Gail Gerhart, Gwendolen Carter, Tom Lodge, Robert Rotberg, Leonard Thompson, and others.

A perennial challenge in writing on contemporary problems is to keep sight of the overall political landscape rather than the distraction of daily headlines. On the surface, the battle lines over power in South Africa seem to shift rapidly. These reform proposals, those arrests, these heated elections, those cross-border raids—all suggest a wild and unpredictable environment. The impression is largely illusion. Essential characteristics of the chief antagonists have proven remarkably durable, though their relative strengths have changed over time. This book is intended to offer a framework in which to analyze current events and measure the balance of forces as civil war intensifies.

Before examining the rise of the African National Congress in

the 1970s and 1980s, readers can track in chapter 1 the ANC's
genesis in 1912 through its fall into paralysis in the 1960s. "Journey
to Soweto" sets the stage for discussion of the contemporary insurgency by reviewing the ANC's early years, when it developed a
distinctive ideological hue, a political base, and, after being outlawed, the experience of underground resistance.

Focus on the present begins then in chapter 2, "Rebellion-in-
Exile," which explores how the ANC leadership, energized by the
Soweto uprisings, staked out sanctuaries across the independent
black-governed states ringing South Africa to train and arm its new
recruits.

Chapter 3, "Linking Protest to Revolt," spotlights the work of
the Congress's domestic network of cells as it tries to coordinate
above-ground campaigns, ranging from consumer boycotts to workplace strikes, with the guerrilla struggle against apartheid. Chapter 4,
"The 'AK–47 Song,'" covers the organization's secret military
wing in its campaign to boost black morale and challenge white
security through assaults and sabotage. Finally, chapter 5, "The
Bunker State," assesses the measures Pretoria has taken to combat
insurgency.

The book concludes in chapter 6, "A Pyrrhic Future," that the
National Party government is losing the battle over minority rule to
black rebellion, but that its fall will likely be far from total and the
ANC's post-apartheid power far from unchallenged.

When both sides stake so much on secrecy, obtaining hard and
accurate information can resemble nothing so much as detective
work. This book is based largely on original material collected over a
period of six years. During several trips to the region I have con-
ducted over three hundred interviews on both sides of the conflict in
seven countries. Many agreed to discuss their views only if their
identities were concealed. Government documents, partisan publications, court records, scholarly papers, and press accounts are supple-
mented with data gleaned from U.S. State Department records
declassified under my Freedom of Information Act request. After
nearly a year of discussions, my wife and I were granted unprecedented access to ANC personnel, and we became the first American
journalists to visit the organization's refugee complex in Tanzania.

This book attempts to gather evidence scattered through these
and other sources to present a balanced and coherent picture of the

war. Inevitably, some points rest more on informed speculation than hard data. In addition, breaks in the flow of information may skew certain sections despite my best efforts. Trial records, for example, provide detailed illustrations of guerrilla operations—but only for those insurgents who had failed in their missions by being captured. Newspaper evidence, while treated cautiously, could introduce other unintended problems stemming from the variable accuracy of different journals and the omnipresent pressures of press censorship. Wherever possible, I have indicated the limitations of evidence and the basis for educated conjecture.

A note about terms is always in order when investigating South Africa, where vocabulary is charged with political connotation. I avoid phrases implying bias, such as "freedom fighter" or "terrorist," except when they are quoted. The term "black," used by some to denote all citizens not born white, refers here only to blacks. Mixed-race coloreds and Indians are identified as such.

Acknowledgments

For all the township fury that characterizes the civil war over apartheid, a plush, pool-side rendezvous in Lusaka, Zambia, hundreds of miles from the South African frontier, acted as my face-to-face introduction to the passions of rebellion. There in 1978, while serving a three-month stint as assistant political officer at the U.S. embassy, I first met African National Congress secretary-general Alfred Nzo. Although graduate research I was performing at the time focused on frontline state coordination in the Rhodesian war, the conflict to the south began to capture more of my attention. Few locales in the work to come would boast the safety and luxury of that first hotel encounter.

An enormous number of people helped me in the course of this work. Not surprisingly for a guerrilla war, many requested anonymity. Space prohibits me from listing others who gave generously of their time and hospitality. But I am delighted to mention those whose efforts were instrumental in the completion of this book.

I owe thanks to the U.S. State Department and Ambassador Stephen Low, who allowed me, during a hectic summer of peace negotiation diplomacy in Lusaka, to pursue my South African interests on the side. The Fletcher School of Law and Diplomacy at Tufts University, and in particular its security studies program grants, generously funded further work, including an extensive journey through the subcontinent. On that same trip I reported on Zimbabwe's independence for the *Boston Globe,* an arrangement for which I must thank my editor, Steve Erlanger.

The support of editors at *Harpers* magazine, most prominently Helen Rogan and Jefferson Morley, enabled me to return with my wife to the region in 1983 after nearly a year of discussions with the ANC concerning access to its sanctuary state camps. I am grateful to Richard F. Schneller, then majority leader of the Connecticut State Senate, for allowing me the time off from my legislative director's post to coproduce the *Harpers* piece, which later formed the basis for sections of this book.

Georgetown University, through the backing of African studies program director Carol Lancaster and professor Herbert Howe, extended me research scholar status, a valuable aid in completing the manuscript.

Among interviewees who can be named, I owe particular thanks to labor activist Tozamile Botha, who consented to a meeting within days of escaping from South Africa; Audrey and Max Coleman, now leaders of the Detainees' Parents Support Committee; Sheena Duncan, former president of the Black Sash; General Michael Geldenhuys, then commissioner of the South African Police; Thabo Mbeki and Johnny Makatini of the ANC; Nthatho Motlana of the Soweto Committee of Ten; editor Percy Qoboza; veteran opposition member of parliament Helen Suzman; Unity Movement president I. B. Tabata; Desmond Tutu, now Archbishop of Cape Town; Neil van Heerden of the South African foreign ministry; and Eddison Zvobgo, cabinet minister in Zimbabwe's government.

In addition, during my journey I was fortunate to be offered the almost boundless hospitality of families around southern Africa and have the utmost gratitude for their many kindnesses. Journalist Lydia Long provided welcome companionship and valuable interviewing assistance.

For the task of reading and reviewing the manuscript, I offer special thanks to Paul Taskier, Jeffrey Kindler, and Geoffrey Norman. In addition, W. Scott Thompson of the Fletcher School, MIT's Willard Johnson and Robert Rotberg, Tom Lodge of the University of the Witwatersrand, Stanley Greenberg of Yale University, and Jeffrey Goldstein and Tony Coles all gave generously of their time in surveying, advising, and commenting on an earlier draft of this study.

Gail Ross of Goldfarb and Singer extended helpful counsel, and Pauline Baker of the Carnegie Endowment for International Peace, Sanford Unger of American University, and Helen Kitchen of the Center for Strategic and International Studies were kind enough to provide constructive advice. Michael and Susan Zur-Szpiro were sources of constant support.

To Marian Neal Ash, my editor at Yale University Press, I owe many thanks for her extraordinary patience and good cheer, her persistent support and editorial wisdom.

On the home front, I am grateful to my in-laws, Marjorie and Avron Douglis, for having furnished office and living space in Washington for several months. My grandmother, Ida Hyman, was a fount of love, and the memory of my late grandparents and uncles provided silent inspiration. Russell Davis, Kim Gutner, and Jerry Davis also helped push this project to completion.

My parents, Jack and Helen Davis, to whom this book is dedicated, gave their all in love, advice, and encouragement. And finally Carole Douglis, my resident editor, writer, and wife, contributed more than she knows to every page of this work.

Sometimes there comes a crack in Time itself.
Sometimes the earth is torn by something blind.
Sometimes an image that has stood so long
It seems implanted as the polar star
Is moved against an unfathomed force
That suddenly will not have it any more.

—Stephen Vincent Benét

1. Journey to Soweto

Sixty-four years span the political evolution of South Africa's black anti-apartheid leadership from "letter to the editor" protest to guerrilla war. In 1912, a genteel African National Congress convened for the first time to propose peaceful reform. But in 1976 the creed of reformism burned with the townships, as the police acted to crush associations dedicated to peaceful change. By the time the body count registered upwards of one thousand victims of the year-long Soweto rebellion, the bulk of black opposition leadership had joined the banned ANC in turning to armed conflict as a legitimate, and even necessary, means of attaining majority rule.

The journey to civil war in South Africa was one of the longest in a continent that had been pocked by violent struggles between white colonial governments and black majorities. But the whites holding onto power at the tip of Africa in 1976 were not expatriates of some far-flung empire; they themselves had become Africans, setting down roots in the subcontinent's soil more than three hundred and twenty years old.

Jan van Reibeeck is thought to have been the first of their number, landing in what was to become the Cape province with a small party of Dutch tradesmen in 1652.[1] Their religious beliefs, business practices, and political views were entirely alien to the indigenous peoples, blacks whose own clan treks five centuries earlier had

I

brought them to Africa's southern extremities. For a time the cultures coexisted. It was not until the European settlers moved eastward out of the confines of the Cape colony, their ranks swelled by Huguenot refugees and their interests turned from trading posts to farmland, that the first major clashes with blacks were to occur.

For many whites, the fighting with Xhosa warriors along the banks of the Fish River helped spread the doctrine that the early Dutch-speaking settlers constituted a unique but embattled culture, a new white tribe in Africa. These Afrikaners, as they came to be known, felt threatened not just by blacks but by the newest wave of immigrants from Europe—the British.

Only five thousand of these imperial English-speakers had arrived to colonize Cape Town in 1820. But they had followed in the wake of British rule, which had supplanted Dutch governance over the Cape colony. London's power provoked a major split in the young Afrikaner nation between those who wished to live and let live with the British and those who yearned for the freedom to farm their land out of reach of "foreign" interference. The dissidents began to strike out in wagon trains from the relative security of the Cape in 1836, pushing the white frontier northward into the heart of black South Africa.

It was a time of turmoil and violence. As the Boers ("farmers" in Afrikaans) fought to establish land claims in the future provinces of Orange Free State, Natal, and Transvaal, the Zulu monarch Shaka was staking out a powerful empire in the east, driving across southern Africa any black communities resisting his rule. But by the time he and his successors had crushed black opposition and consolidated the kingdom, well-armed Europeans had spread throughout the country. The founding of Boer republics in both the Transvaal and Orange Free State, together with the expansion of British sovereignty over Natal as well as the Cape, cast a net of white power that trapped and eventually subdued black armies capable of resistance. A bloody battle at Ulundi in 1879 marked the final capitulation of the Zulus and of black independence in South Africa.

The conflict between white and black did not end at Ulundi, but it did enter a more complex phase. The late 1800s saw massive economic growth in South Africa, fueled by the discovery of diamonds in Kimberley and gold on the Witwatersrand. The sudden conscription of many blacks into industrial labor coincided with the recruitment of many more into Western churches by a gathering vanguard of missionaries. Traditional communal bonds were loosened and often broken entirely by the mounting demands of the booming white economy. Pressed into factories, labor camps, urban hostels, and mine shafts, many blacks found their tribal leaderships incapable of addressing their new circumstances.

Against this background of social upheaval within the black community, the British and Afrikaners spent thirty years following the Zulu defeat at Ulundi alternately fighting and negotiating with each other over the form of white governance in the region. Finally, on the heels of British victory in the Boer War, London called the Union of South Africa into existence on May 31, 1910. Incorporating the self-governing provinces of the Cape, Transvaal, Orange Free State, and Natal into one of Britain's richest dominions, the union was formed without the participation of the majority of its inhabitants, who were black.

The new country could boast only two years of history to its name when two of its chief future antagonists were born within months of each other. One was the South African Natives National Congress (SANNC), later renamed the African National Congress. The other was the South African Defense Force, destined over sixty years later to play the key role in combating ANC guerrillas.

THE ANC: YEARS OF NONVIOLENCE

The SANNC in 1912 betrayed few signs of becoming a formidable opposition to British and Afrikaner power.[2] Its chief distinction was the claim to being the first modern, nontribal organization of blacks formed to discuss black interests under white rule, a testament to the rapid erosion of tribal loyalties in the Union. It was founded by and peopled with Western-educated professionals, many of whom had been schooled abroad.

In an attempt to maintain links with more traditional black communities, founders at first outfitted the SANNC with an "Upper House" of chiefs. But the party was fundamentally an elitist, Western-oriented response to the policies of a European government. Its platform reflected resignation to the reality of white rule, though not to all of its consequences, and the need for blacks to benefit from and work within European frameworks of government, medicine, law, economy, theology, and education.

The administrative seeds of apartheid were sown in the century's first decades by the new Union government, which denied political power to blacks. It was to these laws, which included color bars and racial segregation of land, that the early ANC addressed itself. Under the leadership of Dr. Pixley Seme, the organization first proclaimed its commitment to nonracialism: the peoples of South Africa were to be viewed as one, regardless of skin color.

Conservative in tactics, the ANC nevertheless played a critical role in initiating modern black protest in South Africa. Women sympathizers of the ANC in 1913 organized a modest passive resistance campaign against the new requirement that all blacks in the Orange Free State carry with them domestic identity books. Five years later the ANC's Johannesburg branch, mobilizing against passes required for men, directly organized a Transvaal campaign involving some three thousand blacks and leading to the arrest of seven hundred. Despite these and other demonstrations, however, none of the hated "influx control" laws, designed to monitor and restrict black mobility, were repealed by the provincial administrations.

The 1920s ushered in an era of economic recession brought on by falling gold prices and increased taxes. Black employment fell by nearly 20 percent, a development that choked off postwar optimism concerning improving social conditions. This bitter pill was made all the more difficult to swallow by successful demands on the part of white labor in 1922 for the consolidation and protection of white privilege, particularly in a period of recession. Blacks were made to bear the brunt of economic hardship.

While dissension among black workers led to mass demonstrations, strikes, violence directed against symbols of white power, and hundreds of deaths, the ANC maintained its aloof, constitutionalist approach, and so largely excluded itself from the fray. Until as late as the Second World War, in fact, the middle-class party remained largely apart from the mainstream of high-profile black protest, preferring instead to navigate channels of negotiation marked out by the government. Years of such efforts yielded the ANC few results, but trust in the possibility of compromise persisted.

Such faith reached new heights as South Africa entered World

War II. The government, led by General Jan Smuts, was drifting leftward, and ANC leaders were convinced that the prime minister would move to abolish pass laws as a first step toward equal rights. To provide Smuts with political capital, ANC president Dr. Alfred Bitini Xuma persuaded a reluctant executive board to endorse the alliance against Nazi Germany. It was to be the ANC's last act of faith in white governmental goodwill.

General Smuts, under political fire from the growing pro-Nazi National Party, soon chose to abandon the option of lowering racial barriers. In a bid to retain power in the 1943 general election, Smuts spurned black aspirations, reassuring the whites-only electorate of his government's commitment to white supremacy.

The shock of Smuts's perceived betrayal forced the ANC leadership to recognize the apparent futility of passive negotiation. Peaceful but forceful confrontation seemed the only path available. But with a total national membership of a paltry one thousand, Xuma could not recast the party's strategy without remaking the party itself. Therefore, he had the ANC fitted with a new activist platform, entitled "African Claims," which set out for the first time a comprehensive agenda of demands for political rights such as universal suffrage and equal pay for equal work. Xuma stripped the party of all remnants of official participation by traditional chiefs and reorganized it to encourage democratic selection of leaders and policy. Over thirty years after its founding as an organ of black opinion, the ANC was beginning the work of building a popular national membership amongst South Africa's diverse black population.

Methodically, Xuma sought to position his party as the chief voice of opposition to minority rule, quintupling the number of ANC cardholders to over fifty-five hundred by 1947. Fending off pressure to call mass demonstrations before the party was ready, he worked on building up the organizational skills to overcome communication problems, financial distress, and mounting governmental hostility.

The 1948 general election, however, confronted blacks, coloreds, and Indians with an even higher wall of white power. The Afrikaner-dominated National Party, swept into power by the white electorate for the first time, moved quickly to solidify and formalize the segregationist system it began to label "apartheid." By the time the new mass of legislation passed out of parliament in Cape Town, non-white South Africans faced tight government control over their schools, a ban on unionization, racial segregation by residential and commercial zones under the draconian Group Areas Act, further restrictions on opposition politics under the broadly worded Suppression of Communism Act, prohibitions on all interracial, sexual, and marital relations, and threats by authorities newly empowered summarily to banish urban-dwellers to the rural reserves.

Reverberations from the National Party's apartheid earthquake reached the inner councils of the ANC late in the year in the form of bitter political infighting. A new generation of impatient activists, gathered under the banner of the Congress Youth League, eventually wrested power from the old guard and launched the ANC's first mass protests. The 1952 Defiance Campaign, though marred by violence and near organizational anarchy, proved wildly popular, rocketing party membership past a hundred thousand.

With the new leadership's success came two problems that were to plague the ANC until the 1970s. One was the inflow of police informants among the flood of new members. Because the Congress could carry out few meaningful background checks on its tens of thousands of new constituents, police had no trouble planting agents throughout the ANC's political dominions. Having entered the Congress in the 1952 rush, many subsequently rose in its ranks while in the pay of the security authorities and helped to implicate party executives in the "treason trials" of the late 1950s and early 1960s.

The second problem was a mark of how structurally unprepared the ANC was for the challenge of operating as a mass movement in a hostile environment. Under the weight of its huge new membership, the party proved incapable of maintaining an efficient nationwide network. By 1953, arrests and bannings of the uppermost stratum of ANC leadership threatened the Congress's potential to mobilize its newfound followers to carry out any of its plans.

The near paralysis persuaded Nelson Mandela, a Congress Youth League founding member and a coordinator of the Defiance Campaign's trained volunteers, to launch a foresighted attempt to protect the ANC from repression. His "M-Plan" represented the first practical effort from within the Congress to prepare for the days of underground activity ahead.

The M-Plan's intention was to wean the ANC away from dependence on characteristics of organization most vulnerable to governmental pressure. Mandela envisioned the construction of a discreet but firm cellular network at the grassroots level in constant communication through a hierarchy of middle-level leaders with the national executive. But as it achieved only sporadic success in implementing the M-Plan, the ANC remained largely an undisciplined movement.

Rather than pausing to consolidate its Defiance Campaign gains, the bulk of ANC leadership quickly pressed on with nonviolent mass action in the conviction that the government could be persuaded to change its course away from apartheid. Born of this new activism was the Congress Alliance. Until the early 1950s, chief Youth League executives had so firmly rejected collaboration with communists that some, including Mandela and attorney Oliver Tambo, had proposed expelling the few who belonged to the ANC. However, the gathering momentum of governmental efforts to entrench apartheid spurred the two to seek allies in whatever guise they could be found. The ANC for the first time formed working relationships with communists and nonblacks in the South African Indian Congress, the white radical Congress of Democrats, the small South African Colored People's Organization, and the South African Congress of Trade Unions. In this constellation of congresses, an unprecedented multiracial political coalition, the ANC was the leading light.

In June of 1955 the group organized the Congress of the People in Johannesburg's Kliptown township, in which some three thousand delegates from the alliance's constituent parties adopted the Freedom Charter, later endorsed by the national executive as the ANC's principal political platform.

"We, the people of South Africa," the charter began, "declare for all our country and the world to know . . . that South Africa belongs to all who live in it, black and white, and that no government can justly claim authority unless it is based on the will of the people. . . . " Just as the preamble firmly placed the Congress on the side of multiracialism as opposed to black nationalism, so the remainder of the charter committed the ANC to principles of liberal democracy. It also gave the ANC a tinge of socialism with a nationalization plank which declared that "the mineral wealth beneath the soil, the banks, and monopoly industry shall be transferred to the ownership of the people as a whole. . . . " Yet the charter's provisions did not promise radically to alter South Africa's economic structure.

The work of painting the Congress in ideological colors appealing to the black public was brought to an abrupt end as a result of massive special branch security operations that culminated in the Treason Trial, for which arrests began in December of 1956. Accused initially were some 156 blacks and whites. For over four years, until all were judged innocent of high treason on March 29, 1961, the government was able successfully to withdraw many of the Congress's most important leaders from the political arena.

By 1960, with the Treason Trial grinding toward conclusion, the National Party took further steps to deflect the "winds of change" that were beginning to sweep white colonial governments from the continent. Pretoria abolished indirect black representation in parliament, confining African political participation to the new bantustans, or tribal homelands. These reservations, Prime Minister Hendrik Verwoerd explained, would place "the Natives on the road to self-government in their own areas." The broadened Bantu Education Act ended the academic autonomy of such respected black institutions as Fort Hare University, and the Native Laws Amendment Act equipped the government with new authority to restrict interracial contact. It was not to be long before the Congress itself would be banned in Pretoria's most forceful effort yet to contain black unrest.

COMMUNISTS AND AFRICANISTS

During the nonviolent years of anti-apartheid protest, the ANC was by no means alone in aspiring to leadership of the movement. Among its most important competitors were the South African Communist Party and the Pan Africanist Congress.

The South African Communist Party

Founded by and on behalf of white laborers in 1921 (one of its slogans was "Workers Unite for a White South Africa"), the Communist Party shifted within a few years to the problems and interests of the black proletariat. Yet during its first decades the SACP's leadership was controlled almost exclusively by whites. As a result, the SACP had relatively little impact on opposition black politics until the early 1950s, by which time it was operating underground.

A strictly Soviet-modeled party, the SACP in the 1920s and 1930s closely followed Stalinist doctrines issued in Moscow. Trapped

between the compulsion to win black support by appealing to nationalist sentiments and the need to conform to Soviet class-revolu-
tion tactics, the SACP squirmed from position to position in efforts
to reconcile the two, alienating in the process many anti-apartheid
South African whites and blacks, in addition to the Soviets.

Nevertheless, the SACP drew some two thousand, including 150
whites and 250 Indians, into its ranks to become a disciplined, ideologically driven party armed with some valuable advantages—such
as funds and expertise—derived from its links to Moscow. In time,
the new Youth League powerholders in the ANC began to appreciate
the benefits of an alliance with South Africa's communists. By 1946,
in fact, three black SACP members were members of the Congress's
National Executive Committee. But before any lengthy experience in
cooperation could be accumulated, the Suppression of Communism
Act of June 1950 banished the SACP from legality in South Africa.
Some anticipated the move and planned the party's formal underground reconstruction in 1952. Members began to filter into still law-
ful organizations such as the ANC, the newborn Congress of Democrats, and the South African Congress of Trade Unions (SACTU).

While the Congress of Democrats ran out of political steam by
the early 1960s, SACTU evolved from modest beginnings in 1954
into a tenacious and influential refuge for former communists as well
as a beachhead in the labor movement for the reconstituted Communist Party itself. A new member of the Congress Alliance, SACTU
could boast at its inaugural conference in March 1955 a constituency
of nineteen unions and up to twenty thousand cardholders, a small
but vocal element of South Africa's over two million black workers.
At the height of its above-ground power in 1961, some forty-six
trade unions had voted themselves into the SACTU federation. Although all but a handful of the 53,323 workers they represented were
black, SACTU's leadership remained dominated by whites, many of
them communists.

In fact, through its strong influence in legally sanctioned bodies,
the Communist Party remained a key participant in the protests and
campaigns of the 1950s despite Pretoria's banning orders. Yet the
still-small SACP could claim no popular appeal among the country's
black populace. In order to survive, the leadership officially decided
to hitch the party's future to the ANC and began a process of sharing
people, expertise, and resources. With Moscow's approval, commu-

nists finally adopted in 1962 an overall framework, which remains in effect today, for collaborating with the Congress. The SACP would recognize and assist the ANC as the leading force in a first stage of revolution aimed at destroying white supremacy. Ultimately, the Communist Party would help ignite a second stage that would in turn establish "a socialist South Africa, laying the foundations of a classless, communist society."

The Pan Africanist Congress

If communists considered alliance with the Congress a route to future influence, black nationalists viewed rupture with the ANC as a prerequisite for domination of the liberation movement.

The Pan Africanist Congress (PAC), officially launched at a convention in Soweto's Orlando Community Hall on April 6, 1959, became the institutional heir to a bitter long-standing ideological feud within the African National Congress. To a large extent, of course, the PAC's pre-1959 history is also that of the ANC. But Africanists traced their roots to the writings in the 1940s of the late Anton Lembede, whose black nationalist views and anticommunist positions heavily influenced his contemporaries in the Congress Youth League, later the PAC, and still later the black consciousness movement of the 1970s.

Radically different perceptions of the white race characterized the debate within the postwar ANC between Africanists, who considered anti-apartheid protest a blacks-only affair, and multiracialists, who had faith in achieving change in alliance with philosophically compatible whites. When the ANC joined with the South African Indian Congress in the Defiance Campaign and later linked up with whites, coloreds, and Indians in the Congress Alliance, Africanists feared that the canons of Lembedism were being violated.

Toward the end of 1954, a Congress activist by the name of Potlako Leballo had become disillusioned enough to establish a secret Africanist central committee to act as a watchdog on ANC policy. The political infighting generated by his insubordination weakened provincial and national ANC resources at a time when they were needed to lead the Western Areas protest campaign.

The incipient Africanist rebellion also undermined the 1955 Congress of the People, upon which so many ANC hopes rested. The multiracial nature of the meeting, as well as the openly nonracial tone of the resulting Freedom Charter ("South Africa belongs to all who live in it, black and white"), conflicted with the Africanist aim of psychologically rejuvenating the nation's blacks by having them act alone in reclaiming South Africa from white dominion. In addition, the involvement of communists and former communists in the convention provoked suspicions among Africanists that the national liberation movement would be hijacked by leftists with Soviet objectives in mind.

An opportunity for Africanists to seize power arose when Pretoria ordered widespread detentions and bannings of ANC leaders in advance of the Treason Trial. Within a year the Congress's Africanists were moving to take command of the organizationally disabled party. Throughout 1957 and 1958 the ANC was more preoccupied with a civil war over its own ideological future than any mass anti-apartheid campaigns. Finally, after being shut out of a 1958 ANC conference, the Africanists declared their secession.

The new PAC, led by Robert Sobukwe, did not have the benefit of the ANC's venerable name and tradition, but its impatient activism appealed to younger volunteers. It did not enjoy the Congress's relatively well-developed links with labor, but it had by October of 1959 helped to form the Africanist-oriented Federation of Free African Trade Unions. Within a short time FOFATUSA had drawn to its banner over 18,000 black workers.

The PAC's chief advantage, however, was its ideology. The party's new flag underlined its association with the popular pan-Africanism of Kwame Nkrumah: a green field with a black map of Africa marked by a gold star in the northwest, beaming light from then-revolutionary Ghana. Concluding that attracting mass support quickly was the only way to compete with the ANC for chieftaincy of the liberation struggle, the PAC offered to give vent to pent-up emotions. Whites would be denied a part in the battle against apartheid. Dramatic, nationwide mass protests would be launched. And Sobukwe issued a solemn commitment sure to ignite black excitement: liberation by 1963.

The promise, less conviction than public-relations ploy, was made at the start of the PAC's 1960 anti-pass protests. It helped bring up to 25,000 new members into the party but also encouraged rash action. With virtually no effective advance preparations, the

PAC executive called on all black men to invite arrest by refusing to carry the required passes, and all black women to stay at home rather than go to work or shopping. The ideal outcome would be total paralysis of the South African economy resulting in Pretoria's capitulation to the PAC's demand that passes be abolished. Inheriting the ANC Youth League's passion for mass action over organization, as well as its faith in the power of nonviolent protest, Robert Sobukwe asked his colleagues to kill him if he should attempt to terminate the campaign without having gained concessions.

SHARPEVILLE

Had the police not turned violent in Sharpeville on March 21, 1960, the PAC's effort might never have gained a prominent position in the annals of black protest. In Durban, Port Elizabeth, and East London, there was not a hint of response to Sobukwe's call. In Johannesburg, the PAC leadership courted arrest with a lonely 150 others. In Cape Town and the southern Transvaal, however, crowds of up to 20,000 passless supporters offered themselves to the police. They were enough to detonate a political explosion with reverberations that have lasted for decades.

Squads of troops fired on the demonstrators at Sharpeville, Vanderbijlpark, and Langa, killing seventy-one blacks and wounding another two hundred. Sixty-seven of the dead had been shot at Sharpeville alone. The combination of a poorly disciplined police force, frightened crowds, crude governmental policy, and quick-witted reporters and photographers transformed the PAC's otherwise embarrassing anti-pass protest into a means of focusing worldwide attention on apartheid.

Panic swept South Africa's white community as riots spread rapidly through the nation's black townships. Foreign companies rushed to sell their assets as rumors of revolution jumped from the streets into the boardrooms. Thirty thousand blacks marched on Cape Town, prompting a tottering government to declare a state of emergency and attempt to restore order by detaining thousands of activists.

After parliament hurriedly passed the Unlawful Organizations Act, police began a campaign of violence and intimidation of protesters. Finally, on April 8, Verwoerd issued edicts outlawing both the upstart PAC and the ANC, which had launched its own set of demonstrations in the wake of Sharpeville.

The orders stunned Congress but all but crushed the PAC, whose leaders were already incarcerated as a result of the voluntary arrests of March 21. In fact, South African political history was cruel to the PAC. With just one year of independent existence, the party had not had sufficient time to plant roots of survival deep enough to withstand the winter of Pretoria's 1960 banning decision. It boasted no Africanist M-Plan, no alliance with a ready-made underground organization such as the Communist Party. The PAC had barely made its mark before being banned. Nor did it ever fully recover from the blow. As opposition politics evolved, the ANC found it possible to reconstitute, build upon, and make secure its scattered cells founded in the 1950s. Having been short-changed in time, the PAC possessed no such substantial preexisting network. Its collection of committed supporters was small, relatively unorganized, and rife with police agents.

Africanism as an ideology, however, would not wither with the PAC. Its popularity as an alternative to multiracialism was undiminished and was to manifest itself in later years through intermittent revivals of the PAC and through the rise of black consciousness. But the damage wrought by the 1960 banning order proved that in an environment of unwavering governmental hostility, ideology—no matter how inflammatory—could not by itself sustain a budding resistance movement. In fact, an ideology too racially exclusive could deny a group the considerable benefits of multiethnic alliances.

By contrast, the ANC had developed some important tools that would help it survive the 1960 crackdown. Mandela's M-Plan, even if implemented only on a patchwork scale in the 1950s, represented the blueprint for transition to underground operations. The early Youth League tactic of mass protest would be jettisoned in favor of even earlier Xuma-style discipline. At the same time, cooperation with the Communist Party, whose members had accumulated eight years of experience in the political catacombs, opened up a valuable resource for the time-consuming task of building a network of illegal ANC cells.

Ideologically, the Congress was also better equipped than rival groups to survive in the shadows. The Freedom Charter, with its broad endorsement of democracy, could appeal not just to blacks, but to many coloreds, Indians, and even fringe elements of the white community. As a result, the ANC earned the considerable benefits of cooperation with a variety of constituencies.

By the time it was banned in 1960, in fact, the ANC had taken on a look that would remain largely constant for the coming decades. In addition, it could claim to have tried a multitude of peaceful and legal means to overturn the expanding machinery of apartheid and failed in each effort. It had built a record of justification for the tactic of resistance it was next to adopt: sabotage.

SABOTAGE

Decisiveness, discipline, weaponry, secure underground networks, military competence: none of these was a trademark of the sabotage phase in black opposition politics. Nor were frontline bases or infiltration routes, since every state in the subcontinent was governed by European colonial powers or entrenched white minorities. Conditions were extremely disadvantageous for campaigns of armed resistance in 1961—yet both the ANC and remnants of the PAC launched them.

The period between the emergency bannings of South Africa's two major liberation parties and the first ANC-associated military operation was twenty-one months. In the interim, Congress underwent a supremely reluctant tactical metamorphosis from adamant nonviolence to selective use of force. The switch did not come easily to an organization saddled with a half-century tradition of passive resistance based on faith in the regime's vulnerability to protest. But by mid-1961 the party's rank and file were overwhelmingly in favor of a decision to counter the regime's strong-arm tactics with force.

Still, when ANC and Congress Alliance executives finally agreed to establish a military organization, it was not so much a positive action designed to energize the nonwhite population as a move born of sheer policy desperation. Caught between police repression aimed at destroying the Congress from without and grass roots pressure in favor of violence that threatened to wrack the Congress from within, most leaders perceived no other route that would preserve the anti-apartheid alliance intact. But a vocal faction argued against so abruptly casting off the ANC's nonviolent image, a feature considered to have enhanced the organization's prestige in South Africa and the international community. Moderates had their hand strengthened when Chief Albert Luthuli, president of the ANC, was awarded the Nobel Peace Prize in Oslo in December 1961. His journey to Europe caught the imagination of black South Africans and attracted worldwide publicity to the ANC.

Faced with this high-level internal dissent, the national executive in June of 1961 voted to establish Umkhonto we Sizwe ("Spear of the Nation" in Zulu), or MK for short, as a semi-independent body with a military mission. But the ANC itself would remain a nonviolent political party which, though officially banned, would be available to the regime in the event that it wished to negotiate a rearrangement of power in South Africa.

In practice, maintaining the nominal distinction between the Congress and Umkhonto was confusing and counterproductive, as was the ANC's obvious ambivalence with respect to the use of force. Lack of sophistication in organization and communication proved a barrier to operations between and within both groups. Trial evidence later revealed that ANC cells often received contradictory signals regarding the extent to which Umkhonto operations were to be rendered assistance. Many cells appear not even to have been aware of the ANC's kinship with Umkhonto.

Umkhonto's parental troubles extended also to the Communist Party, which might have been expected to lend the whole of its expertise in underground operations to the mission of planning and launching MK's sabotage campaign. But the sudden split between Soviet and Chinese wings of the worldwide party had profoundly unsettled communist leadership in South Africa, just as it was doing in other parts of the globe, calling into question such issues as the role of force in liberation struggles.

Umkhonto turned to the still legal Congress of Trade Unions to recruit volunteers eager to initiate armed attacks on apartheid. The amorphous General Workers Unions, established under SACTU in 1955 to absorb an overflow of black applicants, served as Umkhonto fronts, channeling volunteers to covert political education classes, local sabotage training, or overseas guerrilla camps. Although the labor federation was still plagued by police surveillance, internal informers, financial problems, and a shortage of experienced personnel, many in SACTU's network were Umkhonto commanders using the union secretariat as cover.

Umkhonto's National High Command viewed sabotage as an introductory tactic in what would have to become a full-scale guerrilla war if its objective of toppling apartheid was not achieved in the first wave of attacks. The new military leadership hoped that bombings of transport and communications networks would throw the economy into disarray and put foreign capital to flight, and that, reeling from such blows, Pretoria would come to its senses and join the ANC at the bargaining table.

To help ready its infant army, the Congress began scouring Europe and Africa for arms, financial support, and training facilities. The ANC established a permanent office in London, while Nelson Mandela and Oliver Tambo collected pledges of assistance at a 1962 Pan-African Freedom Movement conference. At the same time, the SACP's Arthur Goldreich successfully lobbied the Soviet Union and its allies for an estimated $2.8 million in aid. The ANC had to rely heavily on communist channels to ship clandestine foreign funds into South Africa, and on SACP members with war experience to instruct Umkhonto recruits on the manufacture and use of bombs, grenades, and mines.

June 1962 saw Umkhonto's first batch of volunteers escape South Africa for military training in Dar es Salaam. More than a dozen groups made it out over the next twelve months, at first by overland routes through the then colonies of Bechuanaland (Botswana), Rhodesia (Zimbabwe), and Northern Rhodesia (Zambia), and later, as danger grew, by charter aircraft from Francistown, Bechuanaland, to Dar es Salaam. Only a total of some 360 succeeded in reaching ANC camps abroad. Almost as many appear to have been caught by the security forces of South Africa, Bechuanaland, Rhodesia, or Northern Rhodesia. News of the frequent capture of escaping Umkhonto recruits appeared to deter others from joining up.

On December 16, celebrated by Afrikaners as the day a Zulu army was defeated at Blood River in 1838, Umkhonto formally launched its sabotage campaign with bomb attacks on electric power stations and government offices in Port Elizabeth and Johannesburg. Leaflets accompanying the blasts announced Umkhonto's birth, though none made specific reference to the ANC. "The time comes in the life of any nation when there remain two choices: submit or fight . . . we shall not submit and we have no choice but to hit back by all means within our power."

Between June 1961 and July 1963 some 194 scattershot sabotage operations hit such targets as communications and transport facilities, fuel dumps, utilities, and government buildings. Each—according to Pretoria—caused an average of only $125 damage, with the highest reaching $10,000. Insurgents also mounted attacks against suspected police informants, state witnesses in "terrorism" trials, and nonwhites perceived to be collaborators. Many other strikes were acts of random violence. Since neither Umkhonto nor Congress ever initiated any large-scale drive to politicize the black public concerning MK's aims or methods, most of these operations took place unaccompanied by grass-roots support.

Umkhonto was on the whole a low-cost, appropriate technology sabotage campaign that required of its field sections little more than small arsenals of dynamite and gasoline for bomb-making, wire-cutters to slice telephone cables, and other easily obtainable tools. With the assistance of foreign funds and white SACP contacts, however, the high command for obscure reasons purchased a twenty-eight-acre farm by the name of Lilliesleaf in the white Johannesburg suburb of Rivonia as its national headquarters. On the estate, a secret road led to the farmhouse, which was equipped with a radio transmitter, receiving apparatus, and typing and duplicating equipment.

Careful detective work led the security police to the same spot on the eleventh of July 1963. Despite the marginal impact Umkhonto's operations were having on the white community, the government was concentrating much of its power on smashing MK's challenge to its authority.

In June 1962 the National Party herded through parliament the Sabotage Act, which empowered the justice minister to ban individuals he considered to be potential or suspected "terrorists." By such action, the government could restrict a person's political activities and prohibit reproduction of any statements made by someone on the banned list. One year later parliament approved the General Law Amendment Act (1963), which authorized the police to detain individuals for up to ninety days without having to give a reason.

But Pretoria's greatest weapon was its intelligence resources. Taking advantage of the loose membership controls that had characterized the ANC ever since the Defiance Campaign, agents for the security police were able to infiltrate cells or recruit informants throughout lower levels of the organization. "The Congress Alliance was so infiltrated by police spies that the man who kept the post office box key and collected the post every day was a white policeman seconded from the police force," observed I. B. Tabata, head of the rival Unity Movement, after the Rivonia trial.[3] The fact that it took the authorities nineteen months completely to crack the Umkhonto organization suggests, however, that internal M-Plan procedures designed to limit a member's overall knowledge of MK operations had protected the high command for an extended period despite hasty preparations and inadequate implementation of the system.

On the eve of the Rivonia raid, the government could count some 126 convictions under the Sabotage Act, and another 511 cases were sitting on court dockets. The lightning police attack on the too conspicuous Lilliesleaf farm headquarters netted nearly all the Umkhonto high command as well as valuable intelligence information. In the subsequent trial, life sentences were meted out to Nelson Mandela, Walter Sisulu, and Govan Mbeki, the ANC's most prominent leaders still inside the Republic. Even Umkhonto's chief saboteur in Natal turned state's witness and offered detailed testimony against members of the high command.

If the government's banning of the Congress marked the end of nonviolent protest as an accepted ANC strategy, then the smashing of Umkhonto's sabotage campaign signaled what one optimistically called "the death knell of amateurism" in the party's tactic of armed resistance. Postmortems were not hard to find. Joe Matthews, one of the ANC's prominent thinkers and leaders in the 1950s and 1960s, argued that there had been

> no real discussion as to whether timing or conditions were right. There was no discussion of bases and, after all, no nearby states were independent. All of this led to the disruption of the movement and enabled the regime to destroy the ANC's leadership. Meanwhile the masses had no inkling of these events. Here we were embarking on the most important of decisions, and the people knew nothing. We were going to war

without the people with us. The vanguard was isolated, and this allowed the police to easily infiltrate.[4]

The flaws were evident: lack of bases, inadequate organization and discipline, logistical deficiencies, insufficient international support, poor political mobilization, shortages of funds, vulnerability to the regime's counterespionage and counterinsurgency tactics, and an unstable alliance of parent parties. In addition, the apparently minor damage caused by Umkhonto's volunteers was nowhere near effective in bringing South Africa's complex economy to a halt. Nor had the organization demonstrated a talent for attracting national and international media attention sufficient to magnify these incidents into specters of gathering revolution.

The ANC's difficulties in converting to guerrilla warfare were echoed by those of the PAC, which was having an even harder time turning to arms to achieve black revolution. Meeting in Maseru, Basotholand (later Lesotho) in 1961, unjailed members of the PAC's consultative conference elected to move toward armed struggle despite the continued imprisonment of Robert Sobukwe and Potlako Leballo, the group's two top leaders. But it was not until the August 1962 release of Leballo from jail, when he formally reestablished the PAC in Maseru, that the Africanists really began to plan for guerrilla war.

Declaring at a press conference that 1963 would see a PAC-led revolution throughout South Africa in contrast to the "useless . . . isolated explosions" organized by Umkhonto, Leballo estimated the PAC's strength at 150,000 divided into a thousand cells. His statements alerted the security branch, who arrested two PAC couriers heading from Maseru to PAC contact points inside the Republic. Within a week the British colonial police raided Leballo's offices and seized the party's membership lists, which were then handed over at London's order to South African authorities. On June 12, 1963, the minister of justice could announce in parliament the arrest of some 3,246 members of the PAC underground, leaving only "scattered remnants" of the party's organization free. While perhaps exaggerating the extent of the government's triumph, the minister was right in claiming, for at least the time being, the crushing of the PAC's preparations for armed resistance.

Meanwhile, however, renegade PAC elements in the western Cape and Transkei had preempted the party by forming Poqo, a crude sabotage-cum-terrorist group named for the Xhosa word meaning "pure" or "standing alone," a reference to the black exclusivism of Africanist thought. Poqo was a poorly organized, spontaneous grass-roots response to the extreme frustration felt by black backers of the moribund PAC. It had little or no contact with the PAC in Maseru, no clear leadership, no overall strategy, and no foreign support. Incidents perpetrated by Poqo tended to be ad hoc, intermittent, and isolated. It was charged by the authorities with the murder of blacks and coloreds in the western Cape, pro-government chiefs in the Transkei, and seven whites in both Paarl and Transkei. Some of Poqo's attacks seemed premeditated and politically motivated, while others, such as those against the seven whites, appeared contrived to promote terror in the white community. Crushing the group proved to be a relatively simple police task.

The passing of 1963, then, marked the end of the brief sabotage phase of the resistance movement. The year's police victory over Umkhonto, the PAC, and Poqo drove the embattled moderate elements of both the Congress and the PAC to the sidelines. It strengthened the positions of those who advocated full-scale guerrilla war over occasional sabotage as an instrument in countering apartheid. It convinced the leadership of the liberation movements that an unequivocal commitment to armed guerrilla struggle was the only step available to them.

The three sabotage years had wrought vast changes in each of the parties. The PAC was again devastated, with thousands of its internal members now known to and being watched by the police. Its external leadership, though relocated in Dar es Salaam, was in disarray. Sobukwe remained in detention under a special order passed by parliament two days prior to completion of his 1960 sentence. The PAC as the organizational expression of Africanist populism had declined into paralysis.

The security police had virtually beheaded the ANC when it arrested, convicted, and incarcerated such key executives as Nelson Mandela, Walter Sisulu, and Govan Mbeki. With chief Albert Luthuli still under a banning order, the only top Congress leader free to work for the party's survival was Oliver Tambo, who had departed South Africa in 1960 on ANC orders to serve as foreign spokesman.

The Rivonia trial transformed Tambo into the effective head of the ANC, and he soon set up its first command-in-exile. What he inherited was a demoralized domestic network shorn by arrests and tattered by police infiltrators. Its strategy discredited, its leadership captured, its goals unmet, the Congress seemed on the brink of collapse in 1963.

Yet Umkhonto's failure had convinced the ANC leadership of the necessity of regroupment to devise new tactics for the next round. The underground would have to be purged of counterespionage agents and made secure. An external command would have to be formed to conduct operations without fear of capture. Field operatives required more sophisticated training, with better communications between them and superiors. Bases in and infiltration routes through friendly countries would have to be arranged. Leadership would have to be clear and coherent. Political mobilization needed to be coordinated with Umkhonto operations. Politico-military strategy would have to be revised. An extraregional patron was required for greater funding and better supplies.

For much of this to occur, the Congress needed monumental geopolitical changes in the region and; indeed, by the end of the sabotage years they were beginning to surface. Though 1963 had proved disastrous for the South African liberation movements, it had behaved with singular beneficence toward many of Africa's other majority-rule parties. The continent's face was changing dramatically, with more and more states achieving independence from colonial control. These events north of the Limpopo would inevitably alter the tactics and the odds of armed insurgency in South Africa itself.

REGROUPING

The third stage of opposition in South Africa commenced with the aftermath of Rivonia and ended with the violence of Soweto. These events bracketed a twelve-year period characterized by slow-paced reconstruction efforts within the ANC, a building momentum of rage among South African blacks, and increasing governmental repression. Days of peaceful protest had passed with the 1960 bannings, and tactics of politically isolated sabotage had disappeared with the police invasion of Lilliesleaf Farm. The regrouping years, while until 1976 a relatively peaceful period, proved to be only the calm

before the storm rather than the cessation of resistance. At that time
the ANC moved both to create and await the conditions for insurgency which had been absent in 1961–63. By the end of the regrouping
phase, the Congress found itself prepared for the first time to launch
a guerrilla war. At the same time, the PAC and other Africanist rival
groups that emerged during the period continued to demonstrate an
inability to muster the resources to compete.

A titanic leap of faith would have been required in 1963 to
believe in the ultimate resurrection of the ANC. The Congress's own
assessment of its predicament even as late as six years after the
collapse of Umkhonto's sabotage campaign was that the "internal
organization was shattered, grass roots activity [was] limited, communication links were broken, and a gap was evident between the
leadership and the rank and file."[5] Complicating matters was the
length of time it took Tambo to reassemble and take stock of the
various ANC resources and personnel that had made it into exile
during the tumult of the police crackdown. Despite the constant risk
of capture, MK's high command during the sabotage years had made
no comprehensive provisions for transferring overall leadership
abroad. Indeed, until 1963, Tambo had acted merely as the Congress's foreign diplomatic representative. Now, with the smashing of
Umkhonto, Tambo's London office had to be transformed into the
ANC's exile capital.

Tambo presided over an organization cut off from nearly all its
internal sources of funds, necessitating appeals for foreign patrons
that led most frequently, with Communist Party help, to the Soviet
Union and its allies. The executive was now dominated by the Congress's left, in part because of the discrediting of moderate policy
and in part because those members with SACP connections had been
more successful in eluding capture and escaping the country. Under
the new order, the ANC made its commitment to armed struggle
more explicit and its collaboration with the exiled Communist Party
leadership more overt.

In what proved to be a premature effort to signal South Africa's
blacks that the liberation movement was alive and well, Tambo's
executive in 1967 decided to initiate joint military operations with
Joshua Nkomo's Zimbabwe African People's Union (ZAPU), which
was beginning its battle against white rule in Rhodesia. In late July, a
force of Umkhonto soldiers accompanied ZAPU guerrillas across the

Rhodesian frontier from Zambia with orders to fight or smuggle their way through the renegade colony to South Africa. Once inside the Republic, they were to engage in guerrilla activities while being protected by underground ANC cells. In view of the almost total breakdown of communication within the Congress domestic underground and between it and London, it is unlikely that the guerrillas would have gotten far in South Africa before being detected by the police. But before they had the chance to try, Rhodesian security forces intercepted and eventually captured them. It was the last time the Congress would attempt military action against the South African government in the 1960s, marking an admission that the regime's strategy of supporting white colonial buffer states was proving effective in blocking infiltration from abroad. Underscoring Pretoria's success was the 1968 ambush by Portuguese troops of twelve PAC men on their way through Mozambique to South Africa.

Tambo's executive seemed plagued through the 1960s with organizational growing pains characterized by factional fighting and tactical vacillation. This splintering reflected what inside critics argued was Tambo's failure to set goals, unify the small external command structure, maintain troop morale, define the ANC's ideology, and politically mobilize its membership. In these early years of Tambo's directorship, Congress executives acquired a reputation for luxurious living in London.

The ANC finally found the road to recovery from Rivonia some six years after the event at its 1969 Third Consultative Conference in Morogoro, Tanzania. Delegates adopted new policies designed to streamline leadership and infuse the party with purpose. The all-black National Executive Committee was cut in size from twenty-three to nine members in an apparent bid to facilitate decision-making. A new multiracial Revolutionary Council was established to command Umkhonto we Sizwe. A commission was created to resolve complaints and grievances such as those which had sparked a 1968 desertion by dissident trainees. The party also formally endorsed armed struggle and took full responsibility for MK.

Perhaps most important of all was the party's decision to return to the work of methodically building a sturdy infrastructure of resistance. The 1969 conference mandated the reconstruction of the party's shattered underground, with new attention being paid to South

Africa's black youth. The "international solidarity" work that had been the external mission's chief preoccupation would now, on paper at least, be assigned second priority after the work of internal political mobilization.

Although the Morogoro conference was a watershed, it nevertheless did not succeed in eradicating conflict within the ANC's ranks. The continuing discontent over the Congress's close relationship with communists, its acceptance of Soviet aid, and the conspicuous number of whites in military leadership positions led to a chain of Africanist-inspired splits in the early 1970s. Others bolted because they viewed the party as insufficiently radical. But these defections did not appear to hamper significantly the Congress's activities. In the next few years the ANC began the slow process of quietly reconnecting its internal network while waiting for more states in the region to achieve independence from white colonial rule.

AFRICANISM REDUX: THE BLACK CONSCIOUSNESS MOVEMENT

Among blacks inside South Africa the absence of visible spokesmen for the rights of the Republic's majority began to take its toll in frustration in 1973, when an extended period of labor unrest commenced in Durban and quickly spread nationwide. News of foreign landmark events such as the dramatic surrender of Portuguese colonial administrations in Angola and Mozambique to black guerrilla forces energized opposition to apartheid during this period. The ANC, absorbed in the arduous rebuilding process, had little influence in shaping it. In fact, to many frustrated blacks, the Congress was an irritating reminder of an era of political impotence. Activists were searching for a new, effective political weapon with which to challenge apartheid.

What they settled on was the Black Consciousness Movement (BCM), a term generally applied to the myriad of local and national groups federated in the 1970s by a common philosophy. Organizational components of the movement presented an alphabetical patchwork of names—BPC, IDAMASA, ASSECA, BAWU, SASO, SASM, BCP, and AZAPO, to name a few. The threading of all these bodies into a single, wide-ranging philosophical fabric began, however, with the opening of the Black People's Convention in August of 1971 held in a hall in Bloemfontein. Steve Biko, the quiet back-stage designer of the movement, was proclaimed honorary president. The black consciousness philosophy might be described as pragmatic Africanism. While founded upon Anton Lembede's doctrine of black political revival through psychological emancipation, it contained little of his apostles' faith in civil disobedience and armed struggle as a means of reawakening black pride. BCM would legally use existing structures to achieve its goals. "Black man, you are on your own," asserted Barney Pityana, one of BCM's early philosopher-leaders. "The way to the future is not through a directionless multiracialism but through a positive unilateral approach . . . to infuse [the black man] with pride and dignity."6

Black consciousness was vague on the means through which psychological liberation could be achieved, but they would be peaceful. "We are not going to get into armed struggle," asserted Biko. "We'll leave it to the PAC and ANC."7

What BCM did do was to initiate a nationwide, scrupulously law-abiding education and community action campaign designed to work at the grass-roots level toward building a psychology of self-reliance among blacks. At the same time, BCM leaders in all the various constituent groups adopted high public profiles through speeches, interviews, and published articles, in an effort to spread black consciousness widely.

Their stated rule was to use the white-organized system itself to awaken black political influence. Just as the early ANC elite had held fast to the conviction that white domination must weaken in the face of nonviolent black pressure, so the new proponents of black consciousness argued that nonwhites could achieve power through bargaining, and that the strength required for such negotiations could be gathered peacefully from within the apartheid system. Though some activists may privately have assumed that violent opposition would be a natural outgrowth of BCM's black nationalist teachings, the movement itself never engaged in nor prepared for armed resistance.

Along with prying black politics away from dependence on whites—even white liberals—BCM leaders sought to carve out a racially exclusive niche for black laborers. Launched in November of 1972, the Black Allied Workers Union promoted itself as a blacks-only trade union. It was uninterested in organizing strikes for political reasons; rather, BAWU would sponsor training centers, courses for black youths, and other practical programs to psychologically rejuvenate the African community. "We do our own thing and do not confront the government," asserted Black People's Convention Secretary-General Drake Koka, BAWU's most influential leader.[8] But the union had only limited and early success in recruiting affiliates, and its individual membership was estimated in 1975 to be under one thousand.

BAWU's sorry record reflected a basic flaw in the black consciousness movement. Like the early ANC, the pool of BCM activists was numerically small, moderate, and filled with members of the educated middle-class elite. Though skilled in broadcasting their principles, they were ultimately unable to forge an organized network of political opposition through the varied social precincts of black South Africa. At their peak, in fact, the two most important black consciousness groups could count no more than an estimated seven thousand enrollees.[9]

The weakness of BCM's base was particularly dangerous in light of the volcanic expectations it was raising around the country. Promoting a policy that required indictment of apartheid on the one hand and rigid nonconfrontation on the other, black consciousness was preparing the way for an outburst it could neither command nor control. In 1976 something finally gave.

SOWETO AND THE ANC

Twenty thousand marching schoolchildren accompanied the sun into the black Johannesburg satellite township of Soweto on the morning of June sixteenth. Demonstrating against the introduction of compulsory Afrikaans language courses into the curriculum, the students were met by squads of armed police. Placards were ripped away, stones hurled at police, and thirteen-year-old Hector Petersen, lying in a pool of blood, became the uprising's first fatality. Soweto spent that mid-June afternoon ablaze. One hundred and thirty-nine buildings and 143 vehicles, many of them owned by the police or the Bantu Administration Department, were destroyed within a few days. Nearly two hundred people had lost their lives after a week. Within four months rioters had spread the violence well beyond

Soweto to at least 160 black communities in each of the four provinces and all the bantustans. In almost every case the targets of black protest were edifices, personnel, and property symbolic of the National Party government. Widespread spontaneous violence was not to be contained until the end of 1977, by which time between six hundred and a thousand blacks had been killed by security forces. Most prominent among the casualties was Steve Biko, who was beaten and tortured to death by police interrogators in September.

The majority of the 1976 incidents of rebellion were spontaneous rather than organized events. Soweto itself did boast a localized, crudely fashioned group capable of assembling demonstrations, but the Soweto Students Representative Council (SSRC), an offshoot of the South African Students Organization (SASO), was structurally unequipped to provide sustained, skilled direction to what evolved quickly into a national revolt.

Laced together only by the most hastily woven threads of an underground, the council proved highly vulnerable to police counteraction. Key black-consciousness groups such as the Black People's Convention, which might have been expected to assist the students, instead sank into inactivity. A desperate SSRC reacted by repudiating BCM's canons of nonviolence and launching an ill-fated attempt to convert itself into an eleventh-hour liberation army. Twenty-eight-year-old Paul Langa was appointed in mid-1978 to organize an SSRC "suicide squad" to carry out sabotage operations against the state.

Working with perhaps no more than a dozen volunteers, Langa carried out several bomb attacks in Soweto, at least one in conjunction with the equally short-lived South African Freedom Organization. Within a year both hastily assembled urban units were either banned or destroyed. But they served to underline what was viewed by many activist blacks as a verdict of the Soweto revolt: that the tactics of black consciousness had failed as practical weapons against apartheid. The inflexible response of the government in Soweto's wake signaled the collapse of BCM's work-within-the-system approach. Relearning lessons their parents had absorbed in 1960, much of South Africa's township youth concluded that armed resistance was the only choice left to them. But while their elders sixteen years earlier had been unable to find a ready-made liberation group to join, and no nearby friendly countries to which to escape, the radicalized students of 1976 in short order discovered the ANC in the newly independent frontline black states of the subcontinent.

Soweto was indeed to fuel the rehabilitation of the African National Congress. Prior to 1976 the party had neither a widespread student underground nor any large infusions of new blood into its far-flung foreign offices. It was out of touch, a resistance movement-in-waiting. The Congress was in need of a Soweto to drive the black population into active opposition, where it was confident that it alone could mobilize the resources to challenge Pretoria.

On the eve of the Soweto uprisings, however, the Congress was in a delicate position. Its ingrained policies of multiracialism, armed struggle, and accepting material assistance from non-African powers, in particular the Soviet Union and its allies, were in disfavor in BCM-dominated South Africa. Regarded by many blacks as a political relic having little to do with the new wave of ferment, the party had to tread carefully in trying to take advantage of youthful activism.

Trial evidence indicates that by the end of 1975 the ANC had overcome most of the splits and defections that had plagued it for a decade. Moreover, it had succeeded in reactivating a number of cells inside the country, particularly those in the Johannesburg area. But the lack of generational depth in the organization could be seen in the fact that seventy-seven-year-old Martin Mafefo Ramokgadi had to be named as the party's chief internal organizer even as BCM was finding its strength in the young. Major court actions of the period revealed the average age of the ANC guerrilla operating at the time to be thirty-five. Just one year later, after an infusion of youths fleeing the country, the figure dropped to twenty-eight.[10] For the interim, however, the Congress was forced to rely on its aging contacts inside the country to initiate a national recruitment drive. As the Soweto rebellion grew, this task of absorbing the mounting exodus of students into a substantial Umkhonto army became the major preoccupation of Tambo's exiled executive.

On many occasions during this period hasty plans were made by untrained or poorly trained organizers which resulted in the capture by the South African police of several would-be guerrilla units on their way to Botswana. By relying on amateurish internal agents to restart Umkhonto we Sizwe, Tambo risked scaring off potential enlistees, just as had happened in 1962–63. In one case, for example, twelve candidates for military education in Tanzania were arrested near Mafeking in November 1976. The group had planned to reach Botswana, where ANC contacts were waiting to arrange for their transportation to Dar es Salaam, but was never instructed on how to find a way across the border. The driver stopped the minibus twice to ask directions, thereby arousing suspicion and leading to the group's arrest.[11] Despite instances of inept organization, however, impassioned dissidents continued to fill Umkhonto's foreign-based ranks, using the ANC underground or traveling on their own resources across the frontier.

Some ANC funds began trickling into South Africa in conjunction with the organization's new recruitment campaign. Just as the decolonization process had enabled the ANC to employ independent Botswana as a covert frontline transit point for Tanzania-bound trainees, so sovereign Swaziland now came into use as the Congress's channel for inbound finances. Underground chief Martin Ramokgadi himself crossed into Swaziland in April of 1976 to manage the transfers, so that by year's end some $8,600 had been put at his disposal for expenses—such as the purchase of two minibuses for use in transporting recruits.[12] While symbolic of the Congress's renewed commitment to armed struggle, the amount was trivial relative to the financial demands of a growing liberation group, and helped spark charges that ANC executives were using the bulk of donated funds for their own living expenses in London.

Along with recruitment, ANC strategists in 1976 sought to influence, and if possible coopt, the primary activist organizations growing up under the BCM umbrella. The Congress was suspected, for example, of having helped establish the Black Parents Association several days after the first outbreaks of violence in Soweto. Dedicated to lending parental-generation support to the widening protests, the association achieved rapid progress in forging links with comparable groups along the Witwatersrand, thus raising suspicions of ANC underground assistance. In addition, the association was apparently involved with an alleged ANC agent attached to the banned Christian Institute.[13]

Several members of the SSRC executive were also ANC cardholders. For most of the youths, the ANC and PAC had been unknown. "Until I joined," said one of the council's presidents, "the names of these two organizations did not mean anything to me."[14] But in one well-documented Soweto meeting in December 1976, ANC operative Naledi Tsiki secretly held talks with five top SSRC leaders, including then-president Khotso Seathlolo, in order to persuade them to link up with the ANC. He offered the group military training and enticed them with instructions on the use of a Skorpion machine pistol and hand-grenade. While Seathlolo rejected the proposal, the others reportedly agreed to operate privately in a cell under Tsiki's direction.[15] But as Tsiki was arrested only months later, it is unclear whether the ANC was able to make use of its new cell.

At about the same time another student leader sympathetic to the ANC, Elias Masinga, attempted to recruit SSRC cardholders into the ANC and at one stage secretly transported two executives to Swaziland for a meeting with top ANC representatives who offered assistance and cooperation. This December 1976 conference is thought to have boosted ANC influence at the upper levels of the student movement. Some of these activists later underwent local clandestine training in weapons use, and Masinga continued to help establish ANC cells in and around Johannesburg before being arrested.[16]

The SSRC did appear to have received some early, limited military aid from Congress sources in the form of small arms and explosives, most of which later found their way into Paul Langa's Suicide Squad. The fact that the squad was established only three months after the June sixteenth uprising and was operative almost immediately supports the contention that the ANC's expertise "was, quite evidently, speedily transmitted to young men who had no previous training in, or experience of, such techniques."[17] At least three trials over the next two years exposed other ANC efforts to guide student groups across the nation and gather new candidates for Umkhonto training abroad.

The ANC ingratiated itself with the SSRC by cosponsoring on August 23 a successful strike in sympathy with the Soweto protests. On its own, the student group had been largely frustrated in its efforts to organize and coordinate black laborers. But the ANC, through its association with SACTU, had a means to tap labor activism. In doing so that August, its leadership was no doubt attempting to convey to the students how indispensible the ANC would be in broadening protest across South Africa.

While having some underground success in coopting black consciousness agitators and recruiting volunteers, the ANC role most visible to the black public during the uprisings was propagandizing. The Congress tried to salute the angry youths while chiding them for their meek, BCM-inspired tactics. In regular newsletters clandestinely disseminated during the rebellion, the Congress declared, for example, that "we . . . oppose such efforts as the building of clinics, work camps and home industries no matter how well meant. That energy and enthusiasm of the youth must be directed in efforts to destroy the one and only source of our misery and oppression, namely white domination."[18] Congress tacticians were particularly critical of the student focus on black school curricula instead of grievances that would attract a broader constituency for revolt.

Nevertheless, for much of 1976, the Congress recognized the preeminence of student BCM groups. Apart from assisting in limited ways, the ANC concentrated on capturing Soweto's legacy of activism. After years of disfavor, South Africa's oldest black party was preparing to reclaim the mandate of black leadership by making good its promise of armed resistance.

SOWETO AND THE PAC

The Congress was not, however, to be left unchallenged. Black consciousness had been cut from the same Africanist cloth as the PAC, and the rise of one might have been expected to boost the fortunes of the other. But the dormancy of the PAC underground made that all but impossible until 1974, when one of the party's early leaders was released from Robben Island prison.

Zephania Mothopeng had been one of the few top PAC executives to remain in South Africa after Sharpeville, and had paid for his decision in three separate jailings and a period of internal banishment. Mothopeng was sixty-two when in 1974 he secretly began the work of reconstructing an internal PAC. As in the case of the ANC, it is revealing that the PAC's revival had to await the labors of a man two to three times the age of most BCM activists. Steve Biko, for example, was only twenty-eight in 1974.

Whether Mothopeng began organizing under his own initiative or that of the external PAC, the two were in regular communication within a short period of time. While he worked to activate a PAC cell in Krugersdorp, the exiled party leadership, headed by the mercurial

Potlako Leballo, dispatched an agent on a nationwide tour of PAC contacts, ordering them immediately to reassemble their clandestine cells.[19] At least two internal units were founded following the agent's visit, one based in Pretoria to coordinate operations in the Transvaal, another in East London to cover the eastern Cape. In addition, Mothopeng helped to establish the Young African Christian Movement in Kagiso.

For much of 1976 the PAC concentrated on recruitment; virtually no time or funds were spent linking the party to BCM groups. A new courier system improved lines of communication between PAC offices in Botswana and Swaziland, shuttling funds and published party material in, and enlistees for military training out. Couriers also linked Pretoria with East London for policy coordination. In the period between September 1975 and January 1977 the PAC successfully recruited and transported to Botswana or Swaziland at least 130 new members. Hundreds of others found their way into exile on their own, later to be recruited into PAC forces.

While dozens of PAC recruits in the newly christened Azania People's Liberation Army were subsequently trained in guerrilla warfare in China, Ethiopia, Nigeria, and Libya, it was not until 1977 that some began filtering back into South Africa to initiate military operations. By then it was too late. Having met with limited success in building a domestic PAC underground of trustworthy young activists, the party could only steer incoming insurgents to a small group of older-generation organizers to assist their missions. Many of these men and women were known to the security police from 1963 membership lists seized in Maseru. By skillfully using informants and surveillance, the police did not take long to arrest nearly the entire leadership of the reconstituted PAC, trying them together in what became known as the Bethal-18 trial.

Meanwhile the party's exiled executive committee collapsed into internecine conflict. Absorbed in a power struggle, Leballo informed the Swazi government in April 1978 of a PAC guerrilla cell opposed to his presidency and asked that its members be detained.[20] Others were jailed at his request in Botswana.[21] Ten weeks later, the embattled Leballo summoned a consultative conference—the second in PAC history—in Arusha, Tanzania, ostensibly to plan strategy for the post-Soweto era. A bitter clash between the Leballo political wing and the military command backed by new Soweto student members resulted in the expulsion of seven London-based militants and consolidation of central committee control over the PAC army.[22]

Turmoil persisted in the Tanzania-headquartered leadership for the next two years. Leballo himself was ousted in favor of a three-man "presidential council" only eleven months after the consultative conference. David Sibeko, foreign secretary and number two in the party hierarchy, was assassinated one month later in Dar es Salaam.[23] Elected as the PAC's third chief was Vusumzi Make, who barely had time to form a new ten-man central committee before being displaced by former Robben Island prisoner and PAC veteran John Nyati Pokela and an even newer fourteen-man central committee.[24] Upon Pokela's death in July 1985, forty-five-year-old Johnson Mlambo took the helm, pledging to unite the party and continue the competition with the ANC.

Consumed abroad by factional fighting and unstable leadership, and barren at home of an infrastructure capable of translating its dreams of rebellion into reality, the Pan Africanist Congress was not to play a significant part in the post-Soweto era of armed resistance to apartheid. It would retain a place in international diplomatic circles by virtue of its status in the United Nations as one of two recognized liberation movements in South Africa. But after 1978 the story of black military opposition in the Republic is largely the story of the ANC and its allies.

CONCLUSION

Reacting swiftly and characteristically to the Soweto rebellion, Pretoria's security forces mounted a campaign of arrests, raids, detentions, and bannings that all but crushed black consciousness as a force of opposition in South Africa. The police effort also wounded but did not stop underground activities of Congress operatives. Such actions eliminated the ANC's chief rivals for the vanguard position in black politics at the same time that it convinced new sectors of the nonwhite community of the futility of above-ground, peaceful opposition. An era which had begun in 1912 with the ANC as the only black party of peaceful protest ended in 1976 with the Congress as the predominant party of insurgency.

The Congress's survival can be traced in part to its early start over other parties. Having seen all manner of nonviolent protest fall victim to government repression, it had long recognized the necessity for a secure underground and the apparent futility of relying on legal methods of resisting apartheid. While the PAC had reached the same conclusions, it had not been granted sufficient time to organize a covert network. The black consciousness movement, for its part, did not learn the lesson until the Soweto rebellion consumed its plans for peaceful change. As a result, where its competitors had crumbled, the ANC proved structurally capable of withstanding governmental suppression.

A second reason for the Congress's longevity was its controversial relationship with the SACP. While representing only one of a variety of ANC allies, the communists had passed on vital expertise in the art of covert survival, so that the nucleus of an M-Plan underground could be implanted in South Africa's black community prior to the sabotage years. While largely dormant during the 1960s, these cells formed the engine of the 1977 revival. The Communist Party also boosted the Congress's fortunes with intelligence information and a financial tieline to the Soviet Union. No other black movement could boast comparable resources, particularly since other potential foreign patrons, such as China, could not match Moscow in aid or espionage assistance. The ANC was by no means a communist organization itself, but it had come to rely on the SACP during a period when its own resources were sparse.

If the ANC found itself more potent than its partisan rivals, it was still not until other black groups had kindled the fires of black frustration that Umkhonto could launch a sustainable armed rebellion. Committed to violent resistance since 1961, the Congress had shown itself to be administratively disheveled, politically schizophrenic, and militarily amateurish during its sabotage campaign. The following thirteen years, until 1977, were spent rectifying those deficiencies and awaiting events that could be used to renew the struggle.

Indeed, the Congress's strategy of guerrilla war had become far more realistic as a result of the gradual reversal of the geopolitical odds that had been stacked against Umkhonto during the sabotage years. In 1961, not a single state in the region had been governed by black majorities. Consequently, the ANC's sabotage schemes were imperiled, if only for lack of nearby safe havens. In 1976, all but two of South Africa's neighbors were independent; when Zimbabwe joined them in 1980, only Namibia was left under minority rule.

None of these governments could avoid becoming involved in the Congress's efforts to enlist them as front- or rear-base sanctuaries for Umkhonto insurgents.

Prognosticators had been known to forecast black revolution in South Africa for decades. But it was only in the late 1970s that conditions began to converge that could support any serious rebellion. Ponderously in the 1960s, more rapidly in the aftermath of Soweto, South Africa was entering its season of civil war.

2. Rebellion-in-Exile

Trying to direct resistance in South Africa with managers who could not legally set foot in the country was a challenge that forced the ANC to split itself in two. Beyond the Republic's frontier, in states that would permit it, the Congress would establish a government-in-exile. Ideally, from these scattered compounds, the expatriate bureaucracy could freely amass the facilities, weapons, and funds needed to build Umkhonto we Sizwe into a trained guerrilla fighting force. The ANC abroad could act as a kind of borderless welfare state, educating young recruits, providing housing, food, and token wages to its thousands of banished constituents, and focusing all minds on the enterprise of liberation.

At the same time, in principle, another ANC would exist within the hostile environment of South Africa itself. Composed of clandestine cells, this ANC would act as the external command's underground field network, providing reconnaissance, extending cover for infiltrated insurgents, recruiting and testing prospective new volunteers, and attempting to influence the activities of black resistance to apartheid in ways prescribed by the exiled leadership.

South Africa's record of black opposition had demonstrated that a militant anti-apartheid movement needed both foreign resources and a domestic underground to best weather periodic government crackdowns and press on with its objectives. Although the Congress had been slow to reconstruct its internal wing until the turmoil of the Soweto rebellion, it had spent a great deal of effort assembling a bureaucratic superstructure outside South Africa. Much of it had been based in Europe, primarily London, during the wait for black rule in Mozambique, Angola, and Zimbabwe. Critics charged that ANC leaders had been so lulled by the comforts of the developed world that they were seeking to postpone armed insurrection indefinitely in favor of the cushioned exercises of international diplomacy. Indeed, in the decade after Rivonia, the Congress's small coterie of exiles had become professional diplomats and bureaucrats, detached from the daily struggles and perspectives of blacks inside South Africa. As a result, the ANC had had little to do with the upsurge of activism in the early 1970s. But its work abroad did endow the party with the resources to absorb the new wave of recruits and capitalize on the country's political ferment.

To activate those resources the National Executive Committee decided finally to move south into Africa. London would remain the movement's most important post in the West, but it would no longer act as headquarters. Instead, the ANC would position itself in the subcontinent as close as possible to the frontlines of conflict.

RETURN TO THE FRONTLINE

To a large extent, the ANC's tactics of guerrilla warfare were to be shaped not by studied military planning but from the force of circumstances. No better illustration of this process may be found than in the way in which the Congress moved back into southern Africa from Europe. Tambo carried a shopping list of four strategic necessities with him into the subcontinent in the search for facilities close enough to South Africa to enable command of operations inside the country. One was maximum security from cross-border South African attacks. The ANC had determined that it would need ways to protect exiled troops and bureaucrats, either by means of Umkhonto's own military defenses, measures taken by the host state, or by keeping camps beyond the reach of Pretoria's defense force.

Another Congress objective was maximum freedom to maneuver diplomatically and militarily. The Zimbabwean liberation groups during the Rhodesian war had been so dependent on their host states—Zambia, Tanzania, and Mozambique—that frequently the negotiations over their own struggle had been controlled solely by those governments. The ANC wished to avoid being dictated to by nations under pressure from South Africa.

Tambo's third goal was for the party to constitute as small a burden as possible on its host country. In food-short Zambia, when thousands of rebel ZAPU troops were encamped near Lusaka awaiting action in Rhodesia, many locals were outraged at the special supplies the foreigners were thought to be receiving. A crime wave blamed on frustrated ZAPU soldiers also helped to undermine host state support for Joshua Nkomo's exile army. The Congress sorely needed the goodwill of host governments and planned programs to guard against the possibility of its banishment by them.

Finally, the ANC's advance teams sought a large variety of facilities—everything from administrative buildings to schools and military camps. Umkhonto would require routes over which to send arms and guerrillas into South Africa. Key offices would need regular lines of communication with the internal underground.

Seeking a deployment that would most rapidly facilitate the development of armed rebellion in South Africa, Tambo might have considered "the closer the better" a useful maxim. During the period in which white-ruled states provided a buffer against the Republic, no ANC unit could have hoped to establish itself within striking distance of the border. But, by 1975, of the six frontier states, only Namibia and Rhodesia were governed by hostile elites. By 1980, Namibia stood alone. Yet—perhaps to its surprise—the ANC found that it could by no means count on these nations for significant help. All of the five independent frontier states under minority or colonial rule had been securely tied to South Africa's economy, and no change of governments would alter that fact without investments in massive new infrastructure projects.

None was more tightly bound than Lesotho, a kingdom completely surrounded by South Africa. Aptly termed a "captive nation," Lesotho was almost totally reliant on Pretoria for transportation, communications, and energy. Moreover, the country's manufacturing sector accounted for less than 1 percent of its gross national product. Most of the GNP was attributable to wages sent home by migrants laboring in South Africa's mines.[1] Its small neighbor to the north, the kingdom of Swaziland, was similarly situated. Most Swazi trade flowed through South Africa, and an estimated 82 percent of rural homesteads in the country depended on wages earned in the Republic.[2] Pretoria's Electricity Supply Commission provided the kingdom with its electric power.[3]

Botswana, though a member together with Lesotho and Swaziland of the South Africa-controlled Customs Union, was better positioned to diversify its economy. It boasted formidable reserves of natural resources such as diamonds, and a potential to develop transportation lines through other neighboring states. But until Zimbabwe's independence, nearly all of Botswana's food, with the exception of beef, had been imported from South Africa.[4] In addition, most transport and communications facilities were controlled by Pretoria, and between 26 and 50 percent of the country's labor force worked as migrants in South African mines.[5]

Mozambique, until 1975 a Portuguese colony enjoying close relations with Pretoria, depended on South African trade through the port of Maputo for an estimated 40 percent of government revenues.[6] Combined with income from migrant labor, South African trade accounted for 60 percent of the nation's foreign currency earnings.[7] Equally vital was South African aid in managing the skill-short country's ports and railways. Agricultural prosperity in neighboring Zimbabwe held out the prospect of increasing trade with that country. But with its own farm economy in tatters, Mozambique remained in need of South African food imports to feed its people.

Of all the majority-ruled frontier states, Zimbabwe was the least "captive." Although during the civil war the world boycott of Rhodesia had forced virtually all trade through South Africa's open (but premium-priced) rail routes, the newly independent Zimbabwe could consider alternative channels for imports and exports. Nevertheless, each of these was plagued with problems, and up to 80 percent of the country's trade continued to pass through South Africa. In addition, though Zimbabwe's productive farmers could feed the country on their own in good-weather years, South African capital and expertise supported other key sectors such as mining.

In short, each of the five independent frontier states, in varying degrees, stood hostage to South African economic power. Nor was Pretoria shy about using its leverage to prevent those governments from ceding the ANC rights to conduct operations from their territories. In late 1985, for example, Lesotho's economy ground to a near standstill as South Africa sought to oust Chief Leabua Jonathan,

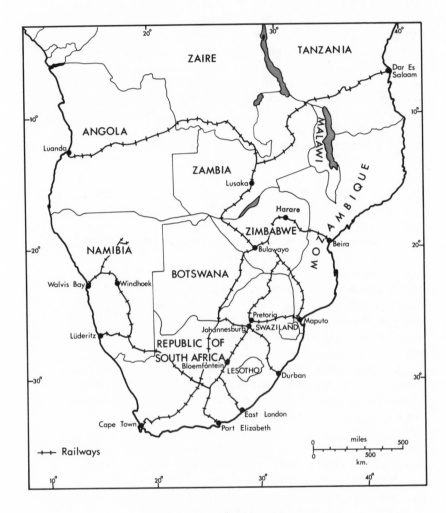

ZAIRE

TANZANIA

Dar Es
Salaam

10°

ANGOLA

Luanda

ZAMBIA

Lusaka

MALAWI

MOZAMBIQUE

Harare

NAMIBIA

ZIMBABWE

Bulawayo

Beira

20°

Walvis Bay

Windhoek

BOTSWANA

Lüderitz

Pretoria
Johannesburg   SWAZILAND   Maputo

REPUBLIC [OF
SOUTH AFRICA
Bloemfontein   LESOTHO   Durban

30°

Cape Town
Port Elizabeth
East London

┼┼┼ Railways

miles
0   500
0   500
km.

Map 2   Southern Africa

whose government had tolerated a low-profile ANC presence. The Republic's unofficial customs boycott was only lifted after the Jonathan administration was overthrown. Less than a week later, ANC personnel were quietly expelled from the country.

Pretoria used the full range of its economic arsenal, including threats to reduce migratory labor, withdrawal of technical experts, trade boycotts, and transportation blockages, to clear the ANC out of border nations. But it also employed more violent methods of coercion.

Three of the five independent states sharing borders with South Africa faced internal resistance movements backed by South African funds, training, or arms. In each case, Pretoria sought to keep the incumbent government off balance, dependent on the Republic to stop the conflict, and even more reliant on South Africa's economic assets to survive.

Mozambique faced a widening guerrilla war organized by the Resistência Nacional de Moçambique, or Renamo, a party formed around members of the defunct Portuguese colonial army. Financed and supplied by South Africa (together with Rhodesia until the collapse of white rule), Renamo's estimated four thousand troops succeeded in crippling the nation's fragile agricultural sector and regularly disabling vital pipe and rail lines to Zimbabwe. As a result, South African food and other assistance to the starved economy became essential. The ruling Marxist FRELIMO government reacted in the only way it could: in March of 1984 the late President Samora Machel signed a formal nonaggression pact with Pretoria, pledging to expel most ANC personnel in return for South Africa's promise to cut off aid to Renamo.

Despite disclosures in 1985 that the South African Defense Force had violated the Nkomati Accord by continuing to supply Renamo, Mozambique could do little but reaffirm its commitment to the treaty. The rightist rebellion continued to grow, threatening to topple the enfeebled FRELIMO government. When President Machel died in a mysterious plane crash on the South African border in 1986, many in the region suspected that Pretoria had engineered the incident in a final effort to bring down the charismatic leader's administration.

Zimbabwe, too, faced a threat to its stability from South African-sponsored dissidents. Prime Minister Robert Mugabe's Zimbabwe

African National Union (ZANU) government, though elected and reelected by large majorities, was by no means free of extremist opposition. In addition to unrepentant whites who had backed the defeated Rhodesian Front regime, many rival ZAPU militants in the west and conservative partisans of Bishop Abel Muzorewa in the east stood bitterly opposed to Mugabe. Some of these could be mobilized by South Africa. An estimated five thousand dissidents trained at South African camps in northern Transvaal have reportedly been the source of numerous clandestine raids and killings.[8] Mugabe was able to display proof of such a connection when, in 1982, a Zimbabwean army patrol killed three white SADF soldiers some twenty miles inside the country. Together with a unit of black troops, the group had apparently been on a mission to sabotage the rail link to Mozambique.

Insurgent pressures had also been applied against Chief Leabua Jonathan's regime in Lesotho, at least up to the time the veteran leader was overthrown by pro-South African army officers in the 1986 coup. The Basotho Congress Party had launched what it termed a "civil war" against Jonathan in 1979, assembling a three hundred-strong Lesotho Liberation Army to carry out a series of bombings and killings from sanctuaries in South Africa's Orange Free State.[9]

"An article of faith in South African foreign policy is non-interference in others' affairs," commented foreign ministry official Neil van Heerden in an interview, "but of course it is always possible that some dirty tricks department is trying to steer things in one direction. . . . " Lesotho, he observed, is "totally in our embrace."[10]

By virtue of their conservative governments and cooperative relations with South Africa, Swaziland and Botswana had not been subjected to the pressures of Pretoria-backed insurgencies. But together with their neighbors, each was vulnerable to yet another form of South African power aimed at keeping the ANC far from the Republic's borders: direct military attack.

With the possible exception of Zimbabwe, none of the five independent frontier nations possessed sufficient military strength to prevent incursions into their territories by South African forces seeking out ANC targets. On occasion, these attacks would be openly acknowledged after the fact by Pretoria and justified as either preventive measures or retaliation for ANC raids inside the Republic. The SADF's brief 1981 ground invasion to destroy an ANC compound on the outskirts of Maputo, Mozambique, was one example. It was followed by the brutal 1982 raid on ANC offices in Lesotho, in which forty-two people were killed; another in 1985 in Gaborone, Botswana, which killed twelve, and a triple 1986 strike against targets in Zambia, Botswana, and Zimbabwe. On other occasions South African military involvement, often unproven but strongly suspected, has been covert in nature. Car bombs, unusual accidents, letter bombs, and mysterious explosions have assassinated ANC officials in each of the frontier states.

Added up, the array of economic and military pressures that Pretoria could apply on neighboring countries to counter the ANC was vast and formidable. "We get our oil, our food, and most of our clothing from South Africa," argued a pragmatic Swazi government minister in 1980. "What benefit would there be from taking an anti-South African position?"[11] As, one by one, the five independent border states came under South African siege, each government was finally forced to discard any initial efforts to assist the ANC. No matter how radical its ideology, each administration officially ordered its territory off-limits to Umkhonto guerrillas.

For an ANC command moving from Europe to southern Africa, the gradual closure of the border states meant that "the closer the better" was a prescription that could not be filled except in the short run. Erecting permanent bases on South Africa's frontier would be lethal policy both for the Congress and host country. ANC executives were left no option but to look farther away, in an outer tier of states, for a place to establish a subcontinental headquarters. The candidates they explored were Angola, Zambia, and Tanzania, the next level of sympathetic countries to the north. Each had acted as a sanctuary state for guerrilla struggles in other nearby nations such as Zimbabwe, Namibia, and Mozambique. None of the three was as reliant as the frontier states on South Africa's economy or transportation systems. Two, indeed, were faced with South African military threats. Nevertheless, the trio represented prime rear-base prospects for the ANC's apparatus.

Unlike the border states, Angola and Tanzania had developed economies outside South Africa's orbit. Angola, as an outpost of the Portuguese empire, had been shaped for trade with Europe rather than the south. Although South African corporate interests were involved in diamond mining, the country's resource exploitation sector had never been dominated by them. With a road system almost entirely self-contained, only one major route linked Angola with the south through Namibia. The country's Benguela rail line, owned by the British-based Tanganyika Concessions, tied Angola to the Zairian and Zambian interior. Its three major airports, four ports, and abundant natural resources reinforced the country's commercial independence of South Africa.

Featuring one of the lowest per capita gross national products in the region, Tanzania's decentralized economy could also claim to be largely free of Pretoria's pressure. Under German and then British colonial rule, Tanzania had evolved as part of an East African economic zone configured for trade through the port of Dar es Salaam with Europe, the Middle East, and India. Until the 1976 opening of the Chinese-built Tazara line to Zambia, no railway had linked the country even circuitously with South Africa. The few roads between Tanzania and the south were poor and unreliable. What commercial ties had existed were almost completely severed under President Julius Nyerere, who instituted a unilateral boycott on trade with the Republic.

South African economic influence over Zambia was greater than in any of the ANC's other rear-base options. Planners and politicians in the capital of Lusaka had long been obsessed with finding transportation routes to the sea for the landlocked country's commerce. On paper, the chief export—copper—and chief import—agricultural products—would seem to be able to traverse rail corridors connecting Lusaka to ports in Angola, Tanzania, and Mozambique, as alternatives to South Africa. In fact, the Angolan and Mozambican routes were regularly sabotaged by South African-backed guerrillas, and the Tazara line to Dar es Salaam was plagued by chronic technical breakdowns. The most reliable route snaked south through Zimbabwe and across the Limpopo to South Africa's efficient docks, thus giving Pretoria important leverage over the country.

Yet Zambia's economy boasted other attributes that provided it a measure of independence from South Africa. The conversion of agriculturally prosperous Zimbabwe from enemy to ally marked the eclipse of South Africa as the chief supplier of corn to Zambian markets in shortfall years. Zimbabwe's development also held out the prospect that it could substitute for South Africa in a variety of other ways, particularly if the rail line to the northern Mozambican port of Beira—guarded by an estimated ten thousand Zimbabwean troops—were made secure. In addition, like its fellow rear-base states, few Zambian migrant workers were dependent on employment in South African industries.

In contrast to its southerly frontier neighbors, therefore, the next three sympathetic states closest to South Africa were far more protected from economic coercion. Even Zambia had proven, when bilateral trade all but shut down during the Rhodesian war between 1973 and 1978, that it could get by with dramatically reduced South African commercial ties. While this economic flexibility granted the three nations greater freedom to host ANC enterprises, Pretoria's military operations added another cost to their involvement with the Congress.

Angola was paying the highest price. Beset with a persistent insurgency led by Jonas Savimbi's American and South African-supported UNITA guerrillas, the Marxist MPLA government in Luanda sought and received large-scale Soviet, East German, and Cuban military assistance. Without the aid of Cuban troops, estimated to number some forty thousand in 1986, and Soviet and East German advisors and weapons, the government would have fallen to Savimbi or succumbed to one of numerous South African invasions. But the foreign troops endowed Angola with a formidable army, giving it the fighting capacity to check, if not defeat, Pretoria's guerrilla allies, and the political license to host ANC bases. At the same time, it placed the country heavily in debt to the Soviet Union.

Tanzania, on account of its distance from South Africa and its more unified political structure, suffered only occasional rumors of insurrections sponsored by Pretoria. It was, however, vulnerable to covert attacks on ANC personnel, or the possibility of long-range South African surgical air raids on ANC compounds. Regardless of this threat, a central tenet of the ruling Chama Cha Mapinduzi party's platform was support for African liberation movements, including both ANC and PAC. The government did not depart from its commitment to guerrilla exiles even when an intoxicated ANC driver was reported to have accidentally killed Tanzanian prime minister Edward Sokoine in April 1984. Dar es Salaam hushed up the incident in a deliberate effort to protect the ANC.[12]

Zambia, being physically nearer to South African military bases both in the Transvaal and in Namibia's Caprivi Strip, had long been

subjected to Pretoria-sponsored destabilization missions and direct
air and ground attacks. South African displeasure at President Kenneth Kaunda stemmed primarily from his offering Western Province
as a sanctuary to SWAPO guerrillas battling defense-force troops
across the border in Namibia. Pretoria's involvement was suspected
or exposed in incidents ranging from a 1976 attack on the town of
Mushala by South African-trained Zambian insurgents[13] to an abor-
tive 1980 coup attempt.[14] "I've warned Kaunda that maybe one day
he will find himself unseated," said South African Prime Minister
John Vorster in 1978 of Zambian threats to seek Cuban military
protection against South African-sponsored raids.[15] Direct SADF
intervention in Zambia occurred several times in 1976 and 1978,
followed by a weeks' long invasion of Western Province in 1980 [16]
and air strikes in 1986. Kaunda's small army was no match for the
mobile and highly trained South African forces.

Any ANC offices in Zambia would clearly represent prime targets for South African counterinsurgency operations, just as Zambia's sponsorship of Joshua Nkomo's ZAPU had attracted periodic
Rhodesian raids. But Kaunda had weathered severe domestic criticism during Zimbabwe's war for independence and appeared willing to do so again by hosting the ANC in its guerrilla campaign
against apartheid.

ANC planners were forced by the geopolitical circumstances of
the subcontinent to abandon hopes for permanent frontier bases.
South African power coursed freely through the border states where
such facilities could have been established, overwhelming commit-
ments of solidarity with the ANC. But Pretoria's anti-ANC influence
ebbed in the three outer-tier nations, where barriers in forms as
varied as Cuban troops and simple distance held it back. Consequently, Oliver Tambo and his fellow Congress leaders adjusted
their strategy for constructing a bureaucracy of rebellion in Africa.
There would have to be a two-tiered approach toward filling Tambo's shopping list.

In the outer arc of "sanctuary states" composed of Angola, Zambia, and Tanzania, the Congress would erect its military camps, administrative offices, and educational institutions. In the inner-tier
"transit states" of Botswana, Zimbabwe, Mozambique, Swaziland,
and Lesotho, the ANC would only set up temporary bases and clandestine infiltration routes to funnel its guerrillas into and recruits out
of South Africa rapidly.

The siting of critical ANC operations as far as a thousand miles from the South African frontier meant that command and control of resistance inside the Republic would be extremely difficult and far less efficient than it could be from a nearby facility. Pretoria would succeed, in this respect, in diffusing the impact of the ANC on domestic black politics. On the other hand, the greater distance from South Africa lent the Congress a measure of physical security it would not have enjoyed closer to the Republic. In addition, being dependent for sanctuary on states less vulnerable to South African coercion meant that fewer restraints would be placed on the ANC by host governments under Pretoria's pressure. The Congress sought to maximize this independence by spreading its administration over all three of the outer-tier states, thus reducing its reliance on any one of them. Umkhonto camps would be located in northern Angola, education and training compounds near Morogoro in Tanzania, and the administrative capital in Lusaka, Zambia.

The independent frontier states would be danger zones for Umkhonto guerrillas, couriers, or arms smugglers traveling between South Africa and the outer command centers. Yet in every border state influential black elites were sympathetic to ANC goals, eager to be on the right side if it were to succeed in overturning apartheid, or sensitive to the criticism of fellow African countries. In varying degrees, they persuaded authorities to "look the other way." Few of the five nations, in any event, possessed sufficient armed forces to patrol, or administrative precision to detect, infiltrators disguised as travelers. "It's very easy to cross from Zimbabwe to South Africa, and if they do, fine," asserted Eddison Zvobgo, minister of legal and parliamentary affairs. "We're not paid by South Africa to be their policemen."[17]

By 1975, the ANC's administrative apparatus had begun to settle into the sanctuary states and expand its links with the internal underground through the transit states. The test of the Congress's future lay, however, in the nature of its changing leadership and the shape of its bureaucracy in Lusaka.

THE CAPITAL

The administrative machinery of the African National Congress has always been shrouded in secrecy. While serving as nerve centers of a growing rebellion some six hundred miles south across the veldt, the

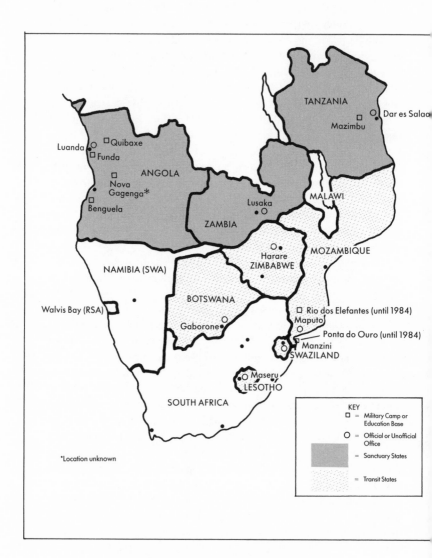

Map 3   ANC Sanctuary and Transit States

low back-street buildings that comprise the ANC's Lusaka headquarters betray their purpose to passersby only by steel gates and tall protecting walls. Congress offices, houses, and farms are dispersed throughout the Zambian capital region in a defensive effort to make the apparatus a difficult target in the event of South African covert or direct attacks. In the 1970s, the ANC was only one of a half-dozen African liberation movements with operation posts in Lusaka. By 1980, however, the Congress was—with Namibia's SWAPO—the most prominent group left. More than one hundred and fifty of its administrators staff at least eleven "cabinet" departments and secretariats and various subdivisions and coordinating committees assigned to different offices in the city. Some eighty cars, many built in South Africa, shuttle workers between party buildings.

Working in austere rooms and living at shifting locations around Lusaka, the ANC's exiled leadership governs a community scattered throughout the subcontinent. At the pinnacle of the bureaucracy is Oliver Tambo, who was reelected to the presidency in 1985 and has served as head of the movement since 1963. But even as some 250 ANC delegates gave their votes to Tambo at the 1985 consultative conference, they also acknowledged their allegiance to Nelson Mandela, then serving his twenty-second year in jail inside South Africa.

Mandela, an attorney by profession, had cofounded the Congress Youth League and worked his way up through the party in the decade preceding Rivonia to chair the ANC's influential Transvaal wing. Having devised the M-Plan and commanded Umkhonto we Sizwe, Mandela had been the most prominent of the police catches when the sabotage campaign collapsed. The drama of his being seized while in disguise was later complemented by the eloquence of his courtroom defense, later memorialized in the book *No Easy Walk to Freedom*. But the image of Nelson Mandela in the 1980s was far different from that of the 1960s.

Through a vigorous public relations campaign focusing on the release of Mandela and other incarcerated activists, the ANC had succeeded in rallying nearly all sectors of black opinion—regardless of party—behind its own charismatic figure. The effort had in effect promoted Mandela in stature from partisan prophet to national saint, and thus the ANC from a prominent caucus to an all-embracing patriotic front. Importantly, he could neither irritate nor alienate anyone since the government would not permit his views to be disseminated. In fact, by the 1980s the idea of Nelson Mandela had become so potent a symbol of black nationalism and such an asset to the ANC that some National Party strategists were promoting his release in hopes of splintering the anti-apartheid opposition by compelling the man to make hard, human decisions.

In Mandela's absence, the person making choices is Tambo. The exacting, hardworking former attorney had been born to a generation troubled by but resigned to the use of force in the resistance effort. Second to Tambo is Alfred Nzo, reelected to the position of secretary-general at the 1985 eight-day consultative conference in the Zambian copperbelt. Having first been promoted to the post at the 1969 conference, Nzo had been responsible for the ANC command's move from Britain to Africa.

In theory, all broad policy directions for the Congress are set by democratically representative consultative conferences, and every ANC officer is accountable to them for his or her actions. But since the party's banning in 1960, only two conferences have taken place: the first in Morogoro, Tanzania, in 1969, and the second in Kabwe, Zambia, in 1985. The third is scheduled for 1990. The Morogoro delegates are credited with the decision to begin moving the ANC back to the region. The eight-day Kabwe convention endorsed the conversion of Umkhonto strategy from sporadic attack to "people's war." Other occasional gatherings of ANC technocrats have issued policy recommendations for various departments.

For all practical purposes the body that controls the African National Congress is the National Executive Committee (NEC), which in its regular meetings operates by standard rules of majority votes by a quorum of members. Each "cabinet" department is accountable to the executive committee for its daily workings. Only the Umkhonto army, with its commanders based far from Lusaka and its operations wrapped in secrecy, is insulated from daily NEC oversight. Tambo and Nzo serve with twenty-eight others on the National Executive Committee. Expanded from twenty-two to thirty at the 1985 convention, the NEC was reorganized to encompass within its ranks nearly every one of the polyglot constituencies that form the ANC, even, for the first time, whites.

Communist Party chairman Joe Slovo became the first white elected to the governing panel. Pretoria claimed that up to twenty-two other executive members could be labeled SACP partisans, making the ANC merely a front for the Soviet Union's South African ally. But others argued that as few as three had been independently documented as communist cardholders. The U.S. Department of State, for its part, estimated in a January 1987 report requested by congressional conservatives that "roughly half" of the NEC's thirty members belonged to the SACP, but that evidence even for this figure "is not conclusive in several cases." The State Department analysis downplayed communist influence in noting that "African nationalism is a strong competitor with orthodox Marxism in ideological appeal."[18]

Determining the precise number of SACP partisans on the African National Congress's top decision-making board is complicated by the fact that the Communist Party keeps its membership strictly secret, partly out of a professed fear of assassination attacks. Longtime ANC expert Thomas Karis, in a 1986 review of declassified CIA biographies of eighteen National Executive Committee members labeled communist by the agency, concluded that only three could definitively be considered members of the SACP based on available data.[19] The men—Slovo, Steve Dlamini, and Dan Tloome—were in any case widely known as active communists. Many others had apparently been placed on the CIA list not as a result of independent research but on the basis of assertions made by South African intelligence agencies, who had an interest in underlining Pretoria's charge that the Soviets manage anti-apartheid resistance.

Interviews with ANC leaders invariably yield the conclusion that communist representation on the NEC, even if exact numbers remain a mystery, gives party members significant but by no means controlling influence in the organization. President Tambo, for example, complains that while no one considered the United States a dupe of the Soviet Union when it was allied with Moscow during World War II, critics often assume that an ANC coalition that includes communists must be controlled by Moscow.

The veterans who still hold the ANC's top posts remain manifestly moderate and Western-oriented. They argue that even if SACP members now occupy important seats on the National Executive Committee, the Communist Party would be a minor factor in a "liberated" South Africa. The 1987 State Department report suggested a similar view. "The SACP appears to have little or no influ-

ence on political and labor groups inside South Africa," it concluded. "This lack of popular support gives non-Communist leaders
of the ANC considerable counterleverage against SACP efforts to
dominate the group."[20]

In addition to communists, the NEC, broadened after the 1985
consultative conference, includes representatives of other Congress
interest groups such as the Indian and colored communities, neither
of which had boasted executive members until Mac Maharaj and
Aziz Pahad joined to speak for Asians and Reg September for mixed-
race South Africans. Women are formally involved through reelected executive member Gertrude Shope, head of the ANC's large
womens' section. The commander of Umkhonto we Sizwe, Joe
Modise, sits on the executive to represent the military, while Steve
Dlamini and John Nkadimeng convey the interests of the South
African Congress of Trade Unions.

Heads of ANC departments were also named to the NEC in
1985. Thabo Mbeki, whose father, Govan, is living out a life sentence in a South African jail, directs the Congress's publicity office.
SACTU secretary-general Nkadimeng, whose son was killed in a
bomb attack in Botswana early in 1985, runs the political department. Johnny Makatini administers the international affairs department, with its twenty-eight foreign posts, after having represented
the ANC at the United Nations in New York. Thomas Nkobi chairs
the department of the treasury. Remaining NEC members were
drawn from MK, educational offices, and ANC missions abroad. A
minority represents the thousands of younger Congress partisans
who fled South Africa during the Soweto period.

Through the eleven "cabinet" departments under the National
Executive Committee the ANC feeds, pays, educates, trains, and
mobilizes the more than ten thousand constituents that now fill its
ranks in the sanctuary states of southern Africa. The ANC, according
to Thabo Mbeki, "is the totality of their lives."[21] A health system
fields a set of clinics of uncertain quality in all three rear-base nations. The education department dispatches its small, insufficient
corps of teachers to ANC schools in Tanzania, Angola, and Zambia.
The arts and culture bureau, belatedly created to emulate the black
consciousness movement's focus on regenerating black pride, re-
produces liberation songs and writings. Barbara Masekela, a former

Rutgers University English professor and brother of singer Hugh Masekela, heads the office.

The treasurer-general administers ANC farms and light factories, each conceived to maximize the movement's self-sufficiency in host nations, and keeps track of the group's real-estate holdings, auto fleets, supplies, and fundraising. From Congress coffers individuals receive between thirteen and twenty-six dollars per month in cash "salaries," though most basic needs, such as clothing, food, housing, and transportation, are arranged for on a communal basis.[22] The womens' section provides staff for day-care and health facilities. The youth section is the chief conduit for transmitting leadership decisions to, and rank-and-file concerns from, the large pool of young South Africans who escaped the Republic after 1975.

The security of ANC operations in sanctuary states is the province of a separate department. The 1985 consultative conference endorsed a rigid code of conduct proposed by security officials for all Congress members to guard against espionage. It includes secrecy and strict limits on social relations with non-ANC people. A form of internal police, the security department also screens proposed new and suspected members to filter out South African agents and inspects parcels for the presence of South African bombs. In addition, its workmen maintain elaborate protective devices, including gates, grilles, walls, and alarms, around Lusaka's ANC buildings. Many high-level Congress personnel are required by security rules to sleep each night in different homes to confound South African intelligence operatives who could direct assassination attacks on them.

Thabo Mbeki's department of information controls everything from press releases claiming credit for bomb attacks to smuggling copies of ANC literature into South Africa. Mbeki, an eloquent British-educated economist, is one of the rising leaders within the ANC. In European and African print shops, his staff produces the periodic *Sechaba* magazine, edited by Francis Meli, which discusses party positions; the *ANC Weekly News Briefing,* a summary of press reports on resistance activities; and dozens of other leaflets and posters. A secret "internal section" operates an underground network to distribute publications and cassette tapes inside South Africa. Mbeki also administers Radio Freedom, which regularly beams ANC news and propaganda into the Republic from broadcasting facilities in Zambia, Ethiopia, Angola, Tanzania, and Madagascar. Nevertheless, Mbeki's efforts to improve the Congress's poor public relations in the United States and Europe have often been blocked by both young and veteran militants distrustful of Western media or opposed to any warming of relations with capitalist countries.

Strategies to promote ideological stability within the Congress are formulated in the political department, while the external missions of the international affairs office aim to explain ANC positions and solicit world support for the organization.

Finally, the bureaucracy of the military wing, Umkhonto we Sizwe, exerts increasing influence within the ANC orbit. Absorbing the bulk of the Congress's sanctuary state personnel and half its money and matériel, MK is nearly an autonomous body. Commander Joe Modise, reported to be a forceful and confident man, only rarely leaves his camps in Angola to consult with the political leadership in Lusaka. His troops are far more combative than the older generation, and their obsession with battle has helped persuade the NEC to make guerrilla warfare the central tactic of resistance to apartheid. At the 1985 consultative conference, amid chants of "Mayhlome," or "Let us go to war," the delegates established a War Council to manage MK operations. At the same time, they directed every ANC member in exile to complete a course in military training in Angola, and declared 1986 "The Year of Umkhonto we Sizwe."[23]

Despite the apparent flow-chart efficiency of the ANC's extensive capital administration, the Congress's work is often undermined both by bureaucratic measures imposed to account for security concerns and by logistical problems characteristic of developing countries. To forestall damage from potential breaches in security, the Congress is thoroughly compartmentalized. Administrators in arts and culture, for example, profess not to know how the resistance songs they produce on Swedish or Soviet-made albums are delivered to the internal underground. Nor, apparently, are they aware of the mechanism by which liberation music constantly springing up in black-labor hostels inside South Africa finds its way into the hands of craftsmen in Lusaka for recording and later broadcast on Radio Freedom. "It is not for us to know who is working on this," asserts department administrator Barbara Masekela.[24] Similarly, other exile bureaucrats are permitted access only to those operations about which they need to know. In the event of capture and torture, such officials would presumably be able to divulge only a limited amount of information about the ANC.

The obsession with security, in fact, has caused the emergence of an entire bureaucratic culture of subterfuge. It extends from prudent assumptions that all phones, offices, and even cars may be tapped, to keeping travel arrangements fluid and confidential to deter kidnappings.

Compartmentalization and secrecy may block South African espionage, but it severely erodes the efficiency of the external ANC. Often major figures depart without notice and reappear without warning, causing permanent confusion in planning. Communications and coordination between leaders and departments or foreign missions are slow and sporadic. Those doing business with the ANC complain that few members below departmental secretary level are confident enough or authorized to act without the approval of superiors, who may be only unpredictably available.

Logistical problems make yet more cumbersome the flow of operations. Because Zambia, Angola, and Tanzania all lack sufficient foreign-currency reserves, all suffer from chronic electrical outages, gas shortages, runs on spare parts, and equipment breakdowns. Congress members complain that vehicles are frequently incapacitated, aircraft grounded, and telephones inoperable.

For some of these reasons, the ANC bureaucracy to many seems slow and inscrutable—at best furtive, at worst incompetent. The ANC "may be one of the world's least effective 'liberation movements,'" concluded *New York Times* correspondent Joseph Lelyveld, who waited in vain for three days in Lusaka to conduct interviews promised by President Tambo.[25]

Ponderous overcaution, in short, appears to protect the activities of the movement from Pretoria's sight, thus giving Umkhonto the potential advantage of surprise in its attacks. It also backfires by undermining the party's attempts to project an image of a responsible and confident contender for power. Were it not for the volcanic impatience of the thousands of youths swelling the Congress's ranks, the weight of bureaucracy might indeed have seriously retarded the ANC's move toward an aggressive buildup of resistance. But that angry new constituency refuses to allow anti-apartheid belligerence to wane as it did in the 1960s. The Soweto generation of South Africa is demonstrating its dissatisfaction with anything less than all-out guerrilla warfare.

THE RANK AND FILE

An account related in Dar es Salaam by ANC official "John Moloise," who asks that his real name remain confidential, symbolizes the rites of passage which each one of thousands of new Congress recruits underwent in the 1970s.

Wielding wire cutters, eight young blacks from the Eastern Cape crouched in the unfamiliar mountain bush listening nervously for South African border patrols. It was 1972, and only the beginning of what would become a mass exodus of students from the Republic. But Moloise was ready to leave. Politically active though only vaguely aware of the ANC, he had succeeded in contacting its underground weeks earlier. A Congress agent, one of many under recent orders to enlist new members, performed quiet background checks to satisfy himself that Moloise was a legitimate activist and not a South African informer. Then, on a day when he could obtain a pickup truck, the agent assembled Moloise and seven others eager to join the liberation movement abroad. The driver motored evenly toward Swaziland, doing nothing to attract police suspicion. Near dusk, Moloise and his fellow recruits scrambled from the truck into the thick frontier bush and waited for nightfall. The driver headed home.

Moloise was frightened as they quickly cut through the barbed wire-topped border fence. Once inside Swaziland, the group walked for hours before finally making contact with the ANC. The head of the Swazi mission dispatched part of the group to Angola for military training. Moloise was assigned to the ANC's transportation pool. For months he worked in Manzini, Swaziland, learning auto mechanics until someone tipped off the police about him. An ANC functionary quickly drove him to the Mozambique border. Climbing over the fence, Moloise made his way to Maputo, where he helped repair and maintain the ANC's fleet of twenty-five vehicles until the Nkomati accord forced all but a skeleton diplomatic staff to leave the country for the sanctuary states in the north.[26]

By 1976 South Africa was shedding rebellious dissidents at the rate of 450 each month. Individually or in organized groups, they were illegally slipping across the borders into Swaziland, Botswana,

Mozambique, or Lesotho. Most were young men and women, like Moloise, who had been attending township schools; but an estimated one-fifth were adults.

The exodus was most telling in Soweto. In 1978 only 14,379 students were registered in township schools compared to 34,656 in the first half of 1976. The black newspaper *World* observed that "Soweto's youth has disappeared." Some of the missing 20,277 had been killed; others were still in detention; more had dropped out altogether or moved to other townships illegally; and others still had escaped abroad.

For those who did leave the country without permission, Justice Minister Jimmy Kruger offered a one-week amnesty—though the program applied only to the offense of illegal departure, not to other crimes. Some parents reportedly traveled to Swaziland and Botswana to urge their offspring to return, but Kruger eventually admitted that only two refugees had taken advantage of the amnesty and come back. Police later charged that some three hundred of the parents who had applied for travel documents were in fact transporting their other children out of the country.[27] The rate of exodus peaked during the period between October 1976 and mid-1977, after which it eased to approximately 250 per month into 1978. By 1979 only some forty to fifty illegal refugees per month were crossing South Africa's borders for sanctuary abroad.

Prior to 1975, the total estimated ANC population outside South Africa was one thousand. Only five years later it stood at nine thousand. Some 75 percent of the twelve thousand escaping blacks had joined the ANC. The remainder had contacted the PAC or elected to fend for themselves.

The Congress was able to reap the harvest of Soweto-era recruits on account of its growing presence in the region and the relative breadth of advantages it could offer. ANC undercover agents helped shepherd youths to the border. ANC officials in frontier states could extend protection and transportation to sanctuary states. Like Moloise, each recruit could be assigned to skilled training, military courses, academic institutions, or administrative offices. In effect, an ANC infrastructure had been put into place, prepared and hoping for just the kind of exodus that started to occur in the mid-1970s.

The outflow of dissidents slowed to a trickle once again after 1979. But the renewal of widespread political unrest in 1985 con-

vinced a new wave of angry blacks to escape their country. This time
domestic Congress cells were under orders from Lusaka to try and
contain the exodus. Its Angolan camps already filled with trained
and impatient soldiers, MK needed more eager recruits to stay at
home to assist returning guerrillas and to learn military techniques
from them. Escape trails in any case were far more hazardous, owing
to new defense force border barriers. Nevertheless, an estimated five
to six thousand left the country, most seeking out the ANC. By
1986, the entire expatriate Congress community totaled between
thirteen and fourteen thousand.

Where exile members are assigned to live and work depends on
whether they are sent to Umkhonto or to the ANC's civil operations.
Umkhonto is thought to claim some 60 percent of the organization's
personnel,[28] giving it, by 1986, approximately eight thousand men
and women under arms. These in turn were divided into combat-
ready troops awaiting missions and new recruits undergoing military
training. The more than five thousand South Africans on the nonmilitary side were either given duties in civil service departments or
enrolled in educational programs.

The majority of those who fled South Africa after 1975 were
young men and women with sufficient initiative to have attended
school, organized anti-apartheid protests, and evaded capture on
their way out of the country. Yet ANC educators observe that a
number of students joining the exile community show signs of severe
mental stress. "Some have been through torture," said Tim Maseko,
principal of the ANC's high school at Mazimbu, Tanzania. "There
are students here who have been chased down and arrested, who've
had their arms and skulls cracked in detention . . . some come here
actually demented."[29] All but a handful escaped alone, with little or
no money, leaving their families at home, making clandestine jour-
neys often described as harrowing owing to the constant danger of
capture by government security patrols.

Such experiences of violence and repression in South Africa
drive most recent exiles not to the extremity of mental breakdown
but to a state of rage their elders in the ANC had nearly forgotten.
The opening of a new generation gap was inevitable. "We were
tolerant, non-violent, convinced we could reason with whites," explained a top ANC veteran in Tanzania who had escaped South
Africa in 1966. "Not the 1976 group. They are very intolerant,
completely violent and ready to fight on the spur of the moment."[30]

The sudden influx of so many new people in so short a time indeed posed a threat to Congress's stability, particularly since most of the Soweto-era exiles had become active through the Africanist black consciousness movement rather than the nonracial ANC. The leadership, by means of a network of political commissars, sought quickly to school the enrollees in ANC political culture to avoid intergenerational skirmishes over traditional controversies such as the role of whites or communists in the alliance. At the Mazimbu complex, for example, commissars are assigned groups of fifteen to twenty students for fortnightly discussions on ANC positions.[31]

The new recruits for the most part appeared to accept nonracialism in the ANC, thereby surprising observers who expected them to echo BCM's persistent criticism of white participation in resistance. But the pages of *Sechaba,* the party's organ for defining strategy, reflect continuing debate over whether the struggle should be a Marxist-oriented proletarian revolution, or one that embraces all classes. The Christian-educated, Rivonia generation leadership has shown that it is prepared to cooperate with any class or race of allies seen as capable of weakening apartheid. Executives buttress their flexible approach by reiterating that the Freedom Charter, far from being a Marxist document, calls for democracy and free enterprise, in addition to a measure of nationalization.

But Marxist theory seems to have attracted increasing support among the young since 1980. Part of the reason is that aid from the Soviet bloc—seen in everything from trucks to East German weapons instructors—is designed to be highly visible, and communist ANC executives such as MK Chief of Staff Joe Slovo have wide influence in the military. "To the students, socialist countries are food, clothes, transport—everything they need," said one ANC instructor.[32] In addition, the Soviets have been able to help define world problems for rank-and file-members through its sympathetic African radio service. To many, therefore, the South African Communist Party and the Soviets have come to be identified as friends of the struggle. Reinforcing this view is Pretoria's unrelenting campaign to portray world communism as its chief adversary, a charge that frightens white constituents but suggests to many activist blacks that communism may be the most effective weapon against apartheid.

The Reagan administration's six-year "constructive engagement" policy of friendly relations with Pretoria also served to disillu-

sion those youths who had seen under President Jimmy Carter some
hope of United States opposition to apartheid. "One can identify an
enemy, as one can identify a friend," explained one student at
Mazimbu. "The Reagan administration has declared itself an enemy
to us. It supports South Africa, which illegally upholds apartheid,
and points to us as terrorists."[33] Many of the angry young, encouraged by Soviet propaganda, do not distinguish between the world's
largest capitalist nation and capitalism itself when they brand the
United States their foe.

The most frequent point of friction between the generations,
however, is the question of how central a role armed resistance
should play in overall ANC strategy. "The older generation is committed only to a controlled armed struggle," asserted a high-placed
Tanzania-based ANC administrator in 1983. "We do not hurt
civilians. Our boys pass through those northern [Transvaal] farms
and don't hurt anyone. We've shown we can hit everywhere, even as
far down as Cape Town. But they are always strategic installations,
not people. It is only a matter of time before the younger men take
over. This is our fear: the wholesale burning of the country. We want
to avoid that. We are not mad. It's easy to destroy, much harder to
rebuild."[34]

But the younger generation now represents the overwhelming
majority, perhaps over two-thirds, of the ANC's external population.
Only a few trusted ones have been admitted to the National Executive Committee, but the impatience of the new generation has made
itself felt in military affairs. At the 1985 consultative conference,
delegates passed a landmark resolution, generated in preconvention
caucuses of the rank and file, to abandon the traditional avoidance of
human casualties in MK missions. "The distinction between 'hard'
and 'soft' targets should disappear," *Sechaba* announced.[35] Shortly
thereafter Radio Freedom urged its followers to carry the war into
white areas. No longer would Umkhonto units pass through farms
with orders prohibiting harm to white owners, a policy proudly imposed by the Rivonia generation. Late in 1985, in fact, MK land-
mines on agricultural properties near the Zimbabwe border began to
erupt, killing or wounding farmers and estate workers.

The worst fears of Congress's veterans are unlikely to be realized,
however, as long as they remain in full control of ANC leadership.
The "old guard" yielded to populist pressure by accepting the 1985

conference resolution dropping the rule against human casualties. But in the day-to-day management of operations, the veterans continued periodically to discourage, and even condemn, attacks by MK guerrillas that specifically targeted civilians. When an underground Umkhonto man planted explosives that killed five whites at a seaside Durban shopping center in 1985, the Lusaka headquarters reacted by characterizing the attack as "inconsistent" with ANC policy. Even if many had interpreted "soft" targets to mean civilians, the leadership had chosen to define them narrowly as military and police personnel.

The Rivonia generation was still trying to limit the armed conflict, hoping to sponsor actions that, while violent, would leave the ANC with a reputation of responsibility and restraint. As the NEC reminded the 1985 consultative conference delegates, in a tone suggestive of the scolding of youths, "if we seriously consider ourselves as the alternative government of our country, then we need to act and operate both as an insurrectionary force and a credible representative of a liberated South Africa."[36] Congress's militants, who are accumulating more power within the movement, do not appear to agree. The question is how long they can be restrained.

WAGING EDUCATION

Lying three-hours' drive west into the bush from Dar es Salaam, Tanzania, is Mazimbu, one of the ANC's largest exile camps. Built since 1979 as a refugee educational center, it is situated on a 3,400-acre abandoned sisal plantation that the Tanzanian government donated to the ANC in the late 1970s. Some seventy standardized concrete and brick buildings topped with metal roofs accommodate South Africans of nearly all ages amid cultivated fields. The project is bounded on three sides by mountains and scattered baobab trees. Plans call for expanding the facility to house 2,400 students. In addition to teaching traditional subjects, Mazimbu represents the leadership's most ambitious scheme to ground its young in the political values of the party.

"After Soweto, when our children saw each other getting shot down in the streets, when they realized the viciousness of what they were up against, they started to pour out of South Africa. We needed somewhere for these young people—adolescents as well as their teachers—to go," explains an ANC official. The Congress concluded that it needed not just barracks, but a means of integrating enlistees into the culture of their new organizational home. It thus founded at Mazimbu the Solomon Mahlangu Freedom College, or SOMAFCO, after the first Umkhonto soldier to be hanged by the South African government. The Mazimbu complex was also constructed with a day-care center for infants five months to three years old, a nursery school, and a primary school. Many parents of the smaller children are based at Umkhonto barracks in Angola.

SOMAFCO is the centerpiece of Mazimbu. In addition, a cluster of buildings forms "Kliptown"—named after the site where the Freedom Charter was signed—where ANC managers have established a variety of manufacturing enterprises designed to maximize the community's self-sufficiency. Mazimbu's farm grows enough corn, sorghum, and beans to stock dormitory kitchens. Other fields are being expanded to provide fruits and vegetables, and sunflower seed for animal feed. ANC workers in a small garment factory manufacture curtains, bedding, and student uniforms. A woodworking factory uses local lumber to construct furniture as well as doors and trim for the buildings. Canning and oil processing plants are scheduled to be introduced in the future. The nearby ten thousand-acre Dakawa farm, developed to house new exiles, is a ready destination for Mazimbu products. The theory promoted by Mazimbu administrators is that each worker in these enterprises should be thoroughly skilled in operations so as to be able to manage a similar factory in South Africa once the ANC assumes power.

Educators are charged with persuading SOMAFCO's students to major in vocational or technical training since the ANC argues it can send no more than 20 percent on to universities in Africa or abroad. An estimated four hundred Congress members, for example, receive scholarships each year to study in Soviet bloc universities. At Mazimbu, however, the campaign to discourage advanced education clashes with the high aspirations of numerous youths who consider the manual arts demeaning. Most expect to transfer to Angola for military training upon completion of their studies, but even reaching that point is an arduous process for blacks whose schooling in South Africa tended to be inadequate, interrupted by boycotts, or altogether nonexistent. Remedial courses are deemed necessary for most exiled students. Ages in the primary school, for example, range from six to as high as nineteen, and in the high school up to the mid-twenties. Because barely one-quarter of the white and black instructors are certified teachers, SOMAFCO cannot meet individual needs effectively, though it claims to do so better than most black education programs inside South Africa.

Another hurdle that administrators face are the resource shortages endemic to Tanzania. In a typical month in 1983, half of the complex's fleet of sixty vehicles were disabled for want of tires and spare parts. Work on a dozen new buildings ground to a halt for lack of cement. No yeast or flour could be found to make bread. Bureaucratic delays of up to six months regularly bottled up critical shipments of supplies and equipment in the congested port of Dar es Salaam.

Though Tanzania's logistical problems lie beyond the control of the Mazimbu administration, the task of political education is well within its reach. In fact, SOMAFCO's students are closely supervised, taught, and guided by a complex-wide network of agents linked directly to Lusaka. Two lines of authority converge in the figure of Mohammed Tikly, director of the ANC's Mazimbu operations. One is the administrative staff of the facility, who are involved in such functions as teaching, supervising cafeterias, managing a health clinic, tracking supplies, keeping accounts, organizing transportation, and planning construction. For each duty, staff are posted to Mazimbu through Lusaka cabinet departments. The clinic, for example, is headed by medics trained by and assigned to the ANC's department of health. Similarly, those responsible for financial records, supplies, and vehicles are dispatched to Mazimbu by the ANC treasurer-general's office. The teaching staff comes from the department of education. While at the complex, the heads of Mazimbu's various offices participate in decision making through a directorate and are accountable through it to Tikly.

A parallel network links SOMAFCO with ideological functionaries guided by the ANC leadership's political department. Unlike the National Executive Committee, which shuns the term "politburo," the chief political body at Mazimbu is known by the Soviet appellation "commissariat." Ironically, one of its prime tasks is to dampen enthusiasm for Marxist radicalism. The staff it fields throughout Mazimbu are known as commissars. Though the com-

missariat works with the complex director, it is also directly accountable to the Regional Political Committee, responsible for all Tanzanian operations, and the country's chief ANC representative.

At the high school, for example, a commissar is appointed to
each eight-person dormitory room. Supervising each is a building
commissar, who in turn is overseen by a unit commissar. Presiding
over this network is a student commissar, who reports in tandem
with his counterpart supervising the staff to the school commissar.
Similar hierarchies exist in Mazimbu's other institutions, making it
unlikely that much could occur at any of them which would escape
the notice of these operatives.

Chief among the orders given to commissars is the task of guid-
ing both staff and students to think and act along Congress-approved
political lines. "The commissar makes sure that everyone receives
ANC publications," explains director Tikly. "He supervises political education, makes sure that meetings are held and that political
activities are right." He is responsible, according to principal Tim
Maseko, for the "political life" of the campus.

The commissar system is the Congress leadership's method of
channeling the wrath and impatience of the young into behavior
consistent with ANC policy. Commissars teach the new generation
lessons drawn by veterans from their decades of anti-apartheid resistance. They also coach students to contain their fervor for controversial ideologies such as black consciousness or Marxism until after
majority rule is achieved. The leadership wants above all to preserve
stability and unity within the ANC. If recent exiles are allowed freely
to espouse ideologies of racial or class exclusivism, it is feared, they
could open movement-wide schisms that, for now, lie buried while
waiting for liberation.

The commissars, therefore, serve as the eyes and ears of Congress's leaders, probing in dorms and overheard discussions for potential sources of ideological unrest and trying to reform politically
wayward behavior. In addition, their work often spills over into
social welfare, as commissars find themselves counseling students
against skipping required duties, drinking, fist fights, or theft. It also
makes them a de facto security force, watching for youths who might
be reporting back to South African intelligence.

SOMAFCO's curriculum is fashioned by commissars and teachers to reflect the ANC's goals for the school. Since most graduates

enter either Umkhonto we Sizwe or one of Congress's administrative departments, political training is considered essential. As a result, along with English, math, biology, agriculture, and geography, the five-year high-school curriculum includes a required course entitled "History of the Struggle," as well as an ANC-oriented survey of world events. From an early age, children housed at the complex are taught the names of Congress leaders. Even nursery schoolers sing black nationalist jingles such as "Solomon Mahlangu / You are a hero / Solomon Mahlangu / Son of Africa," along with Mother Goose rhymes.

"This must be one of the most political spots on earth," observes Rica Hodgson, one of Mazimbu's white administrators. Priding itself on its democratic decision making, SOMAFCO contains a battery of student committees that each day hammer out school policy, discuss resistance affairs, and repeat Radio Moscow news for debate in the evenings. Politics, in fact, dominates almost every aspect of life in Mazimbu during almost every waking hour. The ANC's goal is not only to educate but also to mobilize the community in the enterprise of anti-apartheid resistance. For this reason, though they are situated over a thousand miles north of the Limpopo, Mazimbu's inhabitants consider the complex a "front" in South Africa's civil war. It is not, however, a traditional combat facility. In 1983 there was no evidence of arms, military or paramilitary training, or even such passive defenses as bomb shelters. In fact, the school reportedly requested a small detachment of MK troops for security, but ANC headquarters in Lusaka rejected the idea, reasoning that militarizing the school even to that extent would more likely attract a South African attack than protect against it.

Mazimbu appears to be succeeding in assimilating new exiles into the ANC's political culture. "We have declared ourselves part and parcel of the struggle," said one SOMAFCO senior in 1983. "We have given ourselves to the ANC. Once we finish here, the ANC has the right to put us anywhere we could best serve." He was scheduled to enroll in medical courses and join Umkhonto as what he termed a "doctor-soldier." Mazimbu's schools are annually adding educated, fiercely dedicated men and women like him to the ANC's pool of guerrillas and administrators. Nevertheless, the leadership remains concerned that the Soweto generation's militancy will overpower the ANC's capacity to master it.

SPEARS AND SHIELDS

On the other side of Africa, in the bushlands of Angola, Umkhonto we Sizwe marshals an estimated $50 million in resources to prosecute its widening military challenge to a government over one thousand miles to the south. Controlling more than half of the ANC's external manpower, MK is simultaneously the most secretive and the most important element of the movement's sanctuary-state bureaucracy.

The bulk of MK's estimated eight thousand troops fill barracks in at least four settlements in Angola, if police intelligence evidence introduced at South African security trials is to be believed. The ANC itself reveals little information concerning its military wing. Camps are located at Quibaxe, some one hundred miles northeast of Luanda, Benguela, the coastal railhead town immediately south of the port of Lobito, and Funda, just twenty miles east of Luanda. The fourth is listed as Nova Gagenga, though police testimony does not identify where it lies.[37] Camps formerly used for the training of ZAPU troops in Zimbabwe's war, such as one in Boma township outside Luso and another near Sa' da Bandeira, may also have been made available to the ANC. They are known to be Spartan facilities, and some are in malaria-infested areas. Oliver Tambo observed in 1984 that "a remarkable number of lives" had been lost in MK to the disease.[38]

By 1980, at least five to six hundred MK cadets were believed to be in training at Funda under Soviet, East German, and ANC instructors.[39] The population of other facilities was unknown. To accommodate the influx of new recruits, all the Angolan bases were scheduled to be expanded. Since the Congress places a priority on reducing the burden of its presence on the host country, each of the bases and settlements was ordered to develop agricultural land to provide food, grains, and income. Technical experts were working in the mid-1980s on seeding a new fifteen thousand-acre ANC farm, the first of several planned in various parts of the country.[40] While most MK guerrillas dwell in Angola, commanders are also reported to have assigned some troops to camps in Tanzania.[41] In addition, the more promising soldiers, officers, and future instructors are dispatched to academies in the Soviet Union, East Germany,[42] or Ethiopia[43] for advanced training.

Until 1984, when under the Nkomati accord the late president Samora Machel ejected all but a handful of ANC officials, Umkhonto had operated two bases in Mozambique. Villagelike and hidden in the bush, the encampments occupied a precarious status in a country under a South African economic and military siege designed to compel a break with the Congress. To minimize Mozambique's liability for ANC attacks inside South Africa and to protect its own personnel, MK commanders deployed the frontier state camps as staging areas for troops based elsewhere. Flown or driven into Mozambique, most Umkhonto insurgents would pause in the country only long enough to collect orders and begin the clandestine trek into South Africa.

One of the camps was situated in a lowland area near the coastal village of Ponta do Ouro, just three miles north of Natal.[44] The second, constructed in 1975 as Machel's FRELIMO party was taking power, was reported to be located near the confluence of the Rio dos Elefantes and Limpopo River, within striking distance of the South African border at Kruger National Park in northern Transvaal.[45] In addition to the camps, the Congress occupied a fortified compound in the Maputo suburb of Matola which, in part, was believed to have served as a frontline planning office for military and political operations inside South Africa. It was assaulted by a fifty-man SADF incursion force in 1981, leaving thirteen Congress workers dead and three buildings in ruins.[46]

When the Nkomati accord all but shut down MK's Mozambican bases, the ANC's capacity to infiltrate guerrillas, arms, and communications into South Africa was severely impaired. Like the other border states, Mozambique would now be hostile territory, available only for fewer and riskier transits by Congress operatives.

The only other MK frontier camp known to have existed was a ZAPU base in southwest Zimbabwe, near Bulawayo. In 1979–80, as the Rhodesian war was reaching a climax, Umkhonto had secretly ordered some one hundred soldiers across the Botswana border into a zone occupied by ZAPU troops under the command of ANC ally Joshua Nkomo. Before any guerrilla missions could be launched, however, the new ZANU prime minister, Robert Mugabe, quietly insisted that the insurgents be withdrawn to Zambia.[47]

The Congress, of course, had made the mistake of picking the losing party in Zimbabwe's new order. ZANU had long been associated with the PAC. But Oliver Tambo led a prominent delegation to the country's independence festivities in 1980 and quickly sought to establish a working relationship with ZANU. Mugabe permitted a seven-person office to open in Harare, and he allowed fifty MK veterans who had fought the Rhodesian army with ZAPU soldiers in 1967 to stay. Cautiously, Umkhonto began sending guerrillas through Zimbabwe to South Africa. In 1985 and 1986 its soldiers were believed to have slipped across the Limpopo River to plant explosive mines on northern Transvaal farms. Other border states—Botswana, Swaziland, and Lesotho—have at various times admitted nonmilitary ANC delegations that often included undercover members of an MK transit command staff. Even if Umkhonto could not risk establishing bases in frontier nations, its transit command could organize rapid infiltration of guerrillas, relays of escaping recruits to sanctuary states, and a skeletal courier system to ferry arms into the Republic.

Until a leak revealed his identity in 1982, Umkhonto's top general was known only by the pseudonym "Thabo More." Joe Modise still avoids public contact and only rarely leaves his Angolan bases for ANC headquarters in Lusaka. He is called simply "the Commander," and few details are available about his background apart from his short career as a Johannesburg truck driver and subsequent departure in 1962. He reportedly rose through Umkhonto's ranks, having earned a reputation as a tough fighter by infiltrating South Africa, battling police, and returning to Angola, according to ANC lore.[48] Born in 1931, Modise is considered a forceful, decisive man whose word carries weight inside both Umkhonto and the National Executive Committee.

Whereas other generals in guerrilla wars have welcomed controlled media attention, Modise shuns even the ANC's own propaganda organs, let alone the international press. Officials in the ANC's publicity department have difficulty prying information out of MK. "It is a very closed organization," said one public relations deputy. "When three of our boys were executed recently, our office had no biographies of them. MK did, and it just had no interest or understanding about getting them quickly to Lusaka."[49]

Serving under Modise as chief of staff is Communist Party chairman Joe Slovo, often portrayed by Pretoria as a colonel in the KGB and the genius behind the ANC. A lawyer by profession, Slovo was born in 1926 in Lithuania and moved with his family to South Africa. He helped to found the short-lived Congress of Democrats and acted as defense counsel for a variety of political trials, including, in 1956, his own. Treason charges were dropped two years later, and Slovo stayed politically active. He left for Britain in the wake of Umkhonto's collapse in 1963 and, over a decade later, transferred to Africa to help revive the ANC's guerrilla army. His wife, writer Ruth First, was assassinated in Mozambique in 1982 when a letter-bomb exploded in her university office.

Slovo's charge is administration, a task that presumably involves everything from obtaining weapons, uniforms, and barracks to helping select soldiers and choose sabotage targets. But like Mazimbu, MK is woven together by a parallel web of political commissars who also participate in major decision making. Heading the network is Chris Hani, a veteran member of the ANC's National Executive Committee who fought in Umkhonto's ill-fated incursion into Rhodesia in 1967 and has narrowly missed being assassinated in Lesotho on several occasions. Though little is known of his responsibilities, one can infer from the SOMAFCO model that he presides over a staff of commissars that instructs, monitors, and counsels MK's guerrillas. Political commissars may be appointed for groups as small as eight troops, with each official accountable to unit and base commissars and, ultimately, to Hani. As at Mazimbu, the commissars can be expected to guard against outbreaks of political dissent. Apostasy may be considered especially deadly in the ranks of Umkhonto, where guns are readily available. One rumor suggested that a 1984 camp "rebellion" was harshly suppressed.[50]

In monitoring troops, the MK commissariat no doubt acts as a key line of defense against penetration by South African intelligence agents. Political officials often broadcast warnings to ANC activists over Radio Freedom to be vigilant against infiltrators. But Hani's principal mission is to generate an ideologically charged atmosphere that contains dissatisfaction or impatience and enforces political discipline. Umkhonto's Angola bases probably rival Mazimbu in being "the most political spot[s] on earth."

On a daily basis, MK recruits undergo what the South African government itself describes as "remarkably detailed training" in insurgency tactics.[51] A typical instruction program focuses on techniques of sabotage, covert communication and transportation, and reconnaissance. Soldiers practice using Soviet-bloc firearms, Israeli-made Uzi submachine guns, standard issue SADF weaponry, land mines, and plastic explosives. In January 1986, Chris Hani reported to South Africans over Radio Freedom that MK guerrillas were trained in "the skills of ambushing the enemy . . . raiding for weapons in order to capture them . . . fighting in small groups . . . camouflaging . . . [and] attacking when the enemy least expects you."[52] Called upon to show the court the quality of military training in Angola, captured MK guerrilla James Mange was once asked during his 1979 trial to demonstrate his expertise. Taking over from a befuddled SADF antiaircraft expert, Mange quickly explained how to repair, disassemble, couple to a vehicle, and deploy in firing position a sophisticated Soviet-made antiaircraft cannon.[53]

Only rarely did Umkhonto insurgents field such advanced weapons in actual combat. A normal cluster of arms allotted to a courier or guerrilla from the MK armory would include hand grenades with detonators, blocks of dynamite with detonators, land and limpet mines, timers, and machine pistols with ammunition. Three components—hand grenades, explosives, and small arms—formed the backbone of Umkhonto's weapons resources.

The caches uncovered in recent years by police in South Africa yield a sketch of what Umkhonto's real operational arsenal in the sanctuary states looks like. MK stocks include four basic brands of firearms. Most frequently assigned to troops is the 20-inch-long Czech-made Skorpion VZOR 61 7.65mm machine pistol. Weighing four pounds, it can shoot on automatic up to 840 rounds per minute accurately as far as 219 yards away from the target. The Soviet Tokarev TT-33 7.62mm pistol, half as heavy and as long, is a nonautomatic weapon that fires only 32 rounds per minute at a maximum range of 55 yards. Also supplied is the Makarov SL 9mm pistol, manufactured in the Soviet Union, which is smaller and lighter than the Tokarev but provides comparable power and range. On a larger scale, Umkhonto soldiers often carry the popular AK-47, which at ten pounds and 34 inches long can fire on automatic as many as 600 rounds per minute from 330 yards away.

Four varieties of Soviet-made hand grenades dominate Umkhonto's storerooms of explosives. The RG-42 antipersonnel device is considered by experts to be "defensive" in that it must be hurled from behind cover to guard the thrower against the 75-foot-wide circle of shrapnel the weapon is designed to produce. Even more dangerous is the F1, whose fragmentation radius is up to 600 feet from point of impact. The RGD-5 is lighter and more compact than other Soviet grenades, but is similar in effect to the RG-42. Seen rarely is the RGD Mark II, termed "offensive" because its smaller blast range permits a charging rather than a protected assault on targets.[54]

Only the Makarov and the RGD-5 grenade, of all these weapons, are in active military service in Soviet or East European forces. Manufacture of the Skorpion has ended, so that its appearance suggested a Czech or Soviet policy of drawing down stocks of the machine pistol. The Tokarev is no longer used by the Warsaw Pact, having been replaced by the lighter, smaller Makarov. The AK-47, distributed in various trouble spots around the world, is considered competitive with the later model US M-16. But it has been withdrawn from Warsaw Pact service in favor of the advanced AKM version. The Soviet Union no longer manufactures it, leaving the task to Bulgaria, East Germany, Hungary, Poland, Rumania, and Yugoslavia. Neither the RG-42 nor the F1 grenades have seen active military use in the Warsaw Pact since immediately following World War II.

In short, Umkhonto's arsenal has consisted largely of surplus supplies of outdated Soviet and East European munitions. The weapons also represent a comparatively low level of firepower. The Tokarev and Makarov pistols are essentially protective weapons rather than assault guns. The AK-47, which *is* an assault gun, is not found as frequently as the two pistols, though the trend in recent years is toward increasing use of this reliable weapon. The Skorpion, one of the most common MK guns, is used best in quick surprise attacks such as assassinations rather than in operations that risk battle, since its range is no match against heavier South African machine weapons.

Such armaments help determine specific combat tactics. The range of weapons made available in large quantities to the ANC permit an insurgent to concentrate most effectively on rapid, self-protected assaults on stationary targets. The plastic explosives, mines, and dynamite distributed to MK operatives also enable sabotage attacks. Few of the arms endow guerrillas with the capacity directly to engage units of the South African defense establishment in battle. On occasion, Umkhonto rebels have infiltrated South Af-

rica with sophisticated weaponry such as missiles and rocket-pro-
pelled grenades. But most Soviet-bloc supplies at the Angolan
camps, whether through donor restrictions or ANC request, appeared
to be the more primitive, inexpensive variety.

PAYING THE BILLS

The treasurer-general's department, headed by Thomas Nkobi, administers the funds that keep the Congress's counter-government and
counter-army financially afloat. President Tambo has also assigned
Nkobi the responsibility of developing innovative moneymaking
projects and keeping track of nonmilitary supplies and equipment.
Financial officials estimate the ANC's annual nonmilitary budget at
$50 million. Umkhonto's needs approach an additional $50 million,
according to publicity chief Thabo Mbeki, but most of that is controlled secretly by army budget officials in Angola. Acting as a
borderless welfare state, the ANC supplies food, clothes, housing,
transportation, and health care to its more than thirteen thousand
constituents living outside South Africa. Each also receives a paltry
allowance: about $8.33 per month for a student, or a token salary up
to $26 per month for administrators and soldiers. These direct cash
payments alone must amount to approximately $3.6 million per
year.[55]

The treasury funds the overhead for twenty-eight official foreign
missions in Africa, Europe, Asia, and the United States as well as its
Lusaka headquarters. Transportation costs involve travel to and from
many of these offices by top ANC officials. But they also include the
maintenance and fueling of a fleet of more than two hundred cars,
trucks, and tractors stretched across the sanctuary states. The Congress owns or rents approximately thirty thousand acres of agricultural real estate and hundreds of buildings in southern Africa.
Umkhonto also requires new stocks of weapons to expand its guerrilla war. To pay its way, the ANC depends on its own income-
generating projects and fund-raising, and on major donations, both
cash and in-kind, from governments, international organizations,
and private sources.

Farms and small factories have been started to promote self-
sufficiency in food, clothes, furniture, and construction. In most
cases the ANC deliberately employs host-state nationals, at union

wage, to foster local goodwill. The 3,300-acre Chongella farm, twen-ty-two miles from Lusaka, is worked by Zambian laborers to produce vegetables, corn, poultry, and cattle for the ANC community. Managers channel surpluses into the Zambian market to generate income. Similarly, Mazimbu's furniture factory employs fifty Tan-zanians and twenty Congress students, and its products are built for both community needs and market sales.

In few cases, however, are the projects truly self-sufficient. Chongella has depended on a $500,000 grant and equipment sup-plied by the United Nations High Commission for Refugees. The Mazimbu factory is aided by training provided by East Germany, Denmark, Zambia, and Tanzania. Next door, the complex's garment factory operates Dutch-donated machines using fabric sent from East Germany. Nevertheless, the commercial ventures are nurtured by ANC budget officials as sources of revenue. They also provide an opportunity for vocational training and are a source of pride for a community whose way of life, in most other respects, compels de-pendence on others.

Folded into Nkobi's treasury department is a fund-raising staff which Mbeki claims raises "substantial" sums inside South Africa. Officials sponsor a "Fighting Fund" appeal that encourages com-patriots in exile to support Umkhonto. Crowd-pleasers such as the arts and culture department's singing and dancing "Amandla" troupe are sent abroad on fund-raising tours, as are ANC leaders. In reality, however, the Congress has not undertaken major profession-al grass-roots fund-raising campaigns.

The bulk of the Congress's support comes from governments and international organizations. Of the $50 million nonmilitary budget, as much as $30 million arrives in the form of development special-ists, teachers, tractors, clothing, food, medicines, and other in-kind contributions. The Soviet Union and its allies figure prominently in this category. The remaining $20 million constitutes cash assistance often earmarked, for example, for student scholarships, training pro-grams, or housing. Sweden and Norway top the ANC's list of cash donors, with the Netherlands and Austria following behind. Then, in order of giving, comes UNHCR, the Soviet Union, India, and Ox-fam. Sources have also included the World Council of Churches and the Organization of African Unity's Liberation Committee. In addi-tion, new privately raised money is being channeled into the Con-

74 REBELLION-IN-EXILE

gress's humanitarian aid account through such groups as Bishop Desmond Tutu's refugee fund, politically oriented rock music benefits, and even the cast of the U.S. television series "Cagney and Lacey," who voted to donate their South African royalties. Donations from Western and third-world governments, China, and private institutions are said by ANC officials to have grown significantly in the mid-1980s.[56]

The details of Umkhonto we Sizwe's budget are secret. But given the nature of MK weaponry, it is clear that the Soviet Union, East Germany, and Czechoslovakia are the chief suppliers of in-kind assistance. Because food and clothing for the troops are paid out of the ANC's general fund, other donors also help indirectly to sustain the Congress's guerrilla army.[57]

"We can never have enough money," broods Congress financial deputy Kay Moomsamy. Indeed, the treasury's thinly stretched budget provides only minimal living standards for the ANC's exiled constituency and barely covers all the projects undertaken by its ample sanctuary-state bureaucracy. To help relieve the pressure, President Tambo regularly issues appeals for more funds and has declared his organization's willingness to accept humanitarian and military aid from any source.

CONCLUSION

Few national liberation movements in Africa have waged guerrilla wars under conditions as difficult as those with which the ANC grapples. Pushed by South African power to command posts five hundred to a thousand miles from the target frontier, the Congress attempts to control a nationwide anti-apartheid rebellion with limited resources, outdated weaponry, restless soldiers, and perilous channels into and out of the Republic. Yet its exile bureaucracy has imperfectly but doggedly adapted to the hostile strategic environment of the subcontinent.

In the decade following the Soweto uprisings, the ANC transformed itself in the minds of many black South Africans from distant artifact to neighborhood liberator. Moving back to Africa from Europe was a critical decision that guaranteed the organization's survival. Although Pretoria's economic and military offensive muscled Congress operations out of the border states, the refuge granted by

Angola, Zambia, and Tanzania gave the ANC sufficient room to expand. Command center proximity to South Africa would be unattainable, but other items on Oliver Tambo's shopping list for accommodations—maximum security, freedom of maneuver, host-government support—were available in the arc of sanctuary states. The ANC would not be free of the threat of South African attacks, but it would probably be able to survive them.

Leadership shed its fondness for Western diplomatic forums and adapted not just to tending a rekindled war, but to the militant demands of an impatient new constituency inhabiting the Congress's domains. The bureaucracy built by the National Executive Committee absorbed energy brought out by the angry youth. It also sought to control impatience and apostasy through an elaborate network of watchful commissars. Under the guidance of the Rivonia generation, the political culture of the ANC remained characterized by military moderation, multiracialism, and nationalism. Friendly gestures were made toward factions favoring indiscriminate violence, black exclusivism, or Marxism, but they proved tactical in nature, designed to achieve stability rather than profound change.

An assemblage of rebel resources outside South Africa could mean little, however, without a formidable underground inside the Republic. Guerrillas, couriers, and communications had to flow into South Africa from foreign bases for insurrection to grow, and indeed the Congress's exile bureaucracy had made much of that possible. But success would have to depend most of all on the ANC's ability to build a foundation of public confidence inside the country. If apartheid was to be toppled, it could not be done by any external force but by one rooted at home.

3. Linking Protest to Revolt

Until the imposition of strict controls on foreign television crews, the daily leitmotif of Western television reporting on political unrest would begin with the words "It was another day of violence in South Africa . . ." over videotape of crowds and police murderously clashing. With international audiences more used to scenes of modern long-distance war—missiles blasted at unseen enemies—the personal and brutal nature of this conflict struck a rare note of horror.

Just miles from the township battlefields, South Africans tuning in to the government-owned SABC's nightly news saw far less than viewers abroad. Demonstrations seemed to whites to have occurred spontaneously, with violence usually initiated by young black thugs and abetted by a minority of criminally inclined adults. The toll, to be sure, was high: in 1985 alone there were nearly one thousand deaths, 4,800 detentions, and almost 4,000 buildings damaged or destroyed. But hampered by news censorship, most whites were quick to consider the disturbances the work of agitators taking advantage of naive blacks. To them it was a phase, like others in recent history, which would pass when proper force was applied to put it down.

The unrest of the mid-1980s was, however, neither spontaneous nor transitory. Instead it represented the most visible evidence and consequence of a massive transformation of the black public. The

African National Congress, having established a solid infrastructure abroad, had focused on generating a widening clandestine network of cells to politicize blacks and school them in confrontation. The party could by no means claim to control all anti-apartheid activists or events in the country; but it could take credit for creating an environment of militancy and imparting techniques of organizational survival. This time, white confidence in the government's ability to put down opposition would be unwarranted.

The structural revolution in black politics can perhaps best be seen by freezing a frame from a typical, composited newsreel of township rebellion. At first glance, the scene appears to be a "standard" riot: a maelstrom of police swinging batons and blacks hurling rocks. The same such encounter might have occurred decades ago. On closer inspection, however, differences emerge.

One of the dead on the street, his body burned by a gasoline-soaked tire "necklace" around his head, is a black suspected of having collaborated with the police. His killing was carried out by militants determined to blind the police by preventing access to intelligence information. On other occasions, impromptu "people's courts" in the townships investigate charges of complicity and mete out punishments. Behind the government troops is a row of factories, silent because their black workers have walked out in protest at the "invasion" of the township. Near the empty plants lie white-owned stores, where almost nothing is being sold. Blacks are boycotting them to intensify pressure on white business to lobby against apartheid. Behind the protesters a building is smoldering. Molotov cocktails have gutted the government-run liquor concession that provides the official township authorities with revenue. Black-owned stores on the block remain untouched. In the distance, part of the township police station has been blown apart by a Soviet-manufactured limpet bomb planted late the previous night by a trained insurgent. Officers who man the station, together with the official township councillors and their families, have been forced to abandon their homes nearby for protection outside the community's borders.

The demonstration itself had been banned in advance by Pretoria, but thousands have turned out in defiance of the restriction at the behest of the unofficial civic organization, whose "comrades" have formed street committees throughout the township to mobilize residents. A few urban warriors, hiding in alleyways, aim AK-47s at the charging police. At the center of the melee young men and women are holding up two flags—the ANC's and the South African Communist Party's. Underground members of the groups have smuggled the illegal banners to protesters. The materials may even have been purchased by "taxes" paid now by residents to the civic organization's "comrades" rather than to the government. Students have been excused from their newly "liberated" schools, which now feature anti-apartheid curricula designed by local militants, to swell the demonstration as it collides with the wall of soldiers and armored vehicles. South African Defense Force units wait in the background for the call to reinforce beleaguered policemen. They are aware that in a half-dozen locations throughout South Africa, similar confrontations are taking place at that very moment.

What at first seemed a spontaneous riot is clearly far more significant. The violence in this paradigm skirmish is a consequence of a comprehensive and carefully assembled "united front" of opposition involving labor, consumers, civic organizations, schools, and guerrilla action. The secret domestic ANC, working under orders from its exile leadership, has played the leading role in generating this coalition of rebellion. Though it by no means operates at all times with as much synchrony and intensity as the composite scenario, the alliance is seeking to push effective government power out of black areas in order to convert them into safe havens for Umkhonto insurgents and ANC agents. Once the townships become internal sanctuaries of resistance, the Congress plans to use them as training grounds for further anti-apartheid agitation and as launching pads for attacks on white areas.

Achieving these goals in defiance of a combative enemy depends, first of all, on the skill and influence of the ANC underground: the sturdiness of its structure, the vigilance of its security, and the reliability of its communication links with other internal cells and the Lusaka headquarters. ANC advances depend, too, on the underground's contacts with and control over legal institutions in the fields of labor, education, and township affairs.

Since the Congress is not alone in competing for black allegiances, its capacity to coordinate resistance around the country rests also on its relationships with rival organizations such as Zulu Chief Gatsha Buthelezi's Inkatha movement, homeland parties, and black consciousness groups. To the extent that these competitors shut the

ANC out of important black communities, the less effective and more vulnerable the united-front strategy can be. For the ANC fully to intensify its anti-apartheid campaign, the party would have to control, coopt, or isolate the multitude of organizations claiming to speak for South Africa's aroused blacks.

THE ANC UNDERGROUND

A small, secret ANC network, rusty from a decade of hibernation and still gun-shy as a result of the Rivonia disaster, finally awoke to activism in the midst of the Soweto-era uprisings. Its most important charge from the Lusaka headquarters was to organize the safe exodus of thousands of new recruits for political and military instruction abroad. As escape became more dangerous and the Congress reached a saturation point in the sanctuary states, the internal cells were ordered, by the end of the decade, to step up efforts to establish new clandestine branches across the country to deploy the large number of volunteers at home.

The effort was succeeding only slowly. Laboring under the constraints of government repression and elaborate self-imposed security procedures, the cells were unable to reproduce themselves fast enough to keep pace with the dizzying expansion of black militancy. So serious did the leadership consider the situation that President Oliver Tambo declared 1985 the "Year of the Cadre" in a bid to focus energy on developing the underground. In a frank report to the consultative conference held in June, the National Executive Committee admitted that "our organization inside the country is relatively weak." It described a black populace engaged in revolutionary activities promoted by the Congress, but observed that "what is missing is a strong underground ANC presence."[1] The report recommended that more trained guerrillas be sent back into the country to establish the increased number of cells needed to absorb and organize politicized blacks.

Though the ANC underground may not have grown rapidly, it had nevertheless spread steadily, particularly in urban areas, since the Soweto rebellion. Ironically, its shape was based on a blueprint drawn up by Nelson Mandela nearly a quarter-century earlier, a plan which in turn had borrowed from the Zionist Irgun guerrilla experience in British-occupied Palestine. In recent court testimony, the government's own analysts painted the picture of "a national underground organization, pyramidal in shape and built of cellular units. Each cell is unaware of its brother cells on a horizontal level and is linked vertically to a single member of the cell above, from which orders are received. Security is thus ensured."[2] This is precisely what Mandela had designed in the plan that took his name.

The 1950s scheme had envisioned regional ANC branches consisting of five separate levels of organization, arranged along a ladderlike hierarchy, beginning at the bottom with a cell representing as few as seven homes. The cell leader would be a member of a street committee whose chairman, in turn, would report to a zone chapter covering seven streets. Heads of four zones would convene as a ward committee, with one of their number serving on the top body of the regional branch. Through the chief of the branch, the ANC's national executives could communicate directives and learn of grass-roots action.[3] No one member would be aware of the identities of more than about ten colleagues. While cumbersome, this interlocking system of compartmentalization would protect the bulk of the network in the event of infiltration by the security police or betrayal by a member.

The M-Plan remains the foundation of Congress organization in South Africa. In rural areas, cells consist of as few as five members, and in urban townships, as many as twelve.[4] Their number throughout the country is unknown, though there are believed to be some ten to twelve regional commands. The ANC itself would be unlikely to be aware of the total number of cells.

Propagating the underground has traditionally been considered extremely risky because of the danger of inadvertent recruitment of police informers. To minimize the danger, the Congress adopted rigorous intake screening while prescribing punishment for blacks thought to be assisting the regime. A typical sequence of recruitment would normally begin with a clandestine meeting of the street cell to compile a list of potential enlistees who live on the block. The names may be those of residents who participated in a recent march or school boycott, thereby demonstrating to ANC observers a measure of political consciousness. Members initiate security checks on each candidate to determine his or her reliability and political opinions. One cell member is assigned the task of meeting secretly with each potential recruit. A test, such as acting as a marshal for a funeral protest rally, may be set for the candidate. If the person passes it, he or she may be provisionally invited to join the cell.

Once the recruit accepts, an initiation process begins. The ANC places great emphasis on instructing its members in party history, philosophy, and strategy. "We don't want someone who merely knows how to use a gun," asserts NEC member Thabo Mbeki, "we need a political person, who understands what we stand for."[5] Under the tutelage of his contact, the new cadre is expected to study the Freedom Charter and accept standards of conduct outlined for all members, including the ban on targeting civilians and the need to maintain discipline. Should the recruit pass muster on these points, he or she is normally fully inducted into the ANC underground. The control agent assigns the enlistee a code name and provides training in methods of secret communication with the cell. In addition, the agent gives the new cadre rudimentary instruction in the use of firearms and explosives.

The cell leader, perhaps in consultation with colleagues at higher levels, then assigns the enrollee one of a variety of missions. Prior to 1980, the most promising volunteers would be smuggled out of the country, using ANC vehicles, contact persons, and escape routes, for sophisticated training. In later years, recruits were expected to become involved in community activities, receiving more advanced education in strategy, weaponry, and clandestine operations only from returning Umkhonto insurgents. A new cell member might be assigned to join a labor union, student group, or civic organization to report on its work, influence tactics, recruit members, or relay ANC positions. Alternatively, he or she might be dispatched to a different part of the country to found new underground branches. A third possibility would be assignment to an Umkhonto unit as courier, arms smuggler, or guerrilla fighter.

Secret communication among underground compartments and between them and the Lusaka headquarters hundreds of miles away was perhaps the most complicated problem facing the ANC. In order to best calibrate its policies and reactions to fast-changing developments, the exile leadership hoped regularly to take the pulse of internal black opinion and communicate instructions to its followers at home. Yet links between headquarters and the underground remained sporadic and unreliable as late as the 1985 consultative conference. The NEC complained to delegates that insufficient ties were being maintained with "the many cadres inside the country . . . who are in daily contact with the situation. . . . We have to be in daily contact with our people."[6] Pretoria's increased surveillance of telephone lines, mails, and radio frequencies, together with enhanced border patrols to detect courier transits, made most forms of communication hazardous. On occasion, ANC authorities in Lusaka have had to wait days for confirmation from internal agents that its own guerrillas have attacked a particular target.

To compensate for the information gap, the leadership adopted a decentralized command, setting broad policies in Lusaka and expecting its field workers to make more detailed decisions on their own. For this reason the ANC stresses that cadres be thoroughly grounded in basic party principles so that they implement specific policies in ways that bear the ANC trademark. For example, when Radio Freedom broadcasts an ANC appeal to "make the townships ungovernable," underground leaders in the communities are expected to make decisions regarding alliances and tactics that conform to the current party line.

The Lusaka headquarters also counts on its field activists to distinguish forged from genuine ANC instructions. Taking advantage of the uncertainties surrounding clandestine communication, government agents have periodically fabricated ANC publications in ways designed to confuse and divide the underground and its constituency. In 1983, for example, a false version of the occasional Congress publication *ANC in Combat* suddenly appeared in the townships using language portraying the party as a puppet controlled by Moscow.[7] Three years earlier, in a similar incident, security officials intercepted an underground journal promoting draft resistance among whites and substituted a government-prepared facsimile that crudely urged readers "to sacrifice the lives of your girlfriend, parents or wife for the noble cause of communism."[8] Congress tacticians believe that familiarity with the language, principles, and customs of the ANC enables party members to distinguish real from fabricated instructions.

Outbound communication from the internal cells to Lusaka is handled through the use of couriers—some under Umkhonto's control, others under direction of the secret division of the department of information. These may be people unknown to the security police who possess valid passports and may freely travel into and out of the country. Others carry forged identity documents, while still others have illegally escaped the country over border fences to convey information abroad. Agents also use the mails, but typically with protections such as anonymous post boxes and elaborate codes. In two cases uncovered by the police in 1982, messages sent through the mail by white ANC contacts in South Africa to Congress Alliance members in Botswana were coded based on books owned by the communicants. Barbara Hogan, for example, was given one of two copies of a study in political economy authored by Paul Baran. Using a formula keyed to the page, line, and word numbers of the book, she could pass information on to her ANC agent in Botswana.[9]

Inbound communication was somewhat easier owing to ANC radio facilities. Broadcasting over frequencies in nearby countries, Radio Freedom could alert its underground and the public at large to current tactics and orders. It is not known whether Mbeki's technicians used regular programs to transmit coded instructions to internal contacts. But generally, Radio Freedom proved effective in communicating broad ANC positions, which could then be implemented in specific ways at the discretion of field organizers.

The Congress's department of information also publishes numerous periodicals and documents for domestic distribution. A Soweto-era court trial unveiled one method by which these reached the underground. In Zambia, an ANC press printed a pamphlet entitled "Umkhonto we Sizwe." Packets of them were smuggled into South Africa by clandestine department couriers. One of the messengers secretly delivered a batch to Soweto resident Kerwin Chiya, who in turn passed single copies to a number of contacts, probably members of his cell, including Jan Malatji, who seems to have been the contact person for another cell. Malatji copied the pamphlet on plain paper by hand, possibly to avoid suspicion when later making some twenty to thirty photocopies at an office. Furtively, he distributed half to members of his ANC group by personally slipping them into letter boxes at their homes. Malatji left the remainder with a Congress contact at Johannesburg's University of the Witwatersrand. Presumably cell members at Wits picked up the circulation chain, channeling the document through the university and to black militants in other nearby townships. Malatji and Chiya then manufactured pamphlet bombs—buckets of literature dispersed by means of explosives—and detonated them in Johannesburg's city center as a dramatic means of reminding the public of the ANC's presence.[10] These elaborate practices, however, remained vulnerable to disruption or forgery.

Although government obstacles continued to make communication between the ANC's internal and external wings difficult, the underground had achieved greater progress in ensuring its security from penetration by government informants. During the early 1960s, the South African Police could count on a corps of paid agents posing as legitimate members of the ANC and PAC to keep abreast of opposition politics. It was clear to the Congress's leadership that a subterranean resistance had to be protected against infiltration. Recruits enlisting with the ANC had to know that the leadership would do all it could to shield them. When the Soweto-era revival began, therefore, the Congress sanctioned, not only a rigorous security clearance program, but also a campaign of intimidation and assassination to block police espionage and choke off the number of witnesses willing to testify for the state against accused "terrorists" at trials. The ANC's head of the southern Natal regional committee testified at a 1980 proceeding that one of his standard duties was to order the assassination of court witnesses who had given evidence against Congress operatives.[11] Cells were under regular orders to be on constant watch for infiltrators. In 1980, Brigadier Johan Coetzee, chief of the police security branch, revealed that more than ten of his agents, most of them black, had been killed after infiltrating liberation movements inside South Africa and abroad.[12]

So successful had the ANC become in crippling police intelligence that a judicial commission admitted that "to a large extent the only weapon of the police for anticipating terroristic and other subversive activities" was "information obtained from persons in detention."[13] For many detainees, that meant torture. Even then, the authorities have had difficulty getting convictions through the use of state witnesses. "We have to rely on accomplices," explained Commissioner of Police General Michael Geldenhuys, "and these witnesses are being assassinated . . . so we have to detain witnesses for their own safety and believe me, they're grateful for it."[14] Yet the commissioner admitted that only five informants were in protective custody in May 1980, despite the fact that over twenty-five guerrilla-related trials involving some seventy insurgents were then occurring. As Dr. Nthatho Motlana put it to a judge late in 1985, "state witnesses are regarded in the black community as sellouts and collaborators who do not deserve to live."[15]

It was only a short step to the "necklace" killings that began to be reported in 1985. Youths, acting on rumors in a highly charged political environment, intensified the campaign against those who would assist the government, brutally murdering in just one year some three hundred men and women suspected of having worked as collaborators, according to government statistics.[16] The "comrades'" actions undoubtedly resulted in innocent deaths and allowed the police to exploit the situation by quietly circulating deadly "sellout" rumors concerning legitimate anti-apartheid leaders. But they also made it far more difficult for the police to find anyone willing to provide information about underground activities. The ANC, though it officially disapproved of necklacing, could now operate with more safety than ever before.

SEEKING THE UNITED FRONT

Despite the gains in ANC security, police scrutiny made the task of expanding the underground network a painstakingly slow process. As a result, the Congress leadership's search for a shortcut to power led in the 1980s to an approach that had yielded positive results thirty years earlier: federalism.

The Congress Alliance of the 1950s, affiliating separate colored, Indian, trade union, and communist organizations under the ANC's leadership, had in a stroke conferred on the party political primacy in the nonwhite community. At the same time, the ANC had gained access to new resources and networks it could not have developed easily on its own. The cost for the Congress was a loss of some independence, as each constituent group remained intact, in control over its own institutions, and insistent on having a say on alliance policy. Yet the utility of the federation has never seriously been called into question within the ANC.

Careful students of historical record, party leaders often look to the Congress's past for tactical lessons. To broaden its influence more rapidly and thoroughly than its own cadres could accomplish, therefore, the ANC found ways to, in effect, expand the Congress Alliance. Targeted for affiliation were civic organizations, labor unions, student federations, church bodies, and selected white groups. Through them, the ANC would seek to intensify rebellion, even at the price of diluting its own power.

The UDF

Black townships in 1979 were fertile ground for new institutions opposing apartheid. The violent Soweto-era uprisings had largely ended, but the passions which had fueled them remained. Government action had crushed most black consciousness groups that had dominated resistance in the previous five years, leaving a vacuum in above-ground political activity. In October, in the industrial city of Port Elizabeth, a model for filling that gap was launched when some eight hundred residents voted to establish the Port Elizabeth Black Civic Organization (Pebco).

Pebco was the most prominent and successful of a new breed of local community organizations that sought to battle apartheid at the local level. Each hoped to politicize residents by involving them in specific grass-roots campaigns, such as blocking rent increases. But they planned to avoid taking high-profile national positions that would inevitably attract police attention.

Like many of the urban civic organizations, Pebco found its base of support among worker families and often acted as a township wing of local unions. When Chairman Tozamile Botha was fired from his job at Ford Motor Company for allegedly spending company time on civic matters, Pebco and black Ford workers organized an illegal but effective strike against the company. Inspired by the well-publicized Pebco achievements, civic groups continued to sprout up across the country, forming, in effect, a new front in black opposition to apartheid. While linked to the labor movement, the community organizations represented populist vehicles for black self-determination in parochial issues such as housing, transportation, and schools. But it was not until 1983 that they would become overtly linked to a national body seeking to coordinate their actions.

Cape Town, in August of 1983, hosted one of South Africa's largest anti-apartheid political conferences when some twelve thousand people met to inaugurate the United Democratic Front. Embracing community groups such as Pebco, the UDF was conceived as a means of hitching local mobilization resources to national resistance objectives. In particular, its founders were seeking a vehicle to campaign against the upcoming whites-only referendum concerning the proposed constitution. This "new dispensation," which continued to bar black political rights while providing a limited franchise to coloreds and Indians, had ignited nationwide black indignation.

To protect against governmental repression, the front took on a structural appearance unlike any other major anti-apartheid party in recent history. It would be ultradecentralized and pyramidal in shape; broad policies would be set by a board of recognized leaders, but most of the work would be done by five regional committees and hundreds of local officials in separate but interlocking apparatuses across the country. By the end of 1986, nearly seven hundred community bodies had affiliated with the umbrellalike UDF. In addition to civic organizations, they included womens' groups, labor unions, youth leagues, and religious councils. Responsibility for front campaigns was filtered down to and diffused across the community level, thus involving more of the populace in political agitation and reducing the police's ability to incapacitate them.

Wary of the state's reaction, the UDF from the start took pains to emphasize its independent nature and denied that it was controlled by the African National Congress. Yet its political philosophy, leadership, and strategies all reflected ANC influence.

In its inaugural declaration, the UDF used euphemisms such as "nonracial" and "democratic," which placed it squarely in the Freedom Charter tradition. Dr. Allan Boesak, a minister and prominent anti-apartheid activist, went even further in his keynote address at the 1983 rally. He argued that whites can and should be recruited into the anti-apartheid resistance movement, a position held almost exclusively by the ANC. Like the Congress, the UDF decided that it would avoid prescriptions for the country's post-apartheid future, since debates over such issues could expose the potentially clashing policy agendas of constituent groups and foment disunity. For the purpose of achieving the defeat of minority rule, the front declared itself ready to embrace all races, classes, and ideologies that professed agreement on basic principles such as nonracialism. Most but not all affiliates endorsed the Congress's Freedom Charter, and some openly acknowledged the veteran organization as the leader of black forces opposed to apartheid. Yet in an effort to remain legal, the front continued to emphasize that whereas its philosophy coincided with that of the ANC, its tactics did not. The UDF announced that it would not engage in armed resistance, but would remain a non-violent extraparliamentary opposition.

The UDF's leadership also reflected a Congress background. Among those named as "patrons" were imprisoned ANC chiefs Nelson Mandela, Walter Sisulu, and Govan Mbeki. The active national officials were, in many instances, people long associated with the ANC. Henry Mutile Fazzie, for example, who was banned in 1986 at sixty-five years old, had served as a commander in Umkhonto we Sizwe during the ANC's 1961–63 sabotage campaign. As a UDF leader in Port Elizabeth, he had constructed the country's most successful consumer boycott against white businesses. Other office-holders included such ANC campaign veterans as Archie Gumede and Oscar Mpetha.

It may never be known whether the ANC command was directly responsible for forming the UDF. What is known is that the Congress benefited greatly by its existence and that ANC followers helped to get it off the ground. At an early stage the ANC had demonstrated intense interest in civic groups as legal organs for political mobilization. Days after escaping to Lesotho from South Africa, where he had been banned, Pebco chief Tozamile Botha expressed loyalty to the ANC, announced that he would now openly work in the organization's exile bureaucracy, and implied that he had been following the Congress all along.[17] Through him and other sympathizers in Pebco, the Congress may have hoped to enlarge its underground and its popular constituency. But without a national coordinating body, the myriad of community groups could be isolated, divided from each other, and rendered impotent in the overall effort to combat apartheid. At the time he was banned, in fact, Tozamile Botha had been preparing to initiate the work required to launch a national civic organization, a kind of "super-Pebco" that later emerged in somewhat different form as the UDF. In his view, such a body "would not wish to become a front for another group because it could more readily be harassed, banned and restricted in its activities." At a later stage, however, "it would definitely identify with one organization." He left little doubt which organization that would be.

Pebco's Botha and others conceived of a body such as the UDF as a shadow ANC, acting in concert with but not bound to the outlawed organization. From the perspective of the Lusaka headquarters, on the other hand, the UDF was considered a key component in a multifaceted attack on apartheid that would also involve trade unions and Umkhonto. The success of this strategy depended on the UDF's response to the Congress's call to "make the townships ungovernable."

Internal sanctuaries were what the ANC was after. The movement's inability to establish secure border-state havens was stunting the Congress's domestic growth by limiting infiltration of guerrillas, arms, and communications. Protected base areas inside South Africa would relieve the pressure on cross-border smuggling operations and allow the war to take root at home. ANC tacticians reasoned that racial segregation could be turned to military advantage if the large all-black townships adjacent to white urban centers could be converted into clandestine havens for rebels. Accomplishing that objective had to involve political mobilization of the black populace and ejection of the institutions of white power. The United Democratic Front would be the vehicle to initiate both.

In 1985, ANC headquarters in Lusaka issued a call to activists across the country to rid the townships of governing councils established by the Black Local Authorities Act of 1983. In most black communities, the groups responding were civic organizations under the UDF's umbrella. An unknown number were assisted or directed by underground ANC cadres.

The results were dramatic. Pretoria had intended to have some 103 councils elected and in place by the end of 1984. But one year later, only three were actually functioning. Certainly public support for the councils had been slim from the start: less than 10 percent had voted in Soweto elections, only 12 percent in the Cape townships of Langa, Nyanga, and Guguletu. But it took organized efforts by civic organizations successfully to contest the authority of the official councils.

One of the most dramatic and bloody battles for control of black areas took place in February of 1986 in Alexandra on the outskirts of Johannesburg. Led by four hastily formed youth and civic organizations, all UDF affiliates, militants used their M-Plan-style street and block committees to assemble an urban guerrilla force that fought police and army troops for four days. At the end of the skirmish, with some thirty-one dead, armored vehicles could still patrol the streets—but the township structures imposed by Pretoria had collapsed. Councillors and black policemen had either resigned or fled the community. In their place, the "comrades" set about the task of erecting what they referred to as "people's institutions."

By May, a Residents Joint Committee had been formed to harmonize actions initiated by the different community groups. One of the first tasks activists faced was to provide means for commemorating the dead victims of police assaults. The UDF considered each ceremony an opportunity for mobilization, a testing of discipline, and a vehicle for propagating the political faith. Incongruously, the Mass Funeral Coordinating Committee emerged as the most visible manifestation of the UDF and ANC in Alexandra. At the township stadium in March, between fifty and sixty thousand residents joined in a funeral service for seventeen victims, an event that became a mass rally for the ANC. Marshals patrolled while the crowd sang songs praising Umkhonto we Sizwe and acted out the firing of AK-47s. Banners acclaiming the ANC, Nelson Mandela, and the Communist Party dotted the stadium.

This form of funeral-as-resistance demonstration had been transmitted through the UDF beginning with the 1985 shootings at Uitenhage. As the casualties mounted, and until restricted by new state of emergency regulations in 1986, the tactic was used across the country to channel community outrage into politically constructive behavior. For the banned Congress, the rallies proved a short-lived method of openly "showing the flag" as well as telegraphing its strength to media and international observers. Because legal means of black political expression were so limited, funerals, like boycotts and strikes, became yardsticks by which to measure political support for anti-apartheid sentiment. Much of the daily violence occurring in 1985 and 1986 could be traced to mass funeral marches attacked by police forces, resulting in rioting and more deaths. But in townships controlled by ANC allies, each death was subsequently used to further justify armed resistance.

In Alexandra and other townships the "comrades" sought to gain public trust by establishing alternative courts to review routine disputes, as well as to purge the community of collaborators. "The government must become irrelevant" explained one activist near Pretoria.[18] In Mamelodi, the youth and civic associations assigned street committees the responsibility of dispensing justice and higher bodies the authority to hear appeals. Each committee's primary objective was to teach residents to disregard government-imposed structures and extend their allegiance to the UDF. The committees aired charges of selling out and ordered "re-education" or punishment. To help win over the populace, often dominated by an older generation skeptical of youthful militants, the "comrades" targeted violent crime. In Soweto, for example, the youth congress launched "Operation Root Out Thugs" to round up gangs claiming to represent the liberation movement but thought responsible for criminal assaults. Activists announced plans to rehabilitate such felons through "re-education" in a treatment program.

In communities where the "comrades" were best organized, officials from civic groups collected "taxes," or fees, from residents to help finance protest campaigns or provide municipal services. In contrast, Pretoria's local administration boards in politically active areas faced financially crippling rent boycotts by township dwellers. The Eastern Cape Development Board was reported to be burdened by twelve million Rand in unpaid rents and rates by February of 1986.[19] Its staff were afraid to leave their offices to visit delinquent residents for fear of attack.

Another development in the growing movement to wrest black areas from governmental control was the emergence in 1986 of civic militia units. These self-defense guards were first voted into existence by UDF groups in Transvaal, Cape, and Natal townships as a means of protecting leaders from vigilante and police attacks. But irregular "amabutho" soon began offering auxiliary support for consumer boycotts or worker stayaway actions, thus endowing the UDF groups with a measure of enforcement power. Residents defying UDF campaigns would be subject to coercion and punishment.

To achieve objectives such as rent reductions, detainee releases, and troop withdrawals, the UDF encouraged local affiliates to initiate consumer boycotts against nearby white-owned stores. The first such effort, which began in May of 1985 in the Eastern Cape, had proven that joint action by township groups could convert white businessmen into improbable allies in the struggle for township control. Faced with bankruptcy caused by the drop-off in sales, store owners pressed the police and municipal authorities to grant the protesters' demands. The tactic rapidly spread to black areas nationwide, though without benefit of national coordination of goals or timing. Boycotts flickered frequently across South Africa, illuminating varying levels of black coordination and political sophistication. But where most effective, they won the UDF new ground from Pretoria in the townships. In a successful variant of the strategy, Eastern Cape civic groups led a boycott against community liquor stores, which finance the government-backed administration. Profits plunged from 2.5 million Rand in 1981–82 to 400 thousand Rand in 1984–85, helping to throw the regional board into crisis.[20]

In most parts of the country, a local UDF branch would consist of a civic association composed mostly of adult men and women, a womens' organization, and one or more youth and student groups. If the civic committees lent the township battles leadership, students provided the manpower and enthusiasm that accounted for the increasing intensity of conflict. In 1979, following the banning of a raft of Soweto-period youth organizations, a new group, the Congress of South African Students (COSAS) emerged to don the mantle of youth resistance. By the time it joined the UDF, COSAS had earned a reputation for vigorous efforts to mobilize students against "Bantu education," a term describing the inferior curriculum endorsed by Pretoria for blacks. As part of the front, the COSAS leaders pressed relentlessly for school boycotts, reflecting the militancy of South Africa's young blacks. In 1985, the government reported that over nine hundred schools and 674,000 pupils, or nearly 40 percent of the nation's black students, had been involved in classroom stayaways,[21] most of which were called for by COSAS. Late in the year, Minister of Law and Order Louis le Grange banned the organization.

The ANC itself had been growing uneasy about the extent to which students were dominating the UDF, despite the fact that COSAS was pursuing aims compatible with the Congress's township objectives. To enhance the influence of adults and at the same time prevent a generation from missing out on education altogether, the ANC threw its weight behind the parent-led National Education Crisis Committee. At a March 1986 conference in Durban, the group persuaded students to return to the classroom; but more important, it formulated plans to convert township schools into centers for "people's education," which would serve as another way of replacing Pretoria's authority with community control. Starting by renaming buildings in honor of ANC leaders, UDF groups committed themselves to remaking the curriculum along the lines of an "Education Charter" to serve the goal of political mobilization against apartheid.

To an extent unforeseen by most observers only a few years earlier, the UDF by 1986 had introduced so many such tactics of resistance that it seemed on the verge of supremacy in the nation's black areas. By extension, the ANC appeared to have a unique opportunity to transform the townships into disciplined revolutionary sanctuaries. In fact, however, both the UDF and the ANC faced important hurdles before reaching a point of triumph.

Like every black opposition group before it, the UDF suffered from disruptions in intraleadership communication caused by police harassment and detentions. Ultradecentralization, conceived as the antidote, helped preserve the UDF's presence in the inevitable times of repression or banning. But it made the routine task of coherent and coordinated nationwide policy setting extremely difficult. Federalism with only intermittent central direction resulted in only intermittent harmonization of regional demands and strategies, thus muffling and distorting the UDF's voice of resistance. It also led to a frequent shifting of tones, as constituent groups representing labor, or students, or the middle class—each with different visions of South Africa's future and how to get to it—alternately seemed to gain control of the front's pulpit.

Complicating the UDF's mission was indeed the tension-marking relations among affiliates boasting their own entrenched and independent interests. Most frequently involved in discord were the youth and the trade unions. COSAS branches and youth congresses consistently pushed for more frequent, aggressive, and spontaneous protest action. By focusing narrowly on education-related issues and speaking out against the relative passivity of their parents, the students aroused generational friction. But at the same time they provoked their elders to far greater political involvement. "Previously the struggle was youth-led," observed UDF Transvaal general secretary Mohammed Valli in a 1986 interview. "Now the youth are just one constituent in the struggle."[22]

While an overabundance of zeal was a characteristic of youth participation in the UDF coalition, a wary reticence marked the attitude of trade unions. Black labor groups, worried that worker interests would be lost among what they perceived to be the middle-class concerns of the UDF leadership, stayed away in droves. In 1984 only 3 percent of the nearly six hundred organizations then attached to the UDF were trade unions. Though participation improved over time, the ANC was still exhorting unions to affiliate as late as 1986, some three years into the UDF's life.[23] Ultimately, the formation of COSATU, the Congress of South African Trade Unions, drew many of the politicized worker organizations together into a separate nationwide network. Through COSATU, union leaders felt able to cooperate with the UDF as equals rather than as subjects to assure protection of labor interests. But turf disputes with labor continued to undermine UDF solidarity and implicitly challenged the concept of a federal body that accounted equally for all constituent elements.

The UDF was also plagued by problems of internal discipline. Aspiring to governance in South Africa's black communities, the front had to prove its competence in administration as well as protest in order to win the allegiance of the population. The public looked to the "comrades" in UDF affiliates to curb common crime in addition to the violent excesses of its own inflamed cadres. Yet abuses ranging from theft to necklace killings persisted in the townships, prompting questions as to whether the UDF possessed sufficient control over its own followers to present a responsible alternative to Pretoria. For its part, the ANC expressed anxiety that undisciplined youth gangs, which it optimistically called "mass combat units," be rapidly integrated into Umkhonto to serve rather than complicate the ends of rebellion. But the Congress could not field enough of its own people in the townships to turn its hopes into reality, and consequently found itself unable to exercise authority in many critical situations.

The UDF was under siege from pressures outside its ranks. The state of emergency that Pretoria imposed in 1985 was targeted primarily at the front. By September an estimated 56 percent of UDF national and regional officials had been either detained, charged with offenses, or killed. Others sought safety by staying in hiding. Some two thousand rank-and-file activists had been rounded up by police and detained indefinitely. Thrown off balance by the government's assault, the organization floundered without central direction until second- and third-tier leaders came to the fore. By the start of the second state of emergency in 1986, during which over twenty thousand were rounded up by police, these former middle managers had learned the benefits of going underground, conducting business in clandestine meetings on dark street corners to keep the UDF operating.

LINKING PROTEST TO REVOLT

Nevertheless, affiliates most often found themselves having to make local policy on their own. The national and regional leadership, on the run from police, muzzled by a press censoring itself at Pretoria's order, and endangered by the threat of informers, had difficulty sustaining the UDF as a national force. At the same time, government authorities laid siege to the UDF's township strongholds, cutting off sewage and electric services, trying to eject rent boycotters from their homes, and expelling student militants from schools to win the capitulation of the "comrades." Finally, Inkatha, seeing an opportunity to further cripple an opponent already reeling from the emergency measures, initiated violent attacks on UDF supporters. Unhindered by the police, vigilante groups apparently loyal to Chief Gatsha Buthelezi engaged in clashes throughout Zulu-dominated Natal in 1985 and early 1986.

On the defensive after two years of expansion, the UDF seemed in the midst of a new barrage of repression to have reached a limit to what it could accomplish openly as a legal institution without a significant softening of Pretoria's policies. Affiliates looked now to protecting and consolidating gains, even if that required tactical retreats in some townships. But any assessment of the UDF's impact on black areas in South Africa would have to conclude that profound and lasting effects had been wrought that would boost the ANC's anti-apartheid rebellion.

The United Democratic Front had demonstrated that black groups, when capable of overcoming their differences, had the potential to immobilize white power in the townships. For an underclass afflicted with the trauma of political impotence, this in itself was a liberating lesson. Even the ANC's Lusaka headquarters occasionally betrays more surprise than confidence when its followers inside the country score impressive political achievements. Never before had any opposition movement penetrated so deeply into the black population, recruiting into the fray a wide variety of constituents in a bid to spread the responsibility of resistance. Townships exposed to UDF activity were far more politicized and militant than ever before, yielding the anti-apartheid movement a new wave of activists and sympathizers, and fewer government informants willing to identify them to police intelligence.

Though deliberately weak as a national command, the UDF had functioned effectively as a strategic transmission belt, rapidly passing experience of successful actions to organizers across the country.

Affiliates saw their community tactics and parochial demands suddenly take on national dimensions. The front had proved less an initiator and more a cross-fertilizer of resistance measures adopted at the local level.

In turn, this unique strength at the grass roots lent the African National Congress new possibilities for political mobilization. The townships had become fertile bases for recruitment of underground cells. Even if the authorities could recapture some of their power, a township population influenced by UDF campaigns would likely be more hospitable to ANC guerrillas and less tolerant of those opposed to armed resistance. Equally important for the Congress, each urban center featured through family and ethnic relations "a thousand and one links with the bantustans and rural areas" which could be used "as a springboard to develop our organizational strength and our armed strength within the countryside," according to Umkhonto strategist Ronnie Kasrils.[24] It would take far more battling to transform urban or rural black communities into secure bases for Umkhonto we Sizwe; but in light of the trend toward radicalization in the black population, the chief constraint was the Congress's own shortage of organizers and arms rather than an absence of popular ardor for the cause.

Call to Whites

While the ANC looked to the United Democratic Front chiefly for political agitation in black areas, it also found benefits from the legal movement's success in attracting whites. For more than thirty years the Congress had worked together with anti-apartheid whites on the leftward margins of white public opinion. But from exile the ANC had devised no routine mechanism to link up with the growing number of independent white-dominated groups that were challenging government policies from within the country in a multitude of areas. Nor had it established relations with any mainstream white groups, such as business leaders, who might be susceptible to tactics designed to split the ruling minority.

By 1985, a formal UDF appeal to whites had brought under its federal wing such organizations as the Black Sash, Detainees' Parents Support Committee, Johannesburg Democratic Action Committee, the National Union of South African Students, and the End

Conscription Campaign. Their ties to the front gave Congress operatives within the UDF new access to information generated by white
activists; at the same time the relationship enabled the white organizations to coordinate their actions with those of black groups involved in the overall attack on apartheid. In an effort to reach further
into the ruling race's ranks, the UDF encouraged its white affiliates
to move outside their specialities and communicate broad anti-apartheid goals to their compatriots. In one response, in October 1985,
five white UDF organizations founded a new group with the non-
threatening name "Concerned Citizens" to promote through public
meetings in white suburbs such general UDF themes as "the road to
peace through dismantling apartheid." Though not directly linked to
the ANC, such projects mirrored the Congress's interest in undermining apartheid's constituency.

Mainstream white groups unwilling to cede their independence to
the UDF nevertheless paid close attention to the front's openness to
whites and drew a lesson about the presumed attitude of the ANC
toward them. Beginning in 1985 with a group headed by Anglo-
American chairman Gavin Relly, some of South Africa's most influential business leaders traveled directly to Lusaka to discuss the
nation's ongoing crisis with Congress leaders. Oliver Tambo, risking
the suspicion of ANC militants, assembled top-level delegations to
receive them in formal talks. Moreover, in a policy statement prepared for international audiences marking the ANC's seventy-fifth
anniversary, the executive took pains to emphasize its moderate
position. The January 1987 appeal to whites declared that while an
ANC government would "address the question of ownership, control
and direction of the economy," it would focus on creating rather than
redistributing wealth. At the same time the organization reassured
whites that the Congress supported a multiparty democracy with
basic Western freedoms.[25]

Tambo's welcoming approach unveiled the extent of ANC flexibility in seeking a united front against the National Party government, but the president took care to emphasize for the party's left
that guerrilla warfare remained central to the ANC's strategy. "It is
the armed component which has made them want to come," explained Tambo in remarks broadcast on Radio Freedom after the
much publicized talks with the Relly group. "If they reach the conclusion that indeed, the apartheid system is going to destroy their

interests . . . at that point they will want to . . . even join with forces
that are set to destroy that system . . . [and] that can be an additional
lever, a position which favors our struggle."[26]

Tambo's concept of a realpolitik rebellion assumes that, to succeed, the ANC need not control all elements of opposition, or even
insist on ideological harmony among all anti-apartheid groups.
Rather, the Congress can benefit by any dissension within the apartheid constituency, almost regardless of the quarter from which it
comes. If South Africa's oligarchical white business community,
where only a handful of companies control the bulk of private economic activity, could be encouraged to challenge the National Party
administration, Pretoria would be forced to cope with new fronts of
opposition that the ANC could not have opened on its own.

The Labor Front

The largest and most promising constituency for the ANC was also
among the most politically nettlesome. Though Pretoria first permitted the recognition of black trade unions in 1979, unrecognized labor
organizations had existed for decades in various states of animation.
The ANC's own labor ally, the South African Congress of Trade
Unions, had flourished in the 1950s before going underground and
into exile. Yet three obstacles—extensive unemployment, repression, and a poverty of resources—had taken their toll both by retard-
ing growth and by encouraging fragmentation in the black labor
movement.

Vast black unemployment, usually pegged at a third of the potential black work force, undermines union formation by guaranteeing
the persistence of an employer's market. Management in South Africa has traditionally offered nonwhites low wages and benefits and
poor workplace conditions in the knowledge that replacement labor
would be available in the event of strikes or walkouts. Economic
trends in recent years have only reinforced this barrier to trade unionism. Economists in 1979 calculated that an annual growth rate of
approximately 8 percent would be required merely to absorb the 250
thousand blacks who were leaving school for the labor market each
year.[27] That translated into over 20 thousand new jobs each month.
Yet the scale of investment in labor-intensive industry was clearly
not matching this population growth, particularly in the under-

developed homeland territories. To illustrate the breadth of the problem, the *Rand Daily Mail* published a study one year later which estimated that some 37 thousand new job-seekers were entering the labor market each year in the eastern Cape region comprising Ciskei, southern Transkei, and the border areas between the two reservations. By conservative estimates, an investment of R10,000 was required to create one job. Employing all 37 thousand annual job-seekers in the region, therefore, would absorb some R370 million per year. The fact was, however, that only some R27 million over five years had been channeled into the Ciskei, producing eighteen new factories and 2,160 jobs at Dimbaza at an average cost of R12,500 per job. To absorb its annual crop of would-be workers, the region needed a new Dimbaza complex to open its doors each month. Even this, however, would have left the large existing pool of unemployed untouched.[28]

In addition to economic conditions, government repression acted as a brake on labor organizing. Following a report by the Weihahn Commission, Prime Minister P. W. Botha announced in 1979 that black unions would be brought "under the guidance of the Government" through a new registration process. But by requiring black labor groups to foreswear political issues and conduct business in legally restricted ways, the Industrial Conciliation Amendment Act was perceived by many as an effort to "retract many of the rights enjoyed by black workers under the previous dispensation," according to labor activist Alec Erwin.[29]

At the same time, all work seekers residing in the homelands had to apply for positions at government employment offices, where officials could distribute jobs to "cooperative" blacks and withdraw them from "disruptive workers." Some of the independent homelands went even further. Ciskei authorities in 1980 unveiled a program to "pre-discipline" workers for contract labor in the Republic. Applicants were to be ranked on the wait lists by both skill and obedience. Ciskei undertook to instruct blacks on "discipline at work and the consequences of breaking a contract," as it planned to refuse a second chance for those that did. Said Chief Njokweni to the Legislative Assembly: "to assist in marketing our labor in South Africa, employees must ensure that desertions, walkouts, expulsions and insubordination are eliminated."[30]

Repression could be far more direct. In the 1985 and 1986 states of emergency, the police targeted anti-apartheid union activists across the country for detention. This move only made more visible a shadowy but long-standing police drive to infiltrate unions and harass, jail, or kill labor leaders.

Finally, the sparse resources available to black unions inhibited employee mobilization. In the United States, union strength derives primarily from paid organizers, dues to support strikes and bargaining, and rapid, regular communication within membership ranks through a labor press. In South Africa, black trade unions had never been able to muster either the funds or the freedom to utilize these techniques for growth and survival.

Despite the problems, the surge in political militancy that led to the Soweto uprising also resulted in the spread of labor activism beginning with major strikes in Durban in 1973. By decade's end, three strains of anti-apartheid unions had fought their way to prominence, embracing over 200 thousand black workers. The Federation of South African Trade Unions (FOSATU) specialized in methodical workplace organizing but studiously avoided political alignments. The Confederation of Unions of South Africa (CUSA) emphasized strong labor leadership over rank-and-file participation, while identifying with the black consciousness movement. General workers' unions grouped around the South African Allied Workers' Union (SAAWU) took on a populist approach, soliciting community support and deliberately touching on broad anti-apartheid themes.

Although each gradually began to incorporate the most successful techniques pioneered by the others, FOSATU, CUSA, and SAAWU jealously guarded their own industrial turfs. The rivalry contributed to escalating labor activism, as unions jostled for greater power through confrontation with employers. A membership breakthrough began in 1980; cardholder numbers rocketed through 670 thousand in 1983 to over 1.5 million by 1985. More strikes involving greater numbers of employees and community organizations occurred in 1984 than ever before in the nation's history.

The ANC and its labor wing, SACTU, expressed delight at the phenomenal growth of black unionism, yet the two could claim only partial credit for the labor boom. SACTU's underground network within the black working population appeared too sparse to have engineered, on its own, such a massive transformation. Nevertheless, South African court dockets are sprinkled with cases that purport to expose the extent to which the Congress Alliance sought both to encourage and monitor the process. A 1981 indictment charged that Botswana-based ANC agent Peter Richer had used Rhodes University professor Guy Berger to establish secret contact with FOSATU's eastern Cape branches.[31] One year later the state accused Alan Fine of conveying inside union information, some of it in code, to a SACTU agent in Botswana between 1977 and 1981.[32] A 1985 trial convicted Sipho Binda of coordinating SACTU's underground operations in the Transvaal.[33] A state witness in 1986 testified that members of the populist SAAWU leadership had enjoyed frequent contact with SACTU officials in Lesotho.[34]

The trials, of course, unveiled only a portion of the ANC's efforts to influence labor. In addition to underground contacts that may not have been uncovered by the police, the Lusaka headquarters regularly broadcast commentaries over Radio Freedom and printed reports, instructions, and editorials in publications smuggled into the country. The Communist Party, too, used its small number of internal cells to try to influence union policies. The overriding ANC objective was to unite the various labor movements into one federal union, comparable in structure to the UDF. Such a body would presumably direct energies away from internecine rivalries and toward antilabor practices rooted in the apartheid system. It would also make the ANC's job of providing leadership infinitely easier. Rather than using its thinly stretched underground to coordinate a multitude of worker organizations in competition with each other, the ANC hoped to transmit strategic planning to a single overriding council. From Lusaka's perspective, a united labor movement could act in concert with the UDF as above-ground manifestations of the ANC in a broadening battle against apartheid.

That the task of assembling a united labor front was so protracted can be interpreted as evidence of the weakness of the Congress's influence relative to the powerful lure of territorial competition. For years ANC leaders had issued one appeal after another for trade-union unity, only to be ignored by labor leaders more concerned with the practical pitfalls of federalization. Fearing for the independence of their own unions, officials focused on administrative dilemmas such as how overlapping membership would be counted and demarcated to distribute resources, strategic issues such as which labor bloc's tactics would predominate, and political questions such as whether a bitter rival could gain control over the proposed federation's management. But at a more fundamental level, union leadership was seriously split on how and to what extent black labor should become involved in the politics of the anti-apartheid struggle.

Implicit in the notion of a national federation—particularly the type envisioned by the ANC—was full participation in the overall campaign to overthrow minority rule. Yet the more militant socialists feared that the cost of cheek-by-jowl collaboration with organizations such as the ANC and UDF, for which working-class interests represented only one of many concerns, would be too high for labor. On the eve of the federation's eventual launching, FOSATU's Alec Erwin named the stakes in a position paper. The chief objective of unions is liberation for the specific purpose of restructuring South Africa's economy to benefit black workers, wrote Erwin. But a populist alliance might trade away economic goals in order to broaden the constituency favoring the more limited end of toppling white minority rule.[35] Influential labor leaders argued that the superfederation so lobbied for by the ANC might end up harnessing union power to nonunion objectives unless the new group were designed to be independent of all partisan movements.

COSATU, the Congress of South African Trade Unions, was finally gaveled into existence in Durban in December of 1985. A product of incessant ANC and labor lobbying, it accommodated within months some 600 thousand nonwhite workers and thirty-three unions under its UDF-style federal structure. The new organization represented the largest single union alliance in the nation's history. Pulled in different directions by its autonomous constituent groups, the executive announced socialist aims and principles that reflected lowest-common-denominator agreements. COSATU's agenda appeared broadly coincident with that of the ANC. Yet the leadership took pains to underline COSATU's independence, in part, to be sure, to eliminate justification for police repression; but important internal factions remained convinced that black labor must act as a separate entity in the liberation movement.

As in the case of the UDF, COSATU's arrival was regarded as a milestone in the politics of black resistance. Its largest affiliate, the 220,000-strong National Union of Mineworkers, gave the federation strength derived from the most critical labor market in South Africa. COSATU's national scope made it a legitimate and indispensable player in economic and political developments. But amplifying its importance was COSATU's evident willingness to link labor power explicitly to political goals, putting it in seeming defiance of the union registration law.

COSATU was certainly focusing on labor-specific measures when it promoted both a national unemployed workers organization to reduce strikebreaking and work stoppages on May Day to underline labor solidarity. But President Elijah Barayi announced as early as the founding convention that COSATU's vision of union interest embraced a wide range of political issues. He threatened protest action unless the pass laws were abolished, and urged blacks to stop paying rent for their homes until P. W. Botha decided to negotiate with "leaders of the workers and the people." Other COSATU officials called for a boycott on tax payments, the use of labor action to support student education grievances, and the unbanning of both the ANC and PAC.

In 1986, in a test of COSATU's newfound influence, the federation sponsored nationwide general strikes on May 1, international workers day, and June 16, the tenth anniversary of the Soweto uprising. Involving an estimated 1.5 million laborers, COSATU's call resulted in unprecedented stayaways, ranging from over 30 percent in Natal to 95 percent in the Transvaal and Eastern Cape. By bringing the economy to a near standstill, COSATU had demonstrated a capacity to exact a high toll from the government for maintaining apartheid. But these early successes seemed grounded in the fact that COSATU's national executives were relatively free to organize at the time, that the strikes were of brief duration, and that they marked political events broadly accepted within the black community. It was by no means certain to what extent the union, beset with detentions, bannings, and restrictions, could summon backing for longer strikes or actions on behalf of controversial political objectives such as those promoted by the ANC.

Debates within COSATU regarding the relationship to other anti-apartheid groups reached a climax at summit talks with the ANC and SACTU in Lusaka just four months after the union's founding convention. The joint statement issued at the conclusion of the closed sessions echoed the concerns of labor militants in affirming that "economic emancipation," in addition to "formal political democracy," was an objective central to the liberation movement. Yet the communiqué left open what measures would contribute to economic justice. More importantly, COSATU publicly acknowledged the primacy of the ANC in fighting apartheid, but in language loose enough to placate those favoring an arms-length partnership. The union delegation left Lusaka committed to regular consultations with the ANC and SACTU.

The diplomatic balancing act performed by the Congress and COSATU reflected the fact that while the ANC had long promoted labor unity, the federation had evolved as a delicate coalition of politically diverse unions. COSATU's policies, constituents, and contacts propelled it into an alliance with the Congress, but one in which the union would yield little power to nonlabor political leaders. The executive would coordinate anti-apartheid actions and positions with the ANC and UDF yet guard COSATU as an independent advocate of working-class interests.

COSATU did not, however, enjoy a clear field in organizing black labor. While the federation had registered progressively larger membership gains, unions opposed to the ANC and COSATU continued to receive attention. Most vocal was the United Workers Union of South Africa (UWUSA), launched on May Day 1986 as Zulu Chief Gatsha Buthelezi's counterweight to ANC-oriented labor. Based in Natal, UWUSA's pro–free enterprise, antidivestment platform mirrored that of Buthelezi's Inkatha movement and contrasted sharply with the socialist, pro-sanctions agenda advocated by COSATU. Though observers gave UWUSA little chance of luring non-Natal unions away from the giant COSATU, the new group's tieline to Buthelezi ensured that the active assistance of Inkatha and tacit support of Pretoria would aid UWUSA's survival. For these patrons, the Inkatha union's chief mission would be to deny COSATU the critical advantage of monopoly control over organized black labor. UWUSA would try to check COSATU's gains in the work force, and provide sufficient competition to divert the larger federation's energy and resources away from antigovernment politics.

Another shadow over COSATU's future was police repression. Recognizing the potential for paralyzing the young federation before it could develop administrative sophistication, Pretoria unleashed a multifront campaign against COSATU. Meetings were periodically banned in key cities, leaders were arrested or detained, particularly during the state of emergency proclaimed in June 1986, and censorship laws restricted press coverage of union affairs. The resulting confusion among constituent unions was heightened by divisive rumors and allegations spread, it was believed, by government supporters.

Despite the odds stacked against COSATU, the superfederation served, like the UDF, to give black workers a sense of their power as a united body. Labor had for the first time fashioned a national administrative structure focusing worker attention on apartheid as the ultimate source of shopfloor discontent. Institutionalized through COSATU were new methods of interunion cooperation, new emphasis on rank-and-file debate, and new efforts to coordinate protest action with nonlabor groups in the UDF.

Nevertheless, the federal, decentralized nature of COSATU imposed a political culture of recurrent bargaining and compromise that made the federation vulnerable. No matter how urgent the matter at hand, decisions were slow in coming, dependent as they were on each major partner finding and presenting its own union consensus to the executive. The autonomy of constituent unions also ensured that most national policies would be implemented in sometimes radically different forms across the country, thus blurring whatever message COSATU intended to convey. More importantly, COSATU's unwieldy leadership system made unlikely the development of an efficient labor underground, one that would be authorized both to decide and communicate federation policy in times of repression.

Yet from the ANC's perspective, COSATU served as an instrument for conscripting black workers into the liberation movement. As an ally, COSATU was too balky, independent, and loosely constructed for the ANC's taste. But if treated carefully, the superfederation would operate in concert with the Congress's plans. At the same time, COSATU would promote political activism at the workplace level, converting more factories into potential sources of ANC and Umkhonto recruits. Moreover, the ANC calculated that as government repression made COSATU's work increasingly hazardous, the federation leaders would be compelled to rely more on the ANC and SACTU for the resources of an underground. As in the case of the UDF, the Congress's scheme of benefiting from the political mobilization activities of allied above-ground groups was paying off. The movement's chief concern was racing to meet the demand for its help.

RIVALS

The last piece in the puzzle of black resistance politics comprised groups competing with the ANC for power in post-apartheid South Africa. Some, such as the governing homeland parties, had been fashioned, if not actually founded, by the government to build a black constituency with a stake in white rule. Others such as Inkatha sought a middle ground between the Congress and the National Party. Smaller bodies such as the Azanian People's Organization (AZAPO) claimed a Trotskyite corner at the political extremities. All of these parties shared an interest in halting the increasing popularity of the African National Congress in order to expand their own constituencies and take more prominent roles in defining the nation's future. For its part, the ANC leadership understood that its capacity to coordinate resistance depended upon isolating, discrediting, or destroying its implacable foes.

By far the most serious threat facing the Congress was Chief Gatsha Buthelezi and his well-organized Inkatha movement. Inkatha yeNkululeko yeSizwe (National Cultural Liberation Movement) was founded in 1974 as a modern version of King Dinizulu's Zulu cultural society, launched in 1928. Conceived at first as an exclusively Zulu organization, the group's constitution was revised in 1979 to permit a nonethnic national membership. Despite relatively high entrance fees, which endowed the organization with a large treasury, Inkatha's announced membership grew from a hundred thousand in 1977 to over a million in the mid-1980s.

Periodic surveys confirmed that the party's base of support lay among rural Zulus in Natal, while urban Zulus and members of other black ethnic groups across the country exhibited strong tendencies toward the ANC-oriented camp. Polls also illuminated the conservative ideological profile of Inkatha members. One 1985 study reported that only some 40 percent of Inkatha backers were inclined to endorse strike action, while nearly 80 percent of ANC/UDF supporters would have done so. Under 10 percent of Inkatha members would approve of armed struggle, compared to 70 percent of ANC/UDF partisans who considered it an acceptable tactic. Disinvestment was favored by just 40 percent of Inkatha members but by nearly 70 percent of ANC/UDF backers.[36]

Inkatha has served as Gatsha Buthelezi's personal fiefdom. A controversial personality, Buthelezi is known as an authoritarian with a talent for polish in his approach to supporters, and venom in his relations with competitors. His post, that of chief minister of a geographically fragmented homeland set aside for the Zulu people, had been created by apartheid's master planners as one component of the scheme to separate, not just blacks from whites, but blacks from each other. Buthelezi used his position to seek control over every aspect of the social order in KwaZulu, the nation's most populous bantustan.

Inkatha differed from the ANC in important respects. The KwaZulu party specifically avoided using ideology as a lure for recruitment. "We are not married to any one political system like one-man-one-vote," explained Inkatha executive Peter Davidson. "We are prepared to consider anything as long as it is something we can live with."[37] Instead, Inkatha's political culture was dominated by the personality cult surrounding Buthelezi's populist leadership, and by the traditions of Zulu power. Unlike the outlawed Congress, Buthelezi could openly dispense patronage. The KwaZulu government apparatus, together with the well-funded and legal political machinery of Inkatha itself, provided the chief with thousands of appointments. In a region with high black joblessness, these delivered to Buthelezi a large and loyal constituency. But Inkatha's reliance on homeland institutions guaranteed that the party would remain fundamentally a regional and ethnic body, while the ANC could boast a national, if mostly urban, constituency.

Finally, beneath Inkatha's self-promoted image of moderation and tolerance lay an infrastructure of intimidation unmatched in the ranks of the ANC. Decreeing that "we need to tone up our muscles so that the dove of peace sits easily on the spear," Buthelezi established paramilitary camps to train party regulars "in the employment of anger in an orderly fashion."[38] Wielding wooden staffs known as knobkerries, Inkatha impis (or regiments) endowed local party leaders with authoritarian powers, including the ability to menace students and residents suspected of ANC or UDF sympathies.[39] Inkatha might strike a flexible pose in negotiations with whites, but as a movement it would remain rigidly disciplined.

Although Buthelezi occupied an apartheid-generated post, he refused to follow the next step Pretoria wished him to take: leading KwaZulu to formal national independence apart from South Africa.

But he also eschewed the ANC course of armed resistance, cautioning his followers to "avoid at all costs being made cannon fodder by people who want to use our corpses to stand on in order to be seen as leaders."[40] The KwaZulu chief instead sought to persuade the National Party to negotiate power sharing. By actively contesting the ANC and promoting free enterprise and international investment in South Africa, Buthelezi made himself an attractive candidate for whites seeking a compatible cross-racial alliance. His regional "KwaNatal" experiment, in which Natal whites, Indians, and coloreds and KwaZulu blacks would jointly govern the province, figured as a step toward power sharing.

Publicly condemning armed resistance did not deter Buthelezi from attempting to draw some of the ANC's prestige to Inkatha. The KwaZulu minister regularly reminded audiences of his early relationship with Nelson Mandela. Moreover, he claimed for Inkatha the populist, nonviolent tradition he charged the ANC for abandoning when, in response to the 1960 banning order, it turned to the left and endorsed guerrilla warfare. To underscore the point, Inkatha chose as its official colors green, black, and yellow, the same ones identified with the Congress.

Until as late as 1971 the ANC had underestimated the political ambitions of the Zulu chief, lauding "this great leader of the people" for rallying ethnic opposition to apartheid.[41] Later, when Inkatha entered into heated competition with the Congress for the hearts and minds of Natal blacks, the external leadership faced having to join the contest or seek an accommodation with Buthelezi. A decision was crucial, since Inkatha controlled or monitored virtually all black areas bordering the southern Swazi and Mozambican guerrilla infiltration trails. Unchallenged, Inkatha's hostility could threaten the security of any ANC underground network in Natal.

Risking the wrath of the Congress's domestic supporters, most of whom held Buthelezi in contempt, the Lusaka headquarters chose the path of pragmatism and agreed to two secret 1979 summits with the KwaZulu leader in London. Worried by the regular discovery of MK arms caches by police in Natal, Tambo sought a working relationship with Inkatha that would mute interparty competition and license Umkhonto to operate covertly in eastern South Africa.[42] The meetings, however, were a failure for the ANC. Not only did the delegates disagree on ways to cooperate, but news leaks about their discussions unleashed a storm of criticism from rank-and-file Congress members, who accused the leadership of betrayal. A stunned Tambo at first denied having met with Buthelezi, then confessed the attempt to do business with him.

Buthelezi, on the other hand, emerged from the talks with his status enhanced. His most bitter domestic opponents had been undercut by their own commanders. The venerable ANC had been compelled to treat Inkatha as an equal and seemingly indispensable actor in the anti-apartheid struggle. Infused with a new legitimacy, Inkatha was now more prepared than before to combat the ANC. The Congress "has largely lost touch with the feelings and attitudes of the majority of black people," trumpeted Buthelezi at a 1980 rally near Durban.[43]

Within months the ANC was reported to have responded with a new drive to expand its underground in Buthelezi territory. Feeling swindled, the leadership issued formal denunciations of the KwaZulu chief and signaled its sanction of more overt anti-Inkatha protest. Beginning with unprecedented school boycotts and homeland university demonstrations in 1980, the following years were to see a steady escalation of ANC-Inkatha hostilities in Natal. A new watermark of violence was reached in 1983 when Inkatha impis killed five students suspected of protesting Chief Buthelezi's upcoming address at the University of Zululand. Two years later another Inkatha regiment was accused of killing nineteen mourners at UDF activist Victoria Mxenge's memorial service. An Umkhonto guerrilla was thought to have reciprocated the violence by planting a limpet mine at Durban's Executive Hotel, managed by Inkatha Central Committee member Peter Davidson, because it was known as a favorite rallying point for Inkatha militia. One newspaper counted thirty children injured by the blast.[44]

Still more deaths were reported, this time in the dozens and on both sides, when Inkatha impis armed with spears and knobkerries began an offensive on pro-UDF neighborhoods in townships near Durban late in 1985. "I long for the day when there will be open war between the UDF and Inkatha," declared impi commander Thomas Shabalala. "I will leave hundreds of UDF supporters dead on the battlefield."[45] Like other district leaders under Buthelezi, Shabalala had driven ANC and UDF sympathizers out of his residential camp and funded a small army by levying a militia tax on households.

Blaming the UDF, COSATU, and the Congress for the violence, Buthelezi declared that Inkatha would "banish from our midst the agents of death and destruction who want black to kill black."[46]

The government, meanwhile, was eagerly helping black conservative groups such as Inkatha act as surrogates in its war against the ANC. With repression on the rise, Inkatha-related institutions such as Buthelezi's UWUSA union, together with traditionalist vigilante units, would be given special treatment in matters such as meeting permits, extension of police protection, and virtual immunity from state-of-emergency detentions. Police would either assist or look the other way during impi offensives. Reflecting Pretoria's strategy, Michael Morris of the Institute of Terrorism Research egged on a 1985 Inkatha youth conference. "The ANC regards you as a great threat. You've got to go in there as warriors yourselves."[47] Unable to make headway against the Congress on its own, the Botha government promoted the Inkatha-ANC rivalry in order to distract underground operatives from anti-apartheid action, undermine political support for the guerrillas, and justify its own steady hand at South Africa's turbulent helm. In the absence of an initiative to patch up the feud, ever more deadly clashes between Inkatha and the ANC seemed inevitable.

Meanwhile, however, the Congress could point to greater success in isolating or neutralizing two other sources of competition: the homeland parties and black consciousness groups. Whether formally independent or partially autonomous, the homelands were ruled by chief ministers approved by Pretoria. Moreover, the premiers found their tenures secure owing to boilerplate constitutional provisions granting at least half of the appointments to each homeland parliament either to the chief minister himself or to the South African government. Many MP's were traditional village chiefs on the homeland's payroll. In this way, Venda's Patrick Mphephu, for example, could be soundly defeated at the polls yet remain head of government on the basis of a legislative majority.

However, in many of the impoverished homelands, not just in Venda, the ruling parties could boast only limited popularity. The Quail Commission reported some 60 percent of Ciskei's citizens as opposed to independence for the territory. A group calling itself the Congress People has engaged in violent resistance to the Lebowa government. Following the 1976 burning of Bophutatswana's legislative assembly building, parties critical of the chief minister were banned. Despite the adoption of draconian security measures in nearly all the homelands, a large share of the violence and political unrest sweeping South Africa in the mid-1980s took place in the ethnic reservations.

Though the homelands were ripe for anti-apartheid resistance, the ANC was nevertheless failing to take full advantage of the situation. Veteran Umkhonto officer Ronnie Kasrils, in a 1986 interview published in *Sechaba*, admitted that "we must be aware of our weakness in the countryside and in the bantustans, particularly."[48] He proposed using township people, with their family and ethnic links to the homelands, as springboards for more effective Congress penetration of the rural areas.

Still, the ANC could count some advantages in the homelands. It had built up small but enduring underground networks responsible for a growing number of Umkhonto attacks on bantustan targets. More importantly, the identification of traditional chiefs with unpopular reservation governments had widely discredited ethnic leadership structures, even among the more conservative rural populations. In all the homelands public opinion contained large pro-Congress elements even where the Congress itself was not organizationally well represented.

A major breakthrough for ANC influence in the homelands occurred in March of 1986 when kaNgwane chief minister Enos Mabuza, accompanied by a delegation of twenty-one cabinet members and party leaders, traveled to Lusaka for talks with the Congress. Involved at the time in a bitter land dispute with Pretoria, the group later returned, pledging to urge other bantustan leaders to "be on the side of the ANC."[49]

Mabuza's dramatic gesture opened new possibilities for homeland administrations paying a price in public unrest for collaborating with Pretoria. It also showed the National Party government that traditionalist blacks could not be taken for granted. Overt cooperation with the ANC might help bantustan leaders defuse anti-apartheid insurrection. At the same time, it could promise favored treatment in a future South Africa that might be governed by the Congress. But linkage with the Congress would also invite the varied and dangerous forms of Pretoria's displeasure. By choosing the route to Lusaka, Mabuza had judged the price of not going to be greater than the price of going. Other homeland leaders were reported to be considering similar moves, though the government was expected to discourage them.

For the ANC, friendly relations with cooperative homeland governments offered another shortcut to influence. In bantustans ruled by isolated and hostile elites, the Congress was under pressure to continue building popularity from the ground up. But it simply could not yet field sufficient staff to do so. Where an accord could be struck with territorial leaders, the ANC could gain the fruits of public support with a minimal expenditure of effort. It would be the same political penetration model used with the UDF and COSATU. If successful, allied homelands headed by ministers "looking the other way" could become neutralized sanctuaries for Umkhonto we Sizwe.

The last major source of opposition to the ANC lay in the remnants of black consciousness surviving in AZAPO and related institutions. An heir to the Africanism of the PAC, the Azanian People's Organization had been launched in 1978 with the aim of mobilizing black workers to lead the anti-apartheid struggle. Socialism was the end; the means would involve blacks alone. AZAPO initiated a variety of protests, the most controversial of which was the noisy boycott of U.S. Senator Edward Kennedy's January 1985 tour through South Africa. But the party's doctrinaire approach did not find favor among major union organizations. Even the black consciousness-oriented Confederation of Unions of South Africa betrayed no evident desire to carry AZAPO's militant standard into the workplace. Polls indicated that in most urban townships AZAPO could summon less public support than either ANC-identified figures or Inkatha. Analyst Heribert Adam pegged AZAPO's constituency at only some 10 percent of the black populace nationally in 1986.

In an apparent effort to gain access to a broader audience, AZAPO established the National Forum committee in June 1983. Black consciousness organizers conceived of the group as a vehicle for coordinating protest activities by like-minded groups across South Africa. But the National Forum, arriving on the political scene at the same time the UDF was beginning to coalesce, was seen as a rival federation designed to prevent black consciousness from being swallowed up by the ANC-oriented front. Explicitly socialist, the AZAPO-dominated association soon openly condemned the nonracialism of the UDF and ANC as a scheme to "smuggle whites into the black national liberation struggle."[50] By 1986, forum leaders were committed to "claiming sole rights" to anti-apartheid resistance, and hostility to the UDF had reached a new high. But despite the bombast, neither AZAPO nor the National Forum had shown evidence of popular growth sufficient to check the ANC.

CONCLUSION

By 1986, the proliferation of activist anti-apartheid bodies linking community to workplace in nationwide federations marked an unprecedented evolution of black political sophistication in South Africa. Where previously many small, isolated groups had vied for attention, mechanisms had now developed to institutionalize and coordinate resistance and to spread responsibility for protest down to the grass-roots level. When used to maximum advantage, the structure could produce the composite scene of township insurrection described at the beginning of this chapter: UDF-sponsored boycotts tied to COSATU-ordered strikes, with jointly summoned crowds marching against Pretoria's troops. The lengthening casualty lists served as one measure of the increasing frequency of these clashes.

Responsibility for the radical intensification of protest must be assigned largely to the ANC. In the years following the Soweto uprisings, it had expanded, professionalized, and safeguarded a network of below-ground cells capable of sparking political mobilization activities above ground. The Congress's exile headquarters, in turn, had acted as a bully pulpit of resistance, instructing sympathizers in the broad strategies considered necessary for political advancement. These included formation of the UDF and COSATU, and the exhortation to make townships ungovernable.

Yet the ANC's underground proved too thinly spread across South Africa to take direct advantage of all the upsurge in activism it had itself helped to create. In many townships the roving bands of young blacks that Lusaka preferred to label "mass combat units" remained unintegrated into the liberation movement. The Congress could by no means control all resistance, predict all protest, or even profit through recruitment from all anti-apartheid confrontation. Through its trained agents in the field, the ANC could directly command only selected, mostly urban, areas. To reach the bulk of the black population, the Congress used Radio Freedom and smuggled tracts to convey resistance objectives. But the group's most productive approach was the reliance on allied organizations to bring ANC influence to bear on the black polity.

The shortcut through the UDF and COSATU gave the ANC access to huge numbers of blacks in the townships and on shopfloors with a minimum of effort. Rather than organize from the grass roots up, the Congress underground had merely to work with the union or civic organization leadership. But this federalization of resistance carried grave risks. Neither the UDF nor COSATU, nor most of their affiliates, were controlled by the ANC. While they clearly cooperated with, consulted, and often followed the Congress, even recognized it as preeminent in the nationalist struggle, each had developed separate agendas for the nation's future. They might at times suppress those interests and permit themselves to be subordinate to the Congress during the campaign to overthrow minority rule. But should negotiations begin over the shape of post-apartheid South Africa, they would be bound to assert their independence. Ironically, therefore, the more the ANC's prominence grew through de facto additions to the Congress Alliance, the more its power to control resistance became diffused and subject to the veto of autonomous allies.

To execute greater control, the Congress knew it would have to move beyond shortcut federalism, expanding its own underground web of cadres throughout the UDF and COSATU with the goal of converting the two into clients rather than associates. This tactic could bind the alliance more tightly, giving the Lusaka leadership broader authority to speak and plan on behalf of all component groups. But the intensifying struggle for the political soul of COSATU and the UDF between factions loyal to the Congress and factions committed to independence is likely to be fought out of public sight, in muted tones, and in a language of euphemisms, to avoid giving opponents ammunition. One important factor affecting the outcome will be the National Party government. To the extent that it engages in greater repression, the above-ground groups will be compelled to rely more heavily on underground ANC skills and networks for survival, thus boosting the internal leverage of the pro-Congress lobby. On the other hand, greater freedom might permit the UDF and COSATU to develop on their own, resulting in a more equal—and more rocky—relationship with the ANC.

Pretoria also figures in another, more deadly, aspect of black politics: the rise of violent competition between conservative and ANC-oriented organizations. So-called "black-on-black" conflict, whether involving Inkatha or traditionalists at the Crossroads squatter camp, frequently takes place in an environment of police support for anti-ANC elements. In its search for ways to keep the Congress diverted and on the defensive, denied safe quarter even among blacks, Pretoria nurtures surrogates. Unless the ANC is able to find an accommodation with those groups, ever more brutal warfare will likely result.

In sum, the ANC and its allies have finally embedded in the political terrain a nationwide infrastructure of anti-apartheid resistance. Much of the grid still lies outside the direct command of the Lusaka headquarters; some of it, too, is besieged by Pretoria-backed rivals. Yet its unprecedented success in transmitting the discipline of rebellion to the black grass roots means that the intensity of the struggle is certain to increase. The development also means that, after years of labor, a political context has been created in which guerrilla warfare against apartheid can thrive.

4. The "AK-47 Song"

> Where is Tambo?
> Tambo is in the bush
> He is teaching the soldiers the art of guns
> That they should be one, that they will come.
> —TOWNSHIP SONG, 1986

Over the sounds of grief and anger drifting from more than thirty thousand mourners in Guguletu township, over, too, the methodic rumbling of military vehicles poised at the funeral crowd's edge, a young boy in his early teens could be heard raising his voice in rhythmic cry. Suddenly rising to its feet, the throng joined the youth in the emotionally charged "AK-47 Song," which told of "the boys" returning to liberate South Africa with an arsenal of weapons. Some in the rally waved wood-carved models of the Soviet rifle, while the rest stamped a war-beat in the dust and punctuated the song with chants evoking bullets thudding into targets. A police helicopter circled, unperturbed, above the aroused crowd on this Saturday in March 1986.[1]

Guguletu that afternoon was a showcase of how nonviolence and combat intermingle in modern resistance to apartheid. A peaceful above-ground rally organized by ANC-allied groups memorialized seven alleged Umkhonto soldiers killed by police eleven days earlier on suspicion of attempting an attack on the township constabulary. The funeral's open tribute to the Congress's military wing was choreographed to affirm popular support for guerrilla operations. It was also meant to inspire a new wave of local residents to seek out and enlist in the banned organization's army.

The African National Congress now places guerrilla warfare at the center of its strategy for overcoming apartheid. Advocates argue that military strikes amplify the impact of above-ground protest, lending force to reverse past failures of peaceful resistance. Indeed, it is in the shadowy underground of Umkhonto we Sizwe that the exiled bureaucracy's labors most directly converge with black politics.

MILITARY OBJECTIVES

The Umkhonto that arose in the wake of the 1976 Soweto uprising proved radically different from the one launched fifteen years earlier in a flurry of minor sabotage missions. Where no subcontinental bases had existed in 1961, the new Umkhonto had an arc of countries from which to draw resources. Three hundred poorly instructed saboteurs had been replaced by at least eight thousand well-trained guerrillas. A covert network of cells could now support insurgent operations, whereas in the early 1960s attacks were isolated from the political underground. Homemade bombs had been superseded by Soviet assault rifles and rockets. A deep-cover intelligence service offered the Congress access to the Republic's most sensitive installations. The days of 125-dollar attacks were over.

Strategy, too, had evolved in pace with events. Prior to the Rivonia raid, the black public and an influential faction in the ANC had continued to believe that Pretoria could be brought to negotiations through nonviolent pressure. Umkhonto's scattershot sabotage was meant to represent warning more than warfare. But following the Soweto rebellion a growing majority of blacks had become convinced that arms would have to play a more vital role in anti-apartheid resistance. Umkhonto's strategic mission changed accordingly.

The Congress's ultimate objective in the 1980s was defined as a cataclysmic insurrection guided by trained units of Umkhonto but carried out by black masses armed with whatever weapons they could find. Apartheid's collapse would be speeded by demoralization in the ruling white community and desertions from police and defense forces. Insurrection itself would be the final thunderclap in a growing storm of labor strikes, township rebellion, and armed attacks.[2] Most ANC leaders hoped and expected that the government, when finally convinced of the likelihood of this outcome, would agree to negotiations with the liberation group.

In this context, the Umkhonto underground would be called upon to serve as army, propaganda outfit, and training school. For a burden so large, however, the ANC's military wing seemed woefully undermanned. Even though Umkhonto's estimated troop strength of over eight thousand stood at a historic high, it appeared inadequate on its own to stir political turmoil in a nation of some twenty-five million, particularly since most of the soldiers were based not in South Africa but in Angolan barracks over a thousand miles from the frontier. The number of trained guerrillas infiltrated into the Republic and populating underground cells at any given moment remained secret, with estimates ranging from 350 to 2,000.

But Umkhonto's manpower statistics were misleading. In the immediate aftermath of Soweto, facing a deluge of eager recruits, the ANC leadership had dared to think of Umkhonto as potentially capable of waging a full-scale civil war on its own. Then Pretoria's improved border surveillance cut down on the flow of escapees, while its coercion against neighboring governments made infiltration routes into South Africa from frontline states more hazardous. Congress strategists were forced to rethink Umkhonto's future. Not only could there be no more mass emigrations of enlistees; smuggling those already in sanctuary states back into South Africa would be more dangerous than once anticipated. Pretoria's unexpected Nkomati accord with Mozambique, which dramatically reduced the ANC's presence in the key transit state, made a strategic change of course inevitable.

The Umkhonto soldier trained abroad would now have to act not primarily as a combatant, but rather as one of an elite corps capable of passing military skills on to home-bound cell members in the ANC underground. Placing new value on its best-instructed guerrillas, the Congress leadership announced at its 1985 consultative conference that the Umkhonto command would in the future no longer routinely rely on its small number of infiltrated soldiers for combat missions. "The comrades we are training outside constitute . . . our officer corps," the National Executive Committee reported to delegates. "We cannot deploy them forever as combat units. For obvious reasons, no army in the world fights with combat units composed of officers. Ours will be no exception."[3] The exiles once thought destined to become common soldiers fighting in South Africa under the direct guidance of frontline-based commanders would now shift their focus toward recruiting, training, and commanding units on their own in the field. This landmark reformulation of Umkhonto would likely take an extended period to implement, during which time infiltrated exiles would continue to dominate guerrilla missions.

Once accomplished, however, the shift away from demonstration raids and toward what was called "people's war" promised to have important long-term consequences. Among the most critical was that Umkhonto's top officers in Angola and Zambia would enjoy far less command and control over, and communication with, their underground troops inside South Africa. Ultimately, in fact, headquarters would be unaware even of the identity of people in MK's ranks. By requiring foreign-trained guerrillas to transfer responsibility for fighting to community-based blacks, the ANC leadership was bound to forfeit its capacity to monitor screening, training, and orders given to recruits. Lusaka would be ignorant even of their missions.

The Congress's main links to the Umkhonto underground would be through its small number of infiltrated guerrilla officers; but on account of the difficulties and dangers attending tactical communication with senior commanders based abroad, even this elite would inevitably find itself on its own much of the time. The ANC's training centers in sanctuary states now faced having to sift out for infiltration only those fighters it could trust to pursue Umkhonto strategies even during long periods of isolation from the army high command.

The Congress's decision to transfer combat responsibilities, and to forego the benefit of close supervision of Umkhonto's domestic growth, carried the risk that not all of the principles it taught to govern guerrilla warfare would be adopted by domestic enlistees. The ANC could have little assurance that standards of discipline or restrictions on targets would be obeyed by novice insurgents who lacked months of intensive training at the Angolan barracks. As a result, the dispersion of Umkhonto cells across the country brought greater likelihood of home-grown soldiers carrying out attacks in the ANC's name but contrary to ANC guidelines.

A tragic example of what could occur arose with nineteen-year-old Andrew Zondo's 1985 pre-Christmas bombing of a seaside shopping center in Natal. The guerrilla's action killed five passersby. Later the Congress awkwardly distanced itself from the mission, without issuing an outright condemnation, observing that Zondo had become "deranged" and "shocked beyond endurance" by the government's violence against blacks. Pressed by reporters to explain his movement's position on the attack, President Tambo replied: "If I had been approached by an ANC unit and asked whether they should go and plant a bomb at a supermarket, I would have said 'Of course not.' But when our units are faced with what is happening all around them, it is understandable that some of them should say, 'Well, I may have to face being disciplined, but I am going to do this.'"[4] Renegade fighters might try, in other circumstances, to hold ANC policy hostage by refusing to cease fire when so ordered, by threatening civilians, or by stirring rebellion within the ranks.

Despite these dangers, the tactic of converting Umkhonto into a populist army was a way around Pretoria's efforts to contain the Congress in sanctuary states. The flow of infiltrators back into South Africa might be reduced to a trickle, but each returning guerrilla would now be charged with the task of reproducing himself in new cells of part-time volunteers. These, in turn, would be assembled from among the "comrades" in politically mobilized black areas. Wherever the ANC underground or UDF groups were active, the Congress hoped to create a secret infrastructure of support for Umkhonto units. As military commissar Chris Hani assured listeners on Radio Freedom, MK "will find ways and means of getting in touch with those units which have been created out of the initiative of the people."[5]

The ANC leadership, well aware that its military resources might drain but never defeat the SADF, had long fitted Umkhonto with a politically tailored strategy suitable for guerrilla warfare. Each mission would be a form of "armed propaganda," a way of conveying a variety of messages through military means to two target audiences.

One audience was the natural constituency of anti-apartheid resistance, the nonwhite community. Blacks, Indians, and coloreds already committed to the ANC were judged to need morale-boosting reassurance that the Congress's strength was growing. Others, undecided as to party allegiance, might be inspired to join the ANC camp through demonstrations of support for populist causes. Still other nonwhites opposed to the Congress could be warned that an underground army was capable of striking anyone seeking to damage ANC operations.

The second audience was the white minority. To those who were wavering in their support for apartheid, Congress wished to convey a delicately balanced message: that their security and life-style are at risk, despite all the government's power, for as long as minority rule exists; however, the same ANC responsible for armed resistance is a reasonable, moderate, and nonracial alternative. To those whites implacably opposed to fundamental change, Umkhonto missions would be designed to suggest the futility of fighting against majority rule.

Field commanders would have the authority to select specific targets. Nevertheless, each strike would be required to fall within three sometimes overlapping categories approved by the exile leadership to deliver the party's political messages: "linkage," "retaliation," or "challenge" attacks.

Almost any assault on targets identified with the government could serve to boost the morale of black ANC partisans; but missions directly connected to above-ground confrontations would have the best chance of attracting political agnostics to the Congress's cause. MK units would be directed to seek out bomb opportunities that could serve as linkage targets: corporations involved in bitter disputes with black unions, or rent collection offices trying to break community boycotts, or township constabularies hated by blacks for employing brutal policemen. By bringing force to bear on behalf of the black community, the Congress could advertise both its concern and its power to take action. Retaliation attacks, on the other hand, would be aimed at informers, state witnesses at ANC trials, or government figures particularly detested by blacks. Political assassination, the main instrument of retaliation, would be used to strengthen, in effect, a guerrilla guard around ANC operations.

Finally, challenge attacks would attempt, through audacity, surprise, and persistence, to undermine the government's claim to be able to protect its supporters. Sabotage bombings in white business areas or against power-generating stations that feed white suburbs would be designed to heighten fear and insecurity among the ruling majority. But since the exile leadership sought to portray the ANC as a principled and responsible contender for power, it imposed restrictions against terrorist tactics that specifically targeted noncombatant whites. President Tambo even went to the extent of signing a protocol of the Geneva Convention which legally bound the ANC to avoid attacks on civilian targets, and to "humanitarian conduct of the war," marking the first time a guerrilla group had ever done so. The hoped-for result would be a growing sense among whites that black resistance cannot be stopped, and that things might not be so bad if the ANC were to have a hand at governing. The ANC anticipated that the cordial meetings Tambo began to hold in 1986 with South African businessmen would reinforce the image of the organization's moderation in the minds of many whites. Spreading white demoralization would lead to a decrease in the pro-apartheid constituency, with corresponding increases in emigration, draft resistance, and other trends that would weaken the National Party.

Of all its objectives, Umkhonto experienced the greatest difficulties in carrying out challenge attacks. For one thing, discipline breakdowns in MK's underground ranks led in 1985–86 to more frequent unauthorized strikes against "soft targets," such as restaurant patrons or beach-goers. Lusaka usually maintained an icy silence after such attacks, believing that outright condemnations would risk repelling new enlistees. Yet moderate veterans no doubt squirmed in discomfort as Pretoria proclaimed the "terrorist" nature of the ANC.

A second complication was the government's nearly monopolistic power to define for the white public the circumstances surrounding an ANC challenge attack. Censorship laws gave the police or the bureau for information the right to be the exclusive sources of data about guerrilla actions to be reported in the press or on SABC. As a result, a large number of bombings were simply not covered: as far as most media were concerned, they had not occurred. But in cases where attacks were too significant to be concealed, Pretoria possessed the authority, if it wished to exercise it, to ascribe criminal or accidental causes to events, thus entirely defusing their political effects. Alternatively, the government could put a "spin" on the facts to leave the public with very different impressions from those intended by Umkhonto.

An example of Pretoria's propagandist acumen took place following an October 1976 sabotage operation at the Dikgale railway station near Pietersburg. It had been carried out by foreign-trained ANC guerrilla Naledi Tsiki. Police bulletins, and therefore press reports, emphasized both the damage that might have been caused by the two bombs and the alleged technical incompetence of the saboteurs, which resulted in poor explosive placement and one dud bomb. The impression conveyed by the reports was one of a criminally reckless dullard engaging in terrorism.

Tsiki's subsequent court testimony told a quite different tale. "To a person who lacks the necessary technical know-how," the saboteur explained to the judge, the placement of the dud "may seem to have been the result of miscalculation; but this is not so." In detail Tsiki related how he had intended to cause damage insufficient to derail a train, and had deliberately kept the "dud" bomb's contact switch insulated so that it would not explode. Even though he had had more than enough dynamite and expertise to blow up the track, Tsiki told the court that he had been ordered only to show "the police and army how far we could penetrate if we were forced to do so and what our capabilities were."[6]

Tsiki, a well-trained and carefully instructed guerrilla, had apparently carried out a mission designed to deliver a message to whites about ANC power and restraint. But the only message whites received was that of black incompetence and brutality. With such control over the media, Pretoria could clearly intercept and distort the ANC's propagandist objectives even if it failed to prevent Umkhonto from successfully attacking targets affecting white areas. The problem was particularly acute in challenge attacks because, unlike the black community, whites depended for most news information on the media rather than word-of-mouth networks.

Pressure to surmount the government's media barriers led the Umkhonto high command to order more sensational attacks. While Pretoria might be able to misrepresent a rural railway explosion, ANC strategists reasoned, it could not hide the political message emanating from the successful strike on Sasolburg, the nation's showcase for oil-from-coal technology. Yet such missions were dangerous and required elaborate planning. Moreover, the absence of white casualties seemed to dull their impact on the ruling constituency, in the view of the Congress's militants. If whites began to feel the pain rather than watch the distant smoke of war, the argument went, the conflict would end sooner rather than later. In 1985, therefore, the leadership responded to the internal debate by calling on Umkhonto to carry the conflict into white areas. An angry Radio Freedom commentary aired in October asserted that white soldiers and policemen had been able to conduct the war in black townships as if the communities were foreign countries and "still return to their

homes and spend comfortable nights in the warmth of their beds."
"That myth must . . . be shattered."

> They must be haunted by the mass offensive. We must attack them at
> their homes and holiday resorts just as we have been attacking black
> boot-lickers at their homes. This must now happen to their white col-
> leagues. All along it has only been black mothers who have been mourn-
> ing. . . . The time has come when all of us must mourn. . . . Everyone
> must feel that the country is at war. . . . [7]

The leadership continued to emphasize that attacks, even in white
areas, should be directed only against combatants: soldiers, policemen, and civilians such as border farmers directly integrated into the
government's defense structure. But Pretoria was busy involving
more whites, from students to seniors, in militia and other counterinsurgency duties, thus blurring the line dividing soldiers from civilians. Simultaneously, more MK troops were attributing the persistence of white confidence in governmental power to the paucity of
white casualties. Despite moderation in the exile councils of the
ANC, therefore, the convergence of these trends had already resulted
in a rise in white war deaths.

INFILTRATION TACTICS

Although in 1985 the ANC formally ordered Umkhonto to rely on
domestic recruits rather than foreign-trained guerrillas to expand the
war, nearly all field command and even many missions continued to
depend on infiltrated Umkhonto manpower. These officers carried
with them the military expertise and political strategies the Congress
wanted implanted in the underground township cells. An estimated
forty to fifty were believed to be entering South Africa each month in
1986, far outnumbering those captured or killed in clashes with
security forces.[8] Yet routes into the country from sanctuary states
were becoming increasingly hazardous. Courses at the Angolan
camps taught methods of eluding capture and overcoming border
defenses. Beginning in 1978, Umkhonto appeared to have reduced
the size of the average infiltration unit from five to three, to facilitate
crossings.[9] Nearly every guerrilla was issued between $150 and
$500 in cash in addition to authentic-looking identity documents
forged by experts either in Europe or southern Africa.[10]

To placate the watchful South African government, each of the border states declared its territory off-limits to ANC guerrillas. But in practical terms none possessed the military or administrative resources to block transits by insurgents who arrived with plausible covers describing them, for example, as visiting civilians. "We have no way of knowing whether someone entering the country is an ANC person on his way home," said Eddison Zvobgo, Zimbabwe's minister of legal and parliamentary affairs, in an interview. An absence of political willpower to back crackdowns also played a role. Key bureaucrats and politicians, sympathetic to the ANC, were known to "look the other way" as long as operatives stayed inconspicuous, passed through quickly, and kept guns out of sight. In one case exposed by the South African police, a Botswana government official transported some twenty armed Umkhonto guerrillas over the border himself.[11]

The route through Botswana, one of three major ANC corridors, began to experience significant activity beginning in 1978, perhaps owing to the increasing success of Joshua Nkomo's allied ZAPU troops fighting in neighboring Zimbabwe. Prior to April, most MK guerrillas had entered via Swaziland. But the occupation of much of western Rhodesia by ZAPU must have provided a new buffer zone on the flank between the guerrillas and Rhodesian and South African forces patrolling the region.

Press accounts and trial evidence revealed that the typical Umkhonto unit infiltrating via Botswana would be flown from the Angolan camps to Zambia where, presumably, the soldiers would be given orders and last-minute briefings. From there, the group would be flown to Selibe Pikwe, Botswana, or dispatched across the northern border at Kazungula for the overland journey down the newly constructed road to Francistown, and then along the line of rail to Gaborone. The President Hotel in the capital was often used as a meeting point between incoming insurgents and Botswana-based Umkhonto officers, though as this became conspicuous, private homes came into use. ANC contacts in Gaborone would issue the unit guns, grenades, food, South African currency, and other items from local stocks, before driving it to a remote spot on the South African border. There, in the bushveldt, the group would cut through security fencing and cross the frontier into South Africa.

Traveling farther into the Republic without being detected by police and defense-force patrols entailed varying amounts of risk. Often guerrillas entering on the Botswana corridor had to traverse parts of Bophutatswana, a bleak, impoverished homeland formed of six separate land-blocks and conceived as a reservation for Tswana-born South Africans. The territory's small National Guard, established in 1977 by the SADF in part to deter insurgent transits, posed only occasional threats.[12] The homeland government, having signed a nonaggression pact with Pretoria, took a hostile approach to the ANC. But court cases periodically tracked significant but illegal public support for the Congress, and the movement's popularity was boosted still further in 1986 when Umkhonto guerrillas gunned down a prominent and widely feared Bophutatswana police commander.

Another factor working in the infiltrators' favor was the sympathetic relationship the Congress enjoyed with many Tswana, ethnic compatriots of the homeland's population, back across the border in Botswana. Though long divided by an international frontier, the Tswana people maintain close ties between the two lands. Umkhonto could benefit by assigning Tswana guerrillas to infiltration teams traveling into the territory or by using cross-border family networks to protect its troops.

Guerrillas passing through the northwest Transvaal from Botswana also found it necessary to cross white-owned farmland that formed a buffer between border zones and the industrial heartland of the Witwatersrand. Yet this often proved a surprisingly manageable task in light of the massive depopulation of these regions by whites migrating to urban areas. In 1980 the Transvaal Agricultural Union estimated that over a thousand farms situated between Zeerust, in the northwest, and Messina, on the northern border with Zimbabwe, were entirely unoccupied.[13] Between 1970 and 1978 an estimated ten thousand white farmers had left their properties for the cities.[14] At least a thousand agricultural tracts were being worked only part-time by whites, while "hundreds" of private game farms, country estates, and large ranches were managed only by black supervisors.[15] Messina-area farmers estimated in 1980 that up to 45 percent of the district's estates were unoccupied,[16] and in Thabazimbi in the northwest Transvaal only some eighty of the district's four hundred cattle farms were inhabited by whites.[17]

A worried member of parliament declared in 1978 that "a terrorist could walk unhindered from the Limpopo into Pietersburg without having to cross one farm over which there is proper supervision."[18] Nearly ten years later a crash 32-million-Rand government program could boast only modest success in luring whites back to the border farms with low-interest loans, subsidized security systems, and increased military protection, though the population had at least stabilized. In an apparent effort to provoke a new wave of white flight, Umkhonto insurgents in 1985 began planting landmines on patrol roads. But a vast expansion of defense-force operations to fill the farmowner gap did promise to make guerrilla transits through Transvaal frontier areas dangerous.

A second, though far less traveled, ANC infiltration corridor involved passage through Zimbabwe. Prime Minister Robert Mugabe's ZANU party had never worked closely with the Congress, having been allied instead with the PAC. Even more discouraging for the Congress was the fact that the country's large war-tested military stood alone among border states in its potential to block illicit transit through the narrow Limpopo River frontier that Zimbabwe shares with South Africa. Mugabe until 1986 encouraged trade with Pretoria and, while withholding formal diplomatic ties, sanctioned regular subministerial talks between the two countries on a wide range of bilateral issues, including security.

In this atmosphere, the ANC initially counted itself fortunate to have received permission to open a prominent liaison office in the capital of Harare. Yet Umkhonto's infiltration specialists continued to press for access to the Zimbabwe corridor. By 1985 the ZANU government may have been more sympathetic. In the wake of Mozambique's Nkomati accord, which bound South Africa to cease aiding the Renamo rebels, Mugabe had hoped to reduce Zimbabwe's costly military assistance to Maputo and resume routine trade through the port of Beira. But captured documents had disclosed ongoing South African assistance to Renamo, and sabotage continued to disrupt rail and pipelines. The SADF's surgical strikes against Congress targets in Harare in 1986, followed later in the year by a government order to delay goods transshipped through South Africa for Zimbabwe, helped to bolster those within ZANU who argued for the futility of peaceful relations with the south. Joining in the geopolitical hardball, Mugabe may have authorized the ANC to open an infiltration route into the Republic to give him a bargaining chip in the cold war with Pretoria.

Secrecy makes such speculation impossible to confirm or refute. But what is known is that, beginning late in the year, the SADF reported evidence of ANC guerrillas crossing the frontier. Overcoming sophisticated new entry barriers or sneaking in on some of the ten trains and fifty trucks that traverse the Beit Bridge crossing each day, some units succeeded in planting landmines along unpaved patrol roads before either returning across the border or disappearing into heavily populated Transvaal townships. Others were caught by South African troops.

An advantage enjoyed by Umkhonto was an "ethnic bridge" linking southern Zimbabwe to South Africa. Just as the Tswana straddle Botswana and the Republic, so Venda-born Africans dwell on both sides of the shallow Limpopo: over seventy thousand in Zimbabwe and more than 350 thousand in the "independent" Venda homeland. Chief Mphephu's unpopular territorial government faced a population sympathetic to opposition movements. As a result, Umkhonto operatives could use family ties between Vendas in Zimbabwe and pro-ANC Vendas in South Africa to help smuggle guerrillas into the Republic. To prevent such linkages, Pretoria expropriated from Venda a strip of land running between the homeland and the Limpopo frontier to serve as a military barrier. Measures such as these made infiltration along the Zimbabwe corridor dangerous and infrequent but, as ongoing incidents continued to prove, not impossible.

The third major underground passage into South Africa ran through Mozambique and Swaziland. Prior to the Nkomati accord, guerrillas would regularly fly from Angola or Zambia to Maputo, where ANC agents would take them overland to mission jump-off points near the border with Swaziland. Scrambling over the lightly patrolled frontier fence, insurgents would make contact with ANC operatives in Swaziland, who would issue instructions and weapons from stockpiles located in the town of Manzini. Detachments then would be driven either to the southeastern border with Natal or to the northern frontier with the Transvaal near Jeppe's Reef border post. The highland terrain on Swaziland's broadside western border with South Africa appeared too mountainous for regular Umkhonto crossings.

The 1984 Nkomati agreement threatened to all but shut the ANC out of Mozambique and close down a successful infiltration route.

The accord caught the Congress unaware, leaving it "shocked and stunned," according to President Oliver Tambo. "The enemy has won a point, has gained a very important position, a position none of us thought the enemy would get quite so easily."[19]

For a year, the number of Umkhonto attacks in Natal—missions that normally depended on infiltration, weapons, and guidance from Mozambique and Swaziland—dropped. But by 1985 they were on the rise again, reaching a new high three times the 1984 level. One reason was Umkhonto's reorganization, which emphasized home-based training and command over reliance on incoming guerrillas. But infiltration, too, had apparently resumed, albeit in sharply reduced numbers and with more stealth, at least on the Mozambique side.

The Congress's clandestine return to Mozambique was perhaps predictable for as long as FRELIMO remained in control in Maputo. The ruling party, even before coming to power on the heels of a guerrilla war against the Portuguese, had long cooperated closely with the ANC. The two movements had shared objectives in seeking the overthrow of minority rule, patrons in the Soviet Union, and experiences in the diplomatic wilderness of exile. There were thousands of former FRELIMO fighters working at all levels of the Mozambican civilian and military bureaucracies, who were potential covert accomplices to a quiet ANC return. At the same time, the nation's armed forces were preoccupied with defeating Renamo rather than interdicting Umkhonto insurgents, while the administration was too busy coping with economic crisis to hunt out Congress supporters.

Finally, Pretoria's once secret decision to continue supplying Renamo despite the Nkomati agreement had shattered the previous consensus view within FRELIMO that expelling the Congress would at least bring the benefit of peace. The late President Samora Machel and his successor, Joaquim Chissano, might have reaffirmed pledges to prevent Mozambican territory from being used for ANC infiltration, but after 1985 fully enforcing such a commitment would become a political and practical impossibility.

Umkhonto commanders favor the eastern infiltration corridor through Swaziland despite the kingdom's firm prohibition of any guerrilla forces within its borders. Nearly as vulnerable as any homeland to South African pressure, the landlocked country had secretly entered into an Nkomati-like nonagression accord with Pretoria in February 1982. Periodically, the government ordered roundups of ANC exiles known to be dwelling in the kingdom, but as a practical matter there was little the 1,500-man police force or unruly 3,000-strong army could do to prevent the rapid transit of ANC insurgents from Mozambique through Swaziland into South Africa. Both the main north and south guerrilla trails through the country featured wild, low-veld terrain with vegetation that could be used as cover. Both, too, had the added advantage of ethnic bridges into the Republic.

In the south, some five thousand members of two Swazi clans had trekked from Natal to Swaziland in 1977 when Pretoria had attempted to impose an unwanted chief on them. Settling on farmland purchased from expatriates, the newcomers soon began to raid South African farms across the border. Although arrests on both sides of the frontier brought these to a halt, the group was thought to have forged links with the ANC as a means of demonstrating its hostility to Pretoria. Ethnically related to Natal's Zulus, the settlers and other Zulu-offshoot communities along Swaziland's southern border were thought to have proven especially valuable in helping Umkhonto smuggle guerrillas and arms shipments into South Africa.[20]

Unlike other infiltration corridors, however, the southern Swazi route into Natal terminated in territory more thoroughly under the control of an anti-ANC homeland leader than any other black reservation. Chief Gatsha Buthelezi's Inkatha movement, with networks of representatives lacing nearly every community in the ten landblocks of KwaZulu, had the capacity to uncover local guerrilla contacts, thereby denying insurgents the protection, intelligence information, and sustenance necessary for them to survive undetected by the police. Yet Natal's Durban was listed by the police in 1985 as South Africa's most frequently bombed city,[21] and Pretoria continued to betray anxiety about ongoing infiltration.

Buthelezi may have had a motive to look the other way when Umkhonto guerrillas passed though his realm, despite the chief's much publicized break with the Congress. The more anti-apartheid violence Umkhonto caused, the more whites sought cooperation with Buthelezi as the black leader most willing to leave minority power intact in a post-apartheid South Africa. In the chief minister's calculations, every ANC bombing might deliver him more white votes so he might assume a prominent role in a national power-sharing alliance. Umkhonto infiltration through KwaZulu and Natal, hindered only on a token basis, might hasten the day when the National Party might turn to the Zulu chief to rescue it from spiraling civil war.

Other Swazi infiltration corridors presented different opportunities to the ANC. Welded along the kingdom's northern and western border lay the homeland of kaNgwane, created as a reservation for Swazi-born South Africans. Pretoria had wished to cede the territory to Swaziland, but kaNgwane Chief Minister Enos Mabuza and much of the homeland population opposed the arrangement. Eventually the scheme was tabled, but not before the ANC could capitalize on the widespread dissension by building a base of support within kaNgwane. In 1985 Mabuza traveled to Lusaka to become the first homeland leader since Gatsha Buthelezi to hold talks with the ANC. The chief minister's public recognition of the Congress as the preeminent representative of black political aspirations seemed to signal constituents that assisting Umkhonto's infiltration operations through neighboring Swaziland was acceptable in spite of the legal dangers. With relatives and cultural ties linking kaNgwane's Swazis to those living across the border, Congress agents could hope to shuttle Umkhonto soldiers and weapons through this ethnic "underground railway" into South Africa's Transvaal province.

SANCTUARY

Every successful insurgency in Africa has depended on rebels' converting villages and townships into "liberated" zones. Internal bases of support provide fighters protection against discovery by the enemy; food, water, and shelter they may not be able to obtain on their own; and intelligence regarding enemy targets and movements. Without such sanctuaries, insurgents would be waging an isolated struggle in which the aggrieved population felt it had little at stake and no role. Forced into battle on the government's terms of military rather than political strength, such rebels would find it is only a matter of time before the enemy prevails.

Until 1985, when the ANC command issued its call to free black communities from Pretoria's control, incoming Umkhonto insurgents were relying on a spotty and thinly spread network of cells to sustain them upon entry into the country. The majority of blacks, while sympathetic, felt little compulsion to serve as other than members of a cheering section. Umkhonto was failing to convert passive public approval into active military support. By the time consultative conference delegates assembled in Zambia to debate the movement's future, the ANC leadership had resolved to change course. The war now had to take root at home, even if far from centers of command, and the townships had to be prepared to nourish it.

Meanwhile the United Democratic Front affiliates, with sporadic help from Congress's underground, were proving astonishingly successful in ejecting governmental authority from black communities. In fact, the seizure of power in township after township in 1985 proceeded so rapidly that it caught the ANC unprepared. Strategists had not yet devised a plan for replacing Pretoria's councils with liberation alternatives. Nor had the UDF advised its constituent groups about what to do in the event of triumph. Perhaps neither organization had realistically expected the collapse of apartheid administrations so widely and quickly, for calling upon blacks simply to "make the townships ungovernable" risked inviting chaos rather than "people power."

Predictably, the ascension of civic organizations resulted not in the spread of uniform models of revolutionary government, but in dissimilar and unevenly applied civil administrations. In part, of course, the UDF's problems rested on the incomplete victories it had achieved: Pretoria's councils may have fallen, but patrolling troops brought a dominion of intermittent force over the streets. Revolutionary reign still had to emerge in secret cabals and clandestine cells. Yet the absence of guidance from the Congress for a time compelled UDF affiliates to grope in near political blindness for models of anti-apartheid administration. In many cases indiscipline manifested itself in riots, crime, and marauding youth gangs.

Finally, in April of 1986, the ANC announced principles to harmonize the diverse efforts to create liberated zones. It called for the founding of local "Revolutionary People's Committees," melding together all the ANC-oriented civic groups in each community.[22] Nine months later President Tambo proclaimed 1987 "The Year of Advance to People's Power" to focus energy on building the "organs of people's self rule." But while the Congress urged introduction of "people's courts," "people's education," and democratic decision-making, its chief focus was on establishing sanctuaries for Umkhonto we Sizwe.

Revolutionary People's Committees were charged with "organizing the masses and transforming the no-go areas into strong mass revolutionary bases to provide the ground for the growth and development of our people's army and for the escalation of our people's war."[23] The call represented a de facto acknowledgment that the only practical way for Umkhonto to expand would be to convince many more of the black public to participate in guerrilla warfare. "Our people should not be mere spectators," Umkhonto political commissar Chris Hani pleaded in interviews.

> The doors of the houses of our people should be open to our cadres. Everybody should realize that he has got a role to play to ensure the success of our military operations. To ensure that every cadre, as he throws a grenade in the house of a policeman, into the barracks of the fascist army, that that cadre must be able to get away, must be able to survive in order to be able to fight tomorrow.[24] When the fighters of MK knock at your door, give them food; if they need a change of clothes, give them the clothes. . . . Fighting means . . . collecting information about the enemy. It means surveying his movements and finding a way of conveying this information to an organization in the underground. . . . That is your duty.[25]

In an effort to implant order into the confusion of the townships, the ANC pressed its underground to harness the insurrectionist ardor of what were termed "mass combat units" to Umkhonto we Sizwe. These bands of angry young men were to be organized into cells to harbor incoming guerrillas and man new Umkhonto detachments. Since the limited size of the ANC's domestic network ensured, however, that many such bands would be left unsupervised for an extended period, the Congress urged them over Radio Freedom to train themselves in the interim in guerrilla warfare.[26] Leaders contemplated an underground press and radio curriculum covering such matters as "creating defense structures such as dugouts, tunnels and underground depots; the principles of survival tactics such as the fundamentals of first aid; the principles governing the creation of underground cells; the rudiments of handling basic weaponry such as revolvers, pistols, rifles and hand-grenades; the principles of manufacturing crude weapons such as Molotov cocktails, home-made explosives and how to handle and use them, and other elementaries of military science."[27] According to the ANC's perhaps wishful theory, volunteers thus schooled in military fundamentals would be primed to defend local revolutionary committees as militiamen and, when finally contacted by the ANC underground, to enlist as Umkhonto soldiers.

The Congress by 1986 had in any case already implemented a program of local weapons training where incoming Umkhonto insurgents could found or join underground guerrilla cells. Guerrillas were known to smuggle into the country texts such as "An Elementary Handbook on Explosives" that had been inserted and rebound into the body of inconspicuous novels.[28] "Liberated zones" provided sanctuary for such clandestine coursework.

Security expert Michael Morris informed his colleagues in 1985 that the ANC had established a "grenade instruction school" in the Cape Town area.[29] But nothing so permanent as a school was practical in black areas regularly swept by police forces. Standard operating procedure would more likely have involved brief workshops in shifting locales. One of the few court cases that exposed the operations of an entire ANC cell tracked in testimony some eleven months of undetected Umkhonto training and recruitment in a northern Natal community. Four guerrillas, infiltrating South Africa on the eastern corridor, apparently made contact with two ANC agents in Ingwavuma early in 1984.[30] For the next several months the group worked to enlist local residents into a secret ANC unit, while stowing courier-smuggled weapons in nearby caves and planning some fifty military operations. They appear to have kept in touch with Umkhonto control agents across the border in either Mozambique or Swaziland through coded communications.

At this rudimentary rear base, new recruits learned the use of automatic weapons, explosives, and even rarely seen bazookas and rockets. A captured diary written by twenty-six-year-old Robert Dumisa, who referred to himself as the unit's commander, revealed that locals accepted and aided the guerrillas "because we talk the truth about oppression and we are their children and brothers." But residents harbored grave doubts about the competence of black rebels to strike at the government. "One of the women said we'll start the war and retreat to Swaziland leaving them at the mercy of the police and the army," wrote Dumisa. "Now it is up to us to demonstrate our capability to fight . . .we must not leave them whatever the enemy offensive might be."[31]

Dumisa's experience confirms that Umkhonto guerrillas had to serve as political missionaries as much as warriors, particularly in rural areas where the Congress was less known. Nor could political and military work be separated. Guerrilla raids and recruitment could not succeed without a popular base, and the construction of a popular base depended, in turn, on success in guerrilla warfare. Dumisa's capture, together with twelve others in Ingwavuma, showed that no internal sanctuary, even though operating for nearly a year, could be made absolutely secure against the probing eyes of counterinsurgency authorities. Yet the Congress in the second half of the 1980s had only just begun to experiment with domestic community bases as a means of escalating the war, and Pretoria expected many more to be established.

ARMING THE REBELS

One of the thorniest tactical problems facing Umkhonto's high command was the difficulty in arming its growing ranks of domestic volunteers. Pretoria's crackdown on border security combined with the earlier impact of the Nkomati accord to imperil severely the thin flow of weapons and ammunition being smuggled into the country. Further, the frontier bottleneck coincided precisely with new waves of anti-apartheid resistance that were persuading thousands of blacks to seek enlistment in MK.

Up until 1985, Umkhonto could count on a network of inventive couriers to slip weapons into South Africa. Guerrillas were known to have used forged passports to enter the country through border posts unarmed but prepared to signal couriers when ready to receive weapons. Petrus Molefe, born in the homeland of Qwa-Qwa and trained in guerrilla warfare in East Germany, was one of many MK soldiers dependent for arms on the movement's courier service.

In September of 1977 Molefe reported to the secret Manzini, Swaziland, headquarters of an Umkhonto commander known only by the code name "Dan." The officer ordered Molefe to establish a safe weapons storage and communication system in Kwa Thema township near Springs, one of the Witwatersrand's major industrial centers. The guerrilla was given funds, a forged passport, and a passbook for travel through the Oshoek border post on Swaziland's western frontier, and presumably the name of several ANC sympathizers in Kwa Thema. Molefe entered South Africa in October and made his way to Springs without incident. He apparently found accommodation with one or more of the supporters presumably listed by "Dan," and within ten days had located an appropriate hiding place: an unused water pipe in the township.

On October 16, Molefe used his falsified documents to return to Manzini for a final rendezvous with "Dan." There, he mapped out the Kwa Thema storage location and the two arranged an elaborate communication system. Molefe was to return to South Africa through the border post and, when ready, construct a coded letter requesting the shipment of arms, ammunition, and explosives from Manzini. The letter would be placed in the water pipe, and Molefe would alert an unknown ANC courier of its presence by placing a white sticker on a specified Kwa Thema bus stop. Umkhonto's couriers would then transport the letter to Swaziland and the weapons shipment back to Springs, all without Molefe having to know the identify of any agents apart from "Dan," who was abroad, and his township contacts.

Molefe ordered weapons in November 1977 and was subsequently informed of their arrival by a red marker at the agreed upon bus stop. The arms cache, which included Skorpions, limpet mines, and hand grenades, was later revealed to be the largest single guerrilla arsenal yet found in South Africa. Before Molefe was able to utilize them in any insurgent missions, however, a group of children playing in the area discovered the cache and their find was reported to the police.[32] Molefe was arrested in February 1978, but he could be of little help to the security branch in identifying accomplices and methods of smuggling arms into Kwa Thema.

Umkhonto's courier service had had to use even more creative methods to evade police surveillance. In 1978, government experts demonstrated to the press how cocoa and cookie tins were being used to smuggle plastic explosives, fuses, and ammunition into South Africa.[33] On other occasions, a Botswana-registered car equipped with a false bottom had apparently ferried small arsenals across the border.[34] One of the ANC's weapons of choice, the limpet mine, was favored in part because up to four of them could be strapped to a courier's body underneath clothing without attracting attention.

Despite Umkhonto's success in seeding politically fertile black communities with small stocks of infiltrated arms, the supply was soon hopelessly overwhelmed by demand. "Our aim of arming the people has a long way to go," remarked Umkhonto tactician Ronnie Kasrils in 1986. "Every stone-thrower wants a gun. We have to put guns in their hands."[35] Desire could not substitute for means. Pretoria's improved frontier fortification had made gun-running a more hazardous enterprise. Crowds of eager ANC followers were reduced to marching with wooden replicas of AK-47s to symbolize the scarce weapons, and angry youths continued to hurl rocks and Molotov cocktails at the defense force's armored vehicles.

Umkhonto's dilemma was not without irony. Like "water, water everywhere," South African white society boasted more guns per capita than almost any population in the world; by 1980, over 1.5 million had received firearm licenses, an average of three guns for every four white males in the country.[36] But Pretoria sought to ensure that there was "not a drop to drink" for blacks. Sentences for theft of weapons were severe, often five years in jail, and whites were frequently reminded to lock their arms and ammunition in hiding places inaccessible to housemaids and gardeners. Defense, police, and militia officers insisted on regular inventories of unit armories swiftly to detect any losses.

With its cross-border supply lines incapable of transferring major new arms shipments into the country, the ANC command had to face watching its supporters' frustrations—and casualties—grow. To avert a crisis of unmet expectations, the Lusaka headquarters called in 1985 for "revolutionary creativity" and "self-reliance"; in other words, rather than wait for Angolan AK-47s, blacks had to arm themselves in the only other way possible—by stealing.[37]

> Domestic servants . . . know where their employers keep their weapons and they are the ones who can devise plans for transferring the ownership of the weapons. There are also weapons in the regime's police stations and barracks. Those weapons must be removed. . . . [We] make a clarion call to those of our people who find themselves wearing the murderers' uniforms to use their positions to arm the nation . . . [by] forming some small underground cells right inside the regime's barracks and . . . smuggling weapons out of the armories.[38]

Asking black policemen or domestic servants to purloin guns was asking them to invite joblessness. Only the most plausible alibis could avert layoff and trial on charges of theft. A maid could try to

stage a break-in, have herself bound to a chair, and claim no knowledge of the intruders. A law enforcer could arrange with the "comrades" to be ambushed in a township street. No accounts or statistics
could accurately track how many took such risks, since not all whites
would go through the embarrassment of reporting theft and few such
incidents could be expected to be announced by police and noted by
national newspapers. But by mid-1985 the first scattered stories of
robberies involving firearms had begun to appear.

Black rebels had relieved defense-force troops of five R-4 assault
rifles and ammunition in a Port Elizabeth township in August, reported the *Star*.[39] Seven months later the *Sowetan* described how
five youths trapped a white constable on patrol and stole his service
revolver.[40] In June 1986 a black policeman suffered minor stab
wounds when a group of young men robbed him of a pistol near
Crossroads, according to the *Star*.[41] Seemingly isolated, these cases
formed part of the anti-apartheid community's answer to the Congress's appeal. They probably represented only a small fraction of
the total black response. But Pretoria was as yet betraying little
concern about any hemorrhaging of white arsenals. It would be a
long time yet before Umkhonto could claim to have converted "the
South African mighty war machine into a resource depot for arming
the masses of our people."[42] Fortunately for the Congress, would-be
recruits could find no other black liberation group able to perform
any better.

ESPIONAGE

South Africa's war over apartheid is waged primarily as a shadowy
contest for the intelligence high ground. The ANC, like any guerrilla
movement, needs above all to seal itself off against enemy penetration to preserve its most potent weapon: the surprise attack. Commandos also require information concerning enemy targets so as to
strike with maximum impact and minimum cost. Pretoria, on the
other hand, like any government defending itself against insurgency,
can hope to crush rebellion by uncovering who the guerrillas are,
where they hide, and what they intend to hit before they hit it.

The work of protecting Umkhonto operations from police surveillance involved, more than anything else, public loyalty. But
against the politically unresponsive the movement erected such administrative defenses as security screening and compartmentalized

missions that allowed no one member, if captured, to expose more than a single underground cell. The Congress also assigned political commissars to MK units to guard against infiltrators. The most effective tactic was the Congress's threat to impose punishment on anyone who was thought to be betraying the organization. Umkhonto soldiers could be deployed, in effect, as a counterpolice in service of a countergovernment. Using intimidation and assassination, they sought both to blind Pretoria's military operations and to thwart trials of jailed ANC members. The grisly practice of necklacing, while officially unauthorized, produced the same result: fear of informing on black rebels.

By 1978 South African police authorities had begun to complain publicly about shrinking espionage capabilities.[43] Two years later an alarmed Brigadier Johan Coetzee, chief of the security branch, revealed that "there are many informers who have been murdered and many other agents and informers who have received death threats after they have given evidence in terrorism trials."[44] Moreover, the killings were taking place in spite of a new police program to relocate, and perhaps assign new identities to, the most valuable undercover agents.[45] A 1985 trial of three alleged ANC rebels demonstrated the consequences. One witness after another—three in all—refused to give evidence for fear of ANC reprisals against them, their families, or their property. The judge meted out sentences of up to one year in prison for each of the three.[46]

Mindful of how Rhodesian security had eventually lost its ability to infiltrate rebel organizations, Pretoria tried to stem the tide by offering large cash awards for information.[47] Yet the government's new data on the ANC appeared to have suffered major declines. South African intelligence had failed to unearth Umkhonto's most elaborate and spectacular missions, such as the bombings at the Sasol oil-from-coal plant, the rocket attack on Voortrekkerhoogte base, and the explosions at the Koeberg nuclear complex.

Having shut the police out of most underground operations, ANC commanders could now contemplate using some of the more extravagant pyrotechnics of the spying profession, such as manipulating anxious security authorities by feeding them false rumors or offering them double agents who could pass on misleading information while remaining loyal to the Congress. Whether these tactics actually became part of ANC practice is unknown.

The daily intelligence requirements of South Africa's insurgency more often involved drudgery than pyrotechnics. A unit engaged in "routine" attacks on police stations or government offices had to make tactical decisions based on field reconnaissance. ANC National Executive Committee member Thabo Mbeki described how guerrillas bombed Pretoria's air-force headquarters building at 5:00 P.M. on May 1983.

> Reconnaissance has to be continuous and up to date . . . they need very detailed intelligence information on the street: who is on the street at 5:00 P.M.? Is it military, civilian or both? If both, then in what proportion? Can we carry out the operation without getting caught? . . . The entire area is a military cantonment. You must know what are the security arrangements to safeguard the cantonment. Between 4:00 and 5:00 P.M., 80% of the pedestrians are civilians, so there is a greater chance of not getting caught. From 5:00 P.M. it's 80% security personnel, and we may get caught. . . . Even though the decision may be taken on the outside to go ahead on such and such a day, the Umkhonto unit must do its own reconnaissance.[48]

Agents assigned to the target vicinity, posing perhaps as street cleaners or repairmen, and staking out the scene for a week or more, could provide Umkhonto field commanders with most of the intelligence they needed to plan an attack. The task was not without risk, as numerous court trials revealed. In one typical case of an aborted mission, Thandi Ruth Modise, trained in both Angola and Tanzania, investigated a police station near Krugersdorp, along with a Bantu Affairs Administration Board building, in preparation for two 1978 Umkhonto raids. She was discovered and later convicted.[49]

A second, more advanced intelligence technique used to prepare for assaults on township constabularies was infiltration. Early in 1976, Jeffrey Klaas joined the ANC and received orders to infiltrate the police force. Enlisting in September, Klaas actively recruited other black officers into clandestine cells and passed information on to Umkhonto agents until he was caught and jailed.[50] In another incident, the bold May 1979 Umkhonto operation against Moroka police station in Soweto was assisted by a former policeman who had left the force one year earlier. As an insider, he was able to guide the attack.[51]

More ambitious strikes, the kind that could advertise Umkhonto's presence to whites in spite of press censorship, demanded a more sophisticated intelligence operation managed by the external command rather than field officers. The small number of such incidents suggested that the ANC could deploy relatively few espionage agents in key government institutions. But each case proved to whites that the power structure was penetrable, and often with spectacular results.

The June 1980 explosions at Sasols I and II and the large Natref oil refinery, and simultaneous discovery of an unexploded bomb at Sasol's recruiting office in Springs, are evidence of the ANC's inside contacts in and intelligence on three of the Republic's most closely guarded facilities. The guerrillas overcame a $14 to $20 million security system, and escaped the area despite immediate police cordons and roadblocks, and the mobilization of military, paramilitary, civil defense, and police units throughout the region.[52] Only after a defense-force raid eight months later into Mozambique netted Pretoria an Umkhonto frontline control officer could police finally interrogate a source involved in the attack. The kidnapped agent identified at least one of the saboteurs, David Moisi, who was later captured, convicted, and sentenced to death.[53] The trial confirmed that MK had indeed infiltrated the work force at the plants.

The ANC scored another espionage coup through the offices of the now defunct International University Exchange Fund (IUEF), a nonprofit institution located in Geneva and ostensibly geared toward providing educational scholarships for South African students. Congress agent Frene Ginwala of the party's information department, and Horst Kleinschmidt, an ANC sympathizer and officer of the IUEF, together recruited Renfrew Leslie Christie, a Ph.D. expert in South African energy systems, to act as an internal intelligence gatherer in 1978. While traveling abroad, Christie arranged secret addresses to which information could be forwarded, and he received some $2,600 for expenses, the bulk of which came from the ANC. Returning to South Africa in July 1979, Christie embarked on a covert program to forward data to the addresses in Britain and Switzerland. He obtained documents discussing the regions in which the South African Atomic Energy Board regarded it seismologically safe to detonate nuclear explosive devices. He procured diagrams of Cape Town's Koeberg nuclear facility, as well as blueprints of the Camden electricity generating complex. Christie also reconnoitered power stations near Witbank and Kriel, gathering information to dispatch abroad.

Christie was eventually betrayed by Craig Williamson, one of the IUEF's top administrators and, undercover, a captain in the South African Police. Yet Williamson had not had access to Christie's data, and the prosecution conceded at the spy trial that "the exact nature of this information and the dates on which it was sent are not known to the State . . . it is [also] not known to the State specifically what information and photocopies the accused obtained."[54] Predictably, two years after Christie's reports reached the ANC, Umkhonto blew up parts of the Camden plant in a synchronized triple sabotage mission involving two power facilities and a substation.[55] In December 1982, Umkhonto explosions ripped through the Koeberg nuclear plant, causing over $40 million in damage and delaying its commissioning for over a year. Both operations overcame new layers of security provided to the installations in the wake of the Christie revelations.

Another ANC espionage scheme, this time aimed at the South African Defense Force, aided Umkhonto in less incendiary ways. It was exposed in 1984, when Derek and Patricia Hanekom were accused of recruiting an agent for the ANC in an office of military intelligence. The couple were alleged to have communicated in code with Congress officials in Botswana while enlisting a twenty-five-year-old draftee, Roland Hunter, who served as a clerk in the supersensitive Directorate of Special Operations. By mid-1983, Hunter began providing his contacts with stolen or copied documents listed as highly classified. They included "planning notes on military operations," intelligence "source reports," identifications of Special Operations personnel, and a code book, according to the indictment. Some of these were smuggled to ANC agents in Botswana, while others were hidden in homes or a safe deposit box. The Hanekoms and Hunter were detained in December.[56] How or whether Umkhonto was able to use this informational windfall to improve guerrilla deployment is unknown.

In addition to field-based reconnaissance and scattered spy rings, the ANC was suspected of piloting ongoing espionage activity in the black homelands—Transkei in particular. Minister of Justice D. S. Koyana declared three years after Transkei's "independence" that ANC and PAC exiles were welcome in the territory on condition that they come "unarmed, in peace, and in full recognition of the sovereignty of the state."[57] They came, if not necessarily in sincerest accord with the minister's pledge, and in short order established a beachhead in the homeland's governmental bureaucracy. Much of the Transkei's foreign service, for example, became populated with South African political refugees, despite Umtata's hostility to the liberation movement. One source close to the Congress underground asserted that some of these Transkei technocrats were in fact secret agents reporting on troop movements and political strategies to the ANC.[58]

The ANC's in-house intelligence resources could be augmented by those of like-minded individuals or allied groups. In a celebrated and controversial 1979 case, a seven-year agent for Pretoria's notorious Bureau of State Security (BOSS) defected to Britain, bringing with him some fifty secret documents detailing operations of the Republic's intelligence network. While there were doubts as to Arthur McGiven's credibility (the PAC suggested that he remained a South African spy)[59] and his motives (he sold his information to the *London Observer* for publication), his knowledge of the police was likely to be tapped by the London office of the ANC.[60]

Two other publicly known espionage coups managed by anti-apartheid organizations helped the Congress. In the first, the white group Okhela was believed to have been responsible for obtaining documentation on South Africa's secret nuclear program from diplomatic contacts in West Germany. The information fueled a propaganda drive that tightened controls on Western high technology trade with Pretoria. In the second, an agent in South African Defense Force headquarters in Pretoria smuggled a classified computer list of names and addresses of thousands of conscripts to a foreign-based draft resistance movement. The New York office of SAMRAF, the South African Military Refugees Aid Fund, transferred the list to editors of the underground journal *Omkeer,* which then distributed copies through the South African mails to draftees, urging them either to resist induction or to desert.[61]

The most valuable allied channel of intelligence data for the ANC, however, was the South African Communist Party and, through it, the Soviet Union. Over the years the SACP was thought to have remained adept at tapping agents or sympathizers, particularly in the white community, for inside information. The secretive party could boast what was believed to be a sophisticated, though quite small, underground structure. According to one rumor, a prominent Afrikaner communist, trade-union organizer Elizabeth duToit, had initiated a deep cover espionage program known by the code name "Sleeper." It envisioned the infiltration of government departments and sensitive parastatals by SACP double agents expected to provide the party with intelligence. Launched in the early 1960s, "Sleeper" was said to have been revitalized in the 1970s to supply the external SACP leadership with data of military importance to Umkhonto we Sizwe.[62] No independent verification of the existence of such a program could be found.

In addition to its own underground resources, the SACP was presumed to have served as a conduit for espionage information collected and passed on by Moscow. In 1978, while diplomats were busy moving the South African embassy into new quarters in Paris, top-secret government documents suddenly disappeared. They later resurfaced at ANC headquarters in Zambia. The organizer of the theft was believed to be Henri Curiel, founder of the Egyptian Communist party during World War II and a suspected senior KGB agent.[63] The papers were likely to have been transferred to Communist Party members of the ANC at Soviet orders.

One year later an American newsletter of uncertain reliability reported that Soviet spy vessels equipped with "highly sophisticated electronic gear" had been mixed in with a fleet of Russian fishing trawlers working off the South African coast. "The ships are being used to monitor South African radio transmissions and gather military intelligence," read the story. "The information is in turn fed back to terrorists for use in planning their attack."[64] If the account was as accurate as it was plausible, it is likely that the data was being channeled through the SACP to Umkhonto.

The most sensational Soviet spy operation yet exposed involved an "old school tie" Afrikaner, Commodore Dieter Gerhardt, who for over twenty years supplied Moscow with classified information as he rose through the ranks of the South African Navy. In Gerhardt's 1983 trial, prosecutors charged him with secretly turning to the Soviets in 1962 in frustration over the government's refusal to abandon apartheid. A trusted officer, Gerhardt was posted to Pretoria's defense force headquarters in the 1970s, where he had access to military planning documents for all three services.[65] Later he was promoted to commander of the dockyard at South Africa's sprawling Simonstown naval base. Until discovered in January 1983, Com-

modore Gerhardt and his Swiss-born wife, Ruth, were alleged to
have maintained clandestine contact with Soviet agents by radio
transmission, code letter, and courier, passing on details of the country's most sensitive military secrets.[66] Many were bound to encompass surveillance of southern hemisphere sea-lanes for NATO, a
principal mission of the Simonstown base.

Such information would have interested Moscow but not Umkhonto, which had not once been found to have infiltrated guerrillas
by water. Nevertheless, some of Gerhardt's trove must have covered
counterinsurgency planning data useful to the MK command. Should
Moscow have authorized its transfer to the ANC, the material would
likely have come through South African Communist Party channels.
Insurgent strategists equipped with information on South African
troop movements, base strengths, and military defenses could more
accurately identify attack targets and plan safer postmission escape
routes.

WAR STATISTICS

A statistical portrait of South Africa's rebellion is all but impossible
to paint. The ANC's Lusaka command, for its part, does not always
know what missions Umkhonto guerrillas have undertaken until well
after they are over. In any case, the leadership has adopted the
practice of only occasionally claiming responsibility for strikes, perhaps as a means of bolstering an image of organizational distaste for
warfare. Pretoria, on the other hand, issues periodic updates on
guerrilla activity, but without details, without incorporating incidents in the "independent" homelands, and in a manner designed to
boost confidence in the government's capacity to contain insurgency. Since, as a declassified U.S. State Department cable observed as
early as 1978, "the overwhelming majority of security trials and
incidents are not being reported in the South African press,"[67] there
are no independent means to verify the government's figures.

Even security police statistics, however, trace an outline of
growing warfare. In 1976, authorities attributed an average of just
two incidents every six months to the ANC. Ten years later, the
number had skyrocketed to an average of more than five bombings,
raids, or assassinations each week.[68] The Nkomati accord with Mozambique had cut guerrilla activity from 56 attacks in the whole of

1983 to 44 in 1984. But the effect was only temporary. In 1985, insurgent strikes trebled to a new annual high of 136, a toll that was exceeded again the following year. By August, the official 1986 tally had registered 168.[69]

The government's numbers do not reflect the actual intensity of Umkhonto operations; at best, the "Acts of Terror" index tracks only incidents in which bombs went off or guns were fired. Aborted guerrilla missions, deliberately unexploded bombs, or duds are not counted. For example, Deputy Minister of Information Louis Nel told a press conference in May 1986 that while twelve ANC land-mines had exploded in the preceding decade, thirty more had been unearthed by security forces. Similarly, he listed only seven demolition mines having been detonated by insurgents but eighty-seven others defused by defense patrols.[70] The implication is that for every exploded Umkhonto mine in the decade following the Soweto uprising, between three and twelve others may have been planted by guerrilla units and not included in Pretoria's aggregate figures. If incidents in the "independent homelands" could be added, the barometer of insurgent activity would rise further.

The "Acts of Terror" also do not include other indicators of Umkhonto operations, such as police discoveries of arms caches, accidental explosions in basement bomb factories, arrests of trained guerrillas, industrial sabotage, unsuccessful manhunts for sighted insurgents, and incidents connected with but officially deemed un-linked to the ANC. Anti-apartheid incidents ruled criminal rather than political are not likely to appear on Pretoria's index of rebellion; and, in an unknown number of cases, the government appears to have deliberately suppressed information about successful guerrilla actions.[71] Since the government alone possessed the authority to report on internal security matters, it alone could define the scope of insurgency, and do so in ways that best served its interests.

In short, official statistics on MK operations seriously understate the intensity of guerrilla activity throughout South Africa. The actual number of missions traceable to insurgents could be as much as three times the reported figure.

Not all attacks are equal. Some 19 percent, according to security police, had occurred in and around Durban, the country's most bombed city between 1976 and 1985;[72] the remainder had been scattered throughout the Transvaal, and a lesser number in the Cape province, with only a fraction of the explosions taking place in the Orange Free State.[73] A handful had rocked white residential neighborhoods, though in the first eight months of 1986, in response to the ANC's call to carry the war into white areas, the figure had rocketed to 28 percent of all officially recognized attacks.[74] The rest had hit targets in black townships and homelands or in commercial or industrial areas. And in the government's body count, nearly four hundred officially certified "terror" attacks over ten years had caused some 43 black and 35 white citizens to lose their lives.[75]

Umkhonto missions could be divided into six categories of attacks, according to an analysis made by University of the Witwatersrand professor Tom Lodge. Taking over 150 cases of ANC-linked violence appearing in the press during the six years following Soweto's uprising, Lodge found that only 2 percent of guerrilla attacks were aimed at well-defended SADF targets. By contrast, 37 percent involved sabotage of key economic objectives such as railway machinery and industrial facilities, and 17 percent involved surprise assaults on government buildings and police stations. Shootouts with soldiers or police, which are normally to be avoided by outgunned guerrillas, accounted for 12 percent of incidents in the 1976–82 period. Scattered bombs detonated in public places, usually during nonbusiness hours, amounted to under 10 percent. These offensive missions were balanced by political assassinations of state witnesses and suspected collaborators, a defensive category which reached over 22 percent of Umkhonto's total attacks in the Lodge survey.[76] Lightning raids and sabotage against establishment targets had clearly become the favored tactics of Umkhonto's offensive.

TARGETS

The two main prongs of the rebel charge were aimed at the economy and the government. These, in turn, like all Congress raids, could be divided roughly into national-oriented challenge attacks—those designed to heighten fear and insecurity among whites—and local-oriented linkage attacks—which advertised the ANC's support for black community protest. Strikes against South Africa's economic infrastructure, including energy installations, railway routes, man-

ufacturing plants, and corporate headquarters, constituted the largest
bloc of Umkhonto missions in the decade following Soweto. A 1984
incident was typical of MK challenge attacks on the economy.

Darkness and the thick brush along the ridge above Durban's
Mobil oil refinery complex must have seemed welcome protection to
the guerrillas silently assembling a rocket launcher and automatic
weapons on the night of May 13. Ordered to hit the petroleum
facility, one of the nation's largest, the unit had probably scouted the
area in advance for the best firing position offering the greatest
chance of escape. At 10:22 P.M., they launched a brief attack with a
rocket bombardment and blasts of gunfire. One missile whistled
narrowly over a large oil tank but slammed into a smaller one,
causing explosions and a spectacular fire. For the next two hours
security forces combed the area, later claiming to have killed four
"terrorists" in a gun battle.[77] But it may never be known whether
these victims had been involved in the operations, or whether in fact
they were insurgents at all. The bold Durban raid made front-page
news throughout the country the next morning.

The strongest on the continent, South Africa's economy would
seem an unlikely target for ANC challenge attacks. A complex national infrastructure might be expected to absorb periodic sabotage
without economic tremor, and without the widespread propagandist
reverberations sought by Umkhonto, particularly if white casualties
resulted only rarely. But powerhouse statistics disguised vulnerable
economic foundations. For one thing, the Republic's major industrial centers are few. The economic zone defined by Pretoria in the
north-central Transvaal and Vereeniging in the southern tier of the
province constitutes only some 1 percent of South Africa's land mass
but is responsible for over 50 percent of its gross national product.[78]
Cape Town, the eastern Cape (Port Elizabeth–East London), and
Durban together provide the remainder of the nation's manufacturing
strength.

The concentration of so much industry in a small number of
zones increases the opportunities for sabotage owing to dependence
on common sources of energy, communications, and transport systems. Challenge attacks on any one of these facilities could result in
economic repercussions throughout the zone, just as the accidental
disabling of single power stations caused massive blackouts in the
northeastern United States in 1965 and 1977, or as the destruction by

insurgents of fuel storage facilities at a site near Salisbury forced widespread industrial deceleration in eastern Rhodesia as a consequence of petroleum shortages.

Adding to the regime's vulnerability is, ironically, its quarter-century-old program of import substitution geared to reducing South African dependence on fickle, boycott-prone, and expensive foreign suppliers of key goods. The eastern Cape's automobile industry is a prime example of how more of the nation's industry has become hostage to domestic black labor. To guard against the consequences of a withdrawal of American and European auto giants, a foresighted government stipulated in 1960 that some 12 percent of the mass weight of cars had to be made locally. The figure was hiked to 24 percent in 1962, 45 percent in 1965, 55 percent in 1967, 66 percent in 1978, and 76 percent in 1980.[79] Pretoria could now boast protection against boycotts, but at the cost of exposure to guerrilla operations against sensitive industries carried out under the cover of black unions.

Umkhonto political commissar Chris Hani, in a statement over Radio Freedom, encouraged employees to exploit their positions by assembling workplace MK cells and, in the absence of guns, being "creative and inventive" in attacking the enemy. "If we are working in a factory which produces weapons, vehicles, trucks which are used by the army and police against us . . . you must ensure that there are frequent breakdowns in those machines you operate. You can clog some of them by using sugar and sand. . . . "[80]

The South African economy is also acutely dependent on its mines. Mineral extraction might have accounted for only some 13.6 percent of GNP in 1978, gold alone for just 9 percent; but gold's contribution to export earnings claimed some 43 percent of the nation's total foreign exchange income in 1979.[81] Disruptions in the mines, either in the form of strikes or sabotage, would constitute a grave threat to South Africa's economic health.

Rail lines, in most countries only one of a mix of transportation alternatives, in South Africa hold a near monopoly on internal commerce. They therefore were uniquely effective targets of sabotage. Transport regulations allow any movement of goods by road for over thirty kilometers only by permit, which is only rarely granted.[82] Though burdened with costly and inefficient routes, South African Railways carries virtually all the country's agricultural products, export minerals, locally manufactured goods, and imports between cities and ports. Despite the multiplicity of lines, regular and well-placed sabotage attacks could wreak havoc on important trade routes and cause significant economic hardship.

Finally, South Africa's industrial economy is dependent upon conventional energy systems such as electricity and fossil fuels. In fact, the Republic produces and consumes on its own some 50 percent of the continent's electric power.[83] To help meet its electrical requirements, and to increase water supplies to industrial areas, Pretoria financed a series of hydroelectric projects, including six major dams, numerous tunnels, and other water facilities, under the auspices of the parastatal Electricity Supply Commission (ESCOM).[84] To address the government's fear of sabotage attacks, ESCOM had designed redundant water channels for most of the power stations. But guerrilla attacks could nevertheless result in disruptions either in electric supply or in water provisions for mines, industries, urban areas, or irrigation. As for fossil fuel energy, the Koeberg nuclear plant and three Sasol oil-from-coal facilities had been conceived as local antidotes to the nation's reliance on imports. But Umkhonto bombings at the sites suggested that Pretoria had achieved a measure of energy independence at the price of vulnerability to saboteurs infiltrated through the black labor force.

The Republic's economy, while vigorous, clearly rests on a number of weak pillars. Were they to be hit regularly and effectively, the damage and hardship could undermine white confidence in the government—precisely the objective of challenge attacks. Umkhonto we Sizwe had demonstrated an unmistakable ability to strike at the economy's weak spots, but only infrequently and with inconsistent success. Even in the vastly more violent atmosphere of 1985–86, MK could muster a conservatively estimated average of just one challenge-type attack against economic targets each week.[85] These could cause temporary dislocations but only foreshadow rather than produce a constant assault on white stability. An Umkhonto bid to exploit the Republic's nationwide economic weaknesses on a sustained and effective basis lay in the future.

MK could claim greater success in organizing linkage attacks on the economy. Guerrillas were mounting an average of at least one linkage raid on economic targets each week by 1986.[86] Even if the figure seemed low on a national scale, each incident tended to have a major impact at the local level or in individual industries. In their synchrony with local above-ground campaigns, the salvos were intended to signal the Congress's presence and solidarity with popular resistance to apartheid.

Linking the ANC to local black protest was, for example, the primary mission objective facing an underground Umkhonto cell eyeing economic targets in Durban in the spring of 1985. Trained by infiltrated guerrilla Mduduzi Sithole, the group allegedly received orders and arms from Swaziland-based commanders.[87] In April, according to the police, Sibongiseni Maxwell Dhlomo, a twenty-six-year-old medical doctor, helped another recruit plant a bomb in the Spar Foodliner supermarket. The attack echoed black labor protests against the chain, which had fired employees late in 1984 and refused to rehire them.[88] Two months later Dhlomo allegedly carried out orders from his external commander to support a bitter bread-workers strike with a bombing at Umlazi Bakery. Then, in September, he and two other saboteurs detonated limpet mines in several Durban stores to advertise Umkhonto's backing for a consumer boycott of white-owned enterprises, according to the prosecution's indictment.

Earlier in the year, in a more spectacular linkage attack, a separate guerrilla unit had planted powerful mines inside the Johannesburg headquarters of two of South Africa's largest mining corporations. The explosions had ripped through the two buildings almost simultaneously just after midnight, resulting in extensive damage to several floors of each office block but causing no casualties.[89] The blasts came only days after Anglo-American had fired fourteen thousand black workers at the Vaal Reef gold mine, and after Anglovaal had dismissed three thousand others from its Hartesbeesfontein gold mine. Umkhonto's operation gave violent expression to the rage reported in the National Union of Mineworkers and in the black community as a whole.

Designed as morale-boosters, the bombings seemed to galvanize protest and further popularize the ANC. They also put white employers and shopkeepers on notice that black dissatisfaction contained a sharp edge. White businessmen were forced to understand that defying black public opinion in strikes and boycotts could carry a penalty in destruction of stores and offices. Many could not help but wonder how long it would take before their own lives might pay the price.

Partly as a result, black consumers were winning cooperation from white-owned small businesses in a variety of cities, and unions were achieving some unexpected shopfloor triumphs. Yet such victories left the foundations of minority rule unbroken.

The second prong of the Umkhonto offensive involved attacks on government buildings and police stations. While an average of at least two of every five weekly strikes in 1986 were hitting economic targets, at least one raid each week assailed administrative symbols of apartheid. Constabularies in South Africa's black townships and rural areas take on the appearance of fortresses under siege. Even the smallest is girded with barbed wire and a rampart of sandbags. Bulletproof screens provide armor against the expected.

In an operation typical of the genre, guerrillas overcame defenses at an urban police district headquarters at Roodeport, near Soweto, in 1984. A limpet mine, timed to detonate at 3:20 in the afternoon of August 16, blasted through the third and fourth floors of the City Centre Building. An insurgent had succeeded in planting it, undetected, adjacent to the district commandant's office. Five policemen, including a top-ranking Soweto officer, were injured.[90]

A bolder example of the ANC assault on police institutions took place nineteen months later and twenty miles away in downtown Johannesburg's John Vorster Square, where central command offices are located. A one-kilogram limpet mine, installed in a bathroom by white Umkhonto insurgent Marion Sparg, exploded moments before noon on March 4, 1986. Panicky police and civilians rushed from the building, which suffered damage over four floors. At least four people were injured in the blast, the first guerrillas had been able to mount against the police nerve center.[91]

Other frequently hit government sites included offices of the development boards, which are charged with township administration, the community councils, and any property owned by them. As building defenses multiplied, Umkhonto insurgents in some cases began to plant bombs in more accessible locations such as nearby garbage bins or government vehicles rather than in the offices themselves.

Unlike in early stages of the Algerian civil war, the South African military itself was too strong for the ANC to mount ambushes against government patrols and count on its guerrillas escaping alive. But on infrequent occasions—such as the daring rocket bombardment of the Voortrekkerhoogte base in 1981, the lethal car bombing of Pretoria's air force headquarters in 1983, or the two sabotage explosions at SADF offices in Johannesburg in February and May of 1985—Umkhonto added the military to its list of government targets.

Military and police installations could be attacked in armed assaults only at the risk of reinforcements, quickly summoned, bringing superior firepower and mobility to bear in pursuit of the insurgents. The most effective guerrilla weapon against dangerous targets was the simple limpet mine, easily smuggled into the country, readily concealed. Used with a timer, explosions could be set for hours after the saboteurs' escape.

Umkhonto's offensive against government property and personnel challenged the notion of white invulnerability, conveying to Pretoria a message of growing resistance, and to blacks a sign of encouragement. At the same time, the bombings served a military function, though not one conceived for conventional warfare. ANC commanders hoped that the periodic, unpredictable, and seemingly unstoppable attacks would demoralize civil servants, police officers, and soldiers, particularly blacks and conscripted whites who were presumed to have the least commitment to their work. Insurgent strategists also hoped to compel Pretoria to stretch its defenses across the country, thus increasing the drain on white resources and exposing military weak points.

Government institutions were nowhere more vulnerable than in the black homelands, where Umkhonto was active even though official statistics omitted to tally insurgent operations in the "independent" reservations. By virtue of their reputation as wards of apartheid, most ruling homeland administrations were fragile and unpopular. Even small numbers of high-profile guerrilla attacks proved capable of bolstering public opposition and generating support for the ANC.

From South African "embassy" to its own presidential residence, Venda's emblems of nationhood lie in a quiet enclave in the bush some forty miles south of the Limpopo River and Zimbabwe. In that controversial capital, ruled by a chief minister who had lost 70 percent of the vote in the last election but retained power through appointed legislators, only the small National Force could have been a more critical bureaucracy than the police on the night of October

26, 1981. At 10:50 P.M., a heavily bandaged man walked into the Sibasa police station, less than a mile from Chief Mphephu's quarters, complaining to the three officers present about an injury he had sustained. Suddenly the man drew a hand grenade from his clothes, lobbed it at the policemen, and fled from the explosion into the rainy darkness. Rockets and bullets flared into the building from two nearby points, covering the insurgent's escape, destroying the station, and killing two of the constables. Taking advantage of the thick bush, the Umkhonto guerrillas quickly dispersed, while a heavy downpour covered their tracks.[92]

The Sibasa raid, one of the more vividly chronicled of Umkhonto's missions, provoked a massive homeland-wide crackdown on dissent, a response so much more exaggerated than that normally triggered in Pretoria by a single guerrilla incident that it could only highlight the Venda government's insecurity. Mphephu ordered the detention of respected church, student, and political leaders, a move that later resulted in allegations of beatings, torture, and killings by police and military forces. The chief's overreaction could not have more precisely fulfilled the predictions of revolutionary theorists. It alienated more of Venda's populace at the same time as it magnified Umkhonto's strength and achievement—all without the ANC having to commit more to the operation than a few commandos and a handful of light weapons. Congress commanders now had field-tested proof that low-level warfare in volatile environments could produce valuable political results.

MK soon attempted new ways to exploit homeland instability. Its sabotage bombs gutted Ciskei government offices in both Johannesburg and Pretoria in 1983,[93] and Transkei government quarters near Bloemfontein in 1984.[94] Part of Transkei's Interior Department was wrecked in a 1986 explosion in the territorial capital of Umtata.[95] Three months later, guerrillas killed seven in a late-night assault on one of the city's police stations.[96] Chief Gatsha Buthelezi's KwaZulu administration was hit in a 1983 bombing of development offices near Durban.[97] In June 1986, a nine-month campaign of police assassinations in Bophutatswana came to a head when Umkhonto insurgents shot a tenth victim: Brigadier Makanye Molope, notorious among homeland residents for having ordered his men to fire into a crowd of peaceful protesters at Winterveldt Stadium; eleven had died.[98] Five weeks later, KwaNdebele interior minister

Piet Ntuli switched on his car ignition and within minutes was blown apart in an explosion. News of this hated strongman's death sparked territory-wide festivities and threw into disarray Pretoria's plans to declare KwaNdebele independent.[99] All these attacks served to broaden and reinforce opposition to apartheid, while encouraging more blacks to harbor or seek enlistment in Umkhonto we Sizwe.

CONCLUSION

Guerrilla war is perhaps the most painful and protracted of the many forms of human conflict. Even so, inhospitable terrain, together with the government's massive administrative and military powers, make insurgency in South Africa a peculiarly grueling and cumbersome enterprise. The personal perspective is easy to lose in a shuffle of statistics and reports, but writer Basil Davidson has provided a reminder of the lengths to which rebels must go to achieve their political goals.

> They were realities where strain and weariness, hunger and uncertainty, became a living presence, a drag upon the limbs, a weight upon the mind, a potent enemy among so many other enemies and one, besides, that was almost never absent. For months and even years men and women had to live as the hunters and the hunted, moving as the wild animals they grew to understand so well, sympathizing even with the snakes, enduring every manner of physical and moral test, braving old belief and taboos, fending off the rumors and the intrigues that grow and burgeon under such conditions: often in small groups or even quite alone, sometimes battling for sanity as much as for bodily survival, and always with a host of daily troubles and distractions crowding across their vision of the wider problem, of the contest as a whole.[100]

The ANC's greatest achievement in the decade after Soweto could not best be measured in numbers of weapons, sanctuaries, or explosions, though these were by-products of the Congress's primary work. Rather, the movement's most impressive accomplishment was the recruitment of steadily rising numbers of South Africans into the ranks of the hunters and hunted. Convincing people to endure the hardships of warfare, voluntarily to abandon families and risk their lives, has in any time and country taxed the most magnetic of causes. The best gauge of a political movement is how successfully it can summon, through both ideology and organization, the public to sacrifice. Having been consigned to political antiquity by most blacks prior to the Soweto uprising, the ANC must be judged to have finally developed those crucial powers of persuasion in the late 1970s and 1980s.

The military benefits of political acclaim were obvious. Clandestine bush trails carried volunteers out of and guerrillas back into the Republic. When these channels began to be choked off, the ANC and its allies prepared domestic sanctuaries for insurgent cells. Couriers smuggled weapons and explosives across the frontier from border states. Intelligence agents brought the Congress blueprints of desirable targets. The frequency of bombings, raids, and political assassinations rose a conservatively estimated sixty-two-fold between 1976 and 1986.

Yet the ANC's war, even as it expanded, remained low in intensity. This was not by design. The constriction of infiltration channels bottled up the main body of Umkhonto forces in Angolan barracks a thousand miles north of South Africa's border fences. The numbers that did trickle in were insufficient to screen, recruit, train, arm, and command more than a fraction of the newly restive populace at a time. Sanctuaries chosen to harbor guerrillas proved to be tenuously held and still fraught with risk. Weapons were scarce on account of rising barriers against smuggling and theft. Though intelligence operations could be mounted for accessible targets such as township police stations, espionage coups concerning South Africa's most sensitive and strategic sites were infrequent.

Following ANC guidelines, rebel missions had resulted in remarkably few civilian casualties. But the underground command, ever more diffused and inadequately supervised, had not been able to prevent a rash of terrorist-style attacks by renegade insurgents. At the same time, too many MK troops continued to stumble into shootouts with police and defense forces—some forty-five in the first eight months of 1986, by the government's reckoning;[101] 181 had been either killed or captured in 1985 and 1986.[102] These skirmishes could only rarely be won by guerrillas.

Obstacles compelled the ANC to reach for military consequence not by a swift scramble but by a slow and steady clawing. Armed propaganda had indeed begun to galvanize black resistance and challenge white security; yet the message needed to be more convincing, more deafening, and ceaseless, in order to have a chance of bringing resistance to a climax. What is most significant about ANC progress is not that it had achieved that goal, but that it had finally succeeded in implanting an underground network sufficient to ensure the escalation of rebellion.

5. The Bunker State

In July 1985, as violence was sweeping the country, the South African Brain Research Institute announced a new formula of gases for police to spray at rioters. Scientists labeled the combination of nitrous oxide and oxygen the "Crowdcure Method" and expressed confidence that it would reduce tension and aggression. The institute reported that it had found the substance particularly effective in reducing hostility in the treatment of alcoholics.[1] The laboratory's achievement was promoted only as a technical refinement in riot control, but the scientists' announcement eerily, if unwittingly, echoed Pretoria's actions in combating anti-apartheid resistance. Dissent was looked upon almost as an acute form of illness, suffered by a minority and treatable by extreme and regularly applied therapy even if, as with alcoholism, a complete cure was unattainable.

The government's own counterinsurgency doctrine prescribed quite a different approach to resistance, but over time, theory had proven a meager inoculation against the political demands of the ruling minority. Where strategy dictated a broad combination of meaningful reform and repression, Pretoria could only muster sufficient consensus among whites for a kind of change viewed as superficial by blacks, as well as more frequent resort to force. By the date of the Brain Research Institute's report, in fact, the government's strategy had been reduced to little more than a set of ever more complex technical refinements.

TOTAL STRATEGY

The textbook that military planners originally mined for counterinsurgency doctrine was penned by André Beaufre, a French general whose writings are grounded in the war experiences of Britain, France, and the United States in Malaysia, Algeria, and Vietnam, respectively.[2] He argued that a state may succeed in defeating a guerrilla movement only if it mobilizes all aspects of the power structure, not merely the military, in a sophisticated drive to starve the enemy of psychological resources. The battleground that will determine who is the victor lies in the hearts and minds of the populace. If a government can correctly identify the sources of discontent and undermine them with convincing reforms, then, with a two-pronged campaign of politics and force, it can win sufficient public trust to shrink the popular base upon which guerrilla warfare is built.

A characteristic of Beaufre's counterinsurgency approach, dubbed "total strategy" by Pretoria's generals, is the disappearance of boundaries traditionally separating politicians, bureaucrats, businessmen, journalists, and warriors. All elements of the elite must tie their regular activities to the single overriding objective of defeating the "total onslaught" directed from Moscow. White society has to be militarized, and warfare politicized. To be implemented successfully, "total strategy" requires a high degree of central planning. Not only must the nation's myriad administrative and military structures overcome turf disputes and unite coherently behind a focal leadership; South Africa's economy must also bend to political direction, as must newspapers, radio, and television—the institutions of communication which help to shape the public's political consciousness. Perhaps most important of all, the government must accurately define the causes of rebellion and fashion the reforms most likely to lure important constituents of the opposition onto the path of nonviolent, evolutionary change. Any assessment of Pretoria's potential to defeat its enemies must take these measures into consideration.

THE STATE

High on the apartheid battlement stands the National Party, long the
expression of Afrikanerdom's desire for cultural survival through
political dominance. By providing its supporters with jobs, (approximately 50 percent of all employable Afrikaners depend, directly or
indirectly, on government paychecks)[3] manipulating the symbols of
ethnic pride, and enacting self-serving redistricting laws, the NP has
enjoyed overwhelming majorities in parliament from its first victory
over English-oriented parties in 1948 through the May 1987 election.

Observers have often credited South Africa's white Afrikaans-
speaking tribe with an exceptional degree of unity. It is said to be
nurtured and reinforced by all the overlapping institutions, ranging
from family to school to church, that minister to the group and bind it
to enduring ethnic principles. The Broederbond (Brotherhood), for
example, twelve thousand strong, is a hierarchical, security-ob-
sessed network of branches strung through the Afrikaner community
across the Republic. Established in 1918 for the purpose of wresting
control of South Africa from the British for the Afrikaners, it served
as a secret transmission belt of opinion and policy in tandem with the
National Party. Through it, NP executives remained aware of and
accountable to the Afrikaner elite. Policies announced by Pretoria
were likely to have been generated by the Broederbond, debated and
modified by its members, and finally adopted by it prior to pro-
mulgation. By design, Broeders were filtered into influential positions throughout society, and their disciplined adoption of the party
line had an enormous impact on stifling dissent in the Afrikaner
community in particular, and the white community in general.

Nevertheless, the National Party that State President P. W. Botha
depended on to cut a figure of coherence and strength in "total strategy" was no monolith. Undoubtedly a consensus existed throughout
Afrikanerdom on the desirability of maintaining white supremacy;
but the community was rent with modern and long-standing divisions
that belied the myth of Afrikaner solidarity and endangered the NP's
counterinsurgency schemes. Afrikaners had experienced serious political splits for some a hundred and fifty years, dating from the first
major disagreements over the appropriate reaction to British immi-
gration. The dispute had divided the community so deeply that one

rejectionist faction had launched the 1838 Great Trek to the north, away from British influence, while the rest remained in the Cape with the newcomers.

Later, bitter divisions during the Boer War and in the years prior to the 1948 election over methods of coping with the British continued the tradition of tribal discord. Nor had the feuding abated when blacks overtook English-speakers as the chief perceived threat to Afrikaner survival. Some of the modern factionalism could be traced to unprecedented economic advances within the community. Large numbers of Afrikaners had succeeded in breaking out of the traditional occupation of small farming and had entered the industrial economy dominated by English-speakers. Aided by the government and ethnic networks, these new entrepreneurs and financiers had become the vanguard of a new Afrikaner bourgeoisie less ideological and more materialistic than their rural compatriots.

By the 1980s Afrikanerdom had split four ways. On the left fringe were the few but highly visible members of the opposition Progressive Federal Party, such as former party chairman Frederick van Zyl Slabbert. Within the National Party itself, the ideologically flexible but pro-apartheid "verligtes" controlled the Cape province wing. The National Party's conservative "verkamptes" were an influential force in the Transvaal. On the growing far right stood the Herstigte Nasionale Party (HNP), the Conservative Party, and the neofascist Afrikaner Weerstandsbeweging (AWB), which boasted a party emblem reminiscent of the Nazi swastika. Even the Broederbond faced competition when, in 1984, a former chairman joined with rightists to form the Afrikaner Volkswag, soon to be dubbed the "Counterbond."[4] In short, contrary to the myths predicting a united Afrikaner withdrawal into the "laager" of common defense when under fire, the rise in domestic and international pressure in the aftermath of Soweto resulted not so much in unity as "broedertwis"—bitter fraternal conflict.

The political fragmentation of Afrikanerdom threatened to unravel "total strategy," which had presupposed consensus among the ruling elite on fundamental tactics such as the nature of reform and the extent of repression. The increased popularity of right-wing movements generated pressure on Pretoria to limit the liberalization of racial laws and escalate the use of force to crush dissent. Yet the hardline approach broke with Beaufre's injunction to politicize rather than militarize counterinsurgency. Broedertwis was draining the political content out of total strategy even as the National Party leadership was constructing its form.

Disarray at the political level would prove no barrier to the Botha administration's drive to gather all state institutions under central control for the purpose of conducting the war. "Public service rationalization," for example, began in 1979 at the initiative of incoming Prime Minister P. W. Botha. On the surface, the process appeared to be a straightforward effort to streamline the burgeoning bureaucracy. But included in the plan was a scheme to "rapidly increase the power of the Prime Minister . . . to a phenomenal extent," as the Institute of Race Relations put it.[5] Reshuffling trimmed the cabinet's role in governance and parliament's role in policy deliberation while endowing the prime minister's office with the power of a presidential post. The trend was later enshrined into law when the new 1983 constitution created outright a powerful state presidency with "virtually unlimited executive authority."[6]

The most significant alteration in the cabinet structure was the formal appointment of a standing Committee for National Security, better known as the State Security Council. Although the SSC had been established in 1972, its function until 1979 had been purely advisory. Under the reorganization, it was made explicitly the province of the prime minister, and after 1983 the state president, with the task of "conducting" national strategic planning.[7] For the first time, responsibility for South Africa's overall defense had been largely withdrawn from the cabinet as a whole and vested in the executive.

The energized State Security Council, now dominated by military men, found its jurisdiction broadened to encompass all policy affairs of governmental departments, even parastatals concerned with energy supply and iron and steel sales. The SSC's shift in status was matched in 1980 by a tenfold increase in its staff budget in just one year.[8] Soon after, it flexed its newfound muscle by constructing the secretive National Security Management System. This network of over five hundred community and regional "joint management centers" reporting directly to the SSC shadows civilian administrations at even the most parochial level. Each is staffed by military personnel whose objective is to ensure that nearly every governmental action, particularly in black areas, stems from the state president's "total strategy" perspective.[9] The joint centers operate on the theory that resolving local irritants such as housing shortages and sewage breakdowns can broaden support for Pretoria and undermine the rebel constituency.

Public-service rationalization also gave Botha a new office with vast authority over virtually every major aspect of planning for South Africa's future, including the security, energy, economic, social, and scientific sectors.[10] Finally, new state of emergency measures against black labor and political resistance topped off the chief executive's total strategy powers, granting him the right even to adopt apartheid legislation stalemated in the houses of parliament.

By the mid-1980s, state power was concentrated precisely where Pretoria's counterinsurgency textbook said it should be: in the hands of one person capable of marshaling all resources behind the overriding objective of defeating rebellion. Yet administrative congealment was not to be matched with political cohesion. Botha, a fourteen-year defense minister, found his natural military orientation reinforced by hardliners within and outside the National Party. At the same time, verligte factions pressed for reforms—such as expanding union rights, abolishing passbooks, and permitting racial intermarriage—which they judged would hold black resistance and international sanctions at bay.

Bucking doctrine, Botha refused to choose sides—or perhaps more precisely, chose both sides, since his policies shifted now to one, now to the other, diluting each. Reform suffered most. The new constitution might for the first time permit nonwhite participation in national policy, but only for Indians and coloreds and only in a manner that posed no threat to apartheid; unions might be authorized, but fine-print restrictions threatened to make some weaker than unsanctioned labor groups; passbooks might be eliminated, but new identity cards would serve almost the same purpose; intermarriage might be allowed, but laws barring multiracial housing could prevent such couples from living together. To make matters worse, many lower-level bureaucrats working in politically sensitive departments, such as black affairs or the police, felt unable to keep abeam of the political swerving and reverted to tried-and-true practices of the past. In short, even if the verligte reforms had been sufficient to attract significant black interest, which they were not, Pretoria's new habit of scrambling and contradicting them served mainly to boost mistrust and undermine "total strategy."

THE ECONOMY

Bankruptcies and shortages caused by international sanctions, capital flight, and industrial paralysis caused by bombings and strikes—these were the nightmares of strategists contemplating the economy's vulnerability to an enemy "total onslaught." Crisis in South African commerce would undoubtedly aid insurgency by sapping white confidence and boosting emigration. "Total strategy" sought to avoid defeat on the economic front through measures increasing self-sufficiency, restricting union activity, and guarding sensitive sabotage targets. The institutions of commerce had to be brought under Pretoria's control.

South Africa's business community had always been dominated by English-speakers, though in recent years Afrikaner corporations have become more prominent. Gold, platinum, and other rare minerals constituted the core of the country's economic wealth. But the currency of corporate prosperity continued to be abundant, inexpensive labor and a consumer market sufficiently robust to absorb local products.

Business counted itself as stolidly opposed to communism as the government. It had thrived under apartheid structures facilitating union suppression. But with trade networks extending around the globe, it was far more exposed to international public disapproval of Pretoria's racial policies. Domestically, it complained about suffering directly from shortages in skilled manpower as white military obligations increased. Moreover, the private sector resented having to bear the brunt of black labor and consumer campaigns directed against political grievances. It saw an even greater threat over the long term in the progressive radicalization of the black community: rejection of apartheid had already begun to be equated with rejection of free enterprise.

During the years before Soweto when resistance could be contained, the corporate English community and Afrikaner political elite, otherwise riven by ethnic rivalry, had shared agreement on the desirability of white rule. After Soweto, domestic tumult and world pressures placed new strains on the fragile alliance. Business leaders began tentatively to distance themselves from the Botha administration, seeking instead to link corporate interests to the goal of black power sharing in a system that would preserve free enterprise. A whirlwind of critical declarations, resolutions, and advertisements culminated in a highly publicized 1985 summit of corporate executives and African National Congress delegates in Zambia. Business had acknowledged that its own preservation in a future of growing black influence dictated increasingly vocal independence from Pretoria.

The revelation came just as the government was stepping up its drive to incorporate economic interests into "total strategy." Already in direct control over some 60 percent of the country's fixed capital and, through ministries and parastatals, such key industrial sectors as energy supply, rail transportation, and ports, Pretoria actively intervened to protect the economy against sanctions and disinvestment. It reintroduced a two-Rand monetary system that in effect saddled foreign multinational corporations with huge new losses in the event of their departure. It continued quietly to stockpile critical imports, most notably oil, to cushion the shock of a world boycott. It aided and encouraged industry to blaze clandestine trade routes impervious to sanctions. Most importantly, it promulgated regulations and laws that required growing national self-sufficiency in industries previously dependent on imports.

A siege economy, however, entailed greater reliance on black domestic labor, a prospect relished neither by government nor business. Pretoria's total strategy solution was embodied in the 1979 Industrial Conciliation Amendment Act. Facing an unregulated explosion of black workplace activism, the Botha administration promoted the bill as a major reform that would grant new trade-union rights to blacks. In fact, unions had existed unrecognized for many years. But the legislation forced any labor organization seeking to bargain in the open to undergo a registration process and adhere to strict rules prohibiting involvement in political affairs.

Pretoria hoped by these methods to curb and control black unionism. Instead, membership soared from an estimated seventy-five thousand in 1979 to over one million in 1985. Even more threatening, from the government's viewpoint, was the conglomeration of most unions into a single federation, COSATU, whose leadership traveled to Lusaka to announce its fraternity with the African

National Congress. Perceiving that "reform" had failed to repress, the government's 1986 state of emergency aimed to accomplish the job directly by targeting COSATU members for detention.

The move temporarily disrupted federation operations but, ironically, it also widened the schism between white business and white government. Many corporate managements had achieved a degree of labor calm through carefully cultivated relationships with union leaders. Hundreds of these men were now incarcerated, and in short order industry was hit with wildcat strikes and instability. Business executives responded by regularly and loudly calling for the release of black unionists.

Friction between companies and Pretoria's total strategy command were pronounced, too, in the realm of defense. Legislation enacted in 1980 sought to guard critical industrial sites against sabotage by making the owner responsible for elaborate government-approved security plans. But business, its hands full with labor unrest and a declining economy, considered protection of the 633 declared "national key points" a job for the military and the police.[11] Similarly, corporations working to distance themselves from apartheid policies were dismayed by the implementation of the National Supplies Procurement Act, which authorized the government to seize or order the production of any item deemed necessary for defense purposes.[12]

By the mid-1980s, however, Pretoria had wrestled the economy into a semblance of subordination. As it had done throughout the precincts of state power, the Botha administration had forced the institutions of economic might to recognize the predominant requirements of total strategy. To do so, the government had granted itself more legal authority than ever over labor and capital. At the same time, the onset of international sanctions had driven business into greater dependence on the public sector for help in boycott-busting and building a self-sufficient economy. Protection against sanctions and sabotage were in place, at least in form.

As in the governmental sphere, however, the architecture of total strategy surrounding the economy seemed empty of political coherence. Instead of a united white elite, public and private sectors were pulling against each other on the critical questions of reform and repression. Business agitated for more reform than Pretoria was willing to permit, while government went forward with more repression than most companies felt was necessary. At the same time that the Botha administration was raising ramparts around the economy to defend against insurgency, the vanguard of South African business was sitting down for talks with the outlawed ANC in Zambia. The emerging message was one of political division and confusion.

COMMUNICATION

In the doctrine of total strategy, the side that controls South Africa's organs of communication has an excellent chance of shaping the public's understanding of reality, and thereby winning the psychological war. A tamed press, planners felt, could strengthen the government's hand by downplaying guerrilla strikes, while promoting defense-force strength and the potency of political reform. Uncontrolled media, however, could frighten whites and encourage blacks with detailed reports of rebellion and military failures. The Botha administration was convinced that counterinsurgency could succeed only if the nation's mass communications could be incorporated into "total strategy."

Irritated by the critical stance taken by English-language newspapers, Pretoria had initiated a first wave of attacks on press freedom as early as 1949, when Prime Minister D. F. Malan urged that journalists be licensed like doctors, so that "unethical" conduct could be punished by banishment from the profession.[13] Later, a stream of legislation began to flow from parliament threatening the press with strong restrictions designed to promote the goals and attitudes of the government.

The Bantu Administration Act was used to quarantine black areas in turmoil from reporters. The Criminal Law Amendment Act made it an offense for a news organ to cause a person to break the law. The Criminal Procedure Act of 1955 was fashioned to extract information about sources from reporters. The broad Defense Act simply prohibited the publication of any unauthorized information relating to South Africa's defense. The Internal Security Act (formerly the Suppression of Communism Act) and its amendments empowered the regime to ban any publication that printed information "calculated to endanger the security of the State or the maintenance of public order."[14] The Official Secrets Act blocked the dissemination of any reporting on "the preservation of the internal security of the Republic or the maintenance of law and order by the South Africa Police."[15]

The 1959 Prisons Act withdrew the country's entire penal system from the bounds of press coverage. The sprawling Publications Act of 1974 declared illegal any printed material "harmful to sound relations among the various population groups" or "prejudicial to the safety of the State, the general welfare and peace and good order in the community." Included within this category was "revolt against authority," "attempts to discredit the State . . . in the eyes of non-whites," and "the fomenting of antagonism against whites and the making of propaganda for non-white pressure groups and extremist movements."[16] Similar provisions were incorporated in the Riotous Assemblies, General Law Amendment, and Unlawful Organizations Acts. In addition, the Sabotage and Terrorism acts each defined "incitement" of violence, such as in the form of newspaper articles, as equivalent to committing the actual offense.[17] Under this array of legislation, the government regularly banned articles, books, journals, and whole newspapers, such as the black *World* in 1977.

Pretoria's campaign to coopt the media was sophisticated in that it preserved some of the forms of a free press. Legislation was so broad and ill-defined that editors themselves carried the burden of exercising censorship. The government had only to initiate token criminal cases against the newspapers or reporters and maintain a steady rhetorical offensive based on implicit threats. Proprietors of the nation's papers, fearful of further legislation and costly court defenses, pressed editors to conform to wide and safe definitions of the law.

Apart from imposing self-censorship, Pretoria also injected a fear of intimidation into the journalistic world. Through the Post Office Act, which granted the police the right to intercept or monitor communications by mail, telegram, or phone, the SAP was known to have kept watch on suspect reporters. Some alternative left-wing and student periodicals found themselves under constant surveillance, with visitors conspicuously photographed, distributors harassed, supplies such as newsprint stolen.[18] The more established dailies were infiltrated by police agents, whose mission was less the gathering of inside information than the overt demonstration of police power. "It is an open secret that some reporters on the *Rand Daily Mail* are on the police payroll, and two hold senior positions on the papers," observed one employee.[19]

Other tactics used to manipulate the press were less direct. The government could, for example, ban news access to important opposition figures or outlaw any reference to statements made by them. In an even more resourceful venture, Pretoria's now defunct Information Department had secretly initiated a scheme in cooperation with Afrikaner financier Louis Luyt to buy a controlling interest in the media conglomerate South African Associated Newspapers (SAAN). When that failed, Luyt used a covert government fund to launch *The Citizen,* South Africa's first pro-National Party, English-language daily. Its competitive success helped lead to the 1985 collapse of the venerable, and anti-apartheid, *Rand Daily Mail.*

Responsibility for television and radio was allotted to the South African Broadcasting Corporation, a governmental body established in 1936 on the BBC model. But news coverage on SABC had so fallen under the sway of politics that it had become known as a "mouthpiece" for the National Party administration.[20] The Broederbond, in particular, had made a point of converting the SABC board into a bastion of influence.[21] Confident of his power over the network, P. W. Botha went so far as to announce in parliament in 1980 that "the television service . . . will in future be instructed not to feature reports of the onslaught on South Africa by revolutionary elements as main news items."[22]

Steering clear of news relating to insurrection soon became a characteristic of most media. *Star* parliamentary correspondent Tom Duff observed that "once that wall [of legislation] came down, we generally ignored the issue."[23] Reporters privately admitted that "there are very many guerrilla incidents that the papers know about but don't print." U.S. authorities agreed. In a declassified 1978 cable, embassy officials alerted Washington that "the overwhelming majority of security trials and incidents are not being reported in the South African press."[24]

In 1974, an accord between the police and the press formally obligated editors to refer all national security matters to the government for confirmation and print approval. One journalist described an example of the consequences.

> I might be an eyewitness to a peaceful demonstration where policemen start shooting into the crowd. Even if I gather all the witnesses I want, my editor will still be subject to the agreement and he will bring the story to the police for review. The police will normally give the standard statement: "A group of policemen were attacked by slogan-chanting,

fist-waving youths. The police asked them to dispel. They were given a chance to do so. The youths threw stones, and the police fired. A number were killed and some were arrested." Sure enough, the night editor will change my story so that it will read "Police were forced to open fire on slogan-chanting youths throwing stones, and two were killed."[25]

It is a tribute to the legal ingenuity and courage of journalists and editors that a good deal of unauthorized information regarding insurgency continued to appear in newspapers. But the Soweto uprisings triggered a second, even more intensive, assault on the media as "total strategy" swept through the Botha administration. Government would no longer settle for excluding bad news from the airwaves and newspaper pages; its own policies would now have to be presented in a positive light.

The germ of Pretoria's new approach first surfaced in the secret ranks of the Broederbond. "Masterplan for a White Country: The Strategy" was drafted and circulated late in 1976 as a crash attempt to formulate a broad plan for Afrikanerdom's future security through apartheid. The document placed great emphasis on the use of propaganda to defuse opposition. Through it, "radical action will have to be stigmatised," and "resistance to radicalism . . . engendered on a broad front."[26] Upon the shoulders of the propaganda managers would be placed the task of strengthening tribal identities among South Africa's blacks in order to divide them and undermine the ANC's appeal.[27] In particular, the report said, the SABC's radio and television services for blacks had to create "a public opinion sympathetic with the homelands."[28]

In a 1979 paper, the SADF's Brigadier C. J. Lloyd wrote that "the news media," along with the private and public sectors, would have to be incorporated into a "national counter-insurgency strategy" designed to "secure the support of the local population through indoctrination, propaganda and counter-propaganda."[29] But it was the landmark 1980 Steyn Commission which set the context of the new policy first mooted in the Broederbond. Arguing that Soviet communism in the guise of the ANC was seeking to use "terrorist" incidents to wage psychological war against South Africa, the report asserted that newspapers had to orient news coverage to downplay radical opposition. They had also to observe the veil of secrecy around the SAP and SADF, while at the same time promoting trust in both. "Opposition" would be tolerated, but only in a context which could be seen as placing the security of the state ahead of all other objectives. The media could not be permitted to "promote terror and revolution by means of coverage and prominence they afford such occurrences," declared the report.[30]

The Steyn Commission recommended a series of actions to withdraw the media's last vestiges of freedom to cover radical resistance to apartheid. Within months of the report's release, two bills and several regulatory directives were issued complying with and even exceeding Steyn's recommendations. The National Key Points Act prohibited publication of information on any guerrilla attacks on classified installations. Had the act been in force in June 1980, the public might not have learned of the ANC's strikes against Sasols I and II and the Natref refinery, or if it had, then only in a form prescribed by the government. The Second Police Amendment Act went further, flatly outlawing unauthorized publication of information on all insurgency and counterinsurgency activities. The widest possible definition of "terrorism" was used in the act, and the government made clear that it would enforce its new laws as never before, now in the context of "total strategy." "When necessary, we can talk in great friendship with a sword in our hands," commented Minister of Police Louis Le Grange of negotiations with the press over the new restrictions.[31]

Pretoria's sword was sharpened to a still finer edge in the states of emergency in 1985 and 1986. Expansive new regulations barred reporters from "unrest areas" and ordered them to evacuate a location if even the possibility of disturbances arose. For all intents and purposes, the only permitted source of information on rebellion was the official government briefing, which the authorities used most frequently to reassure the public that events were firmly under control.

If "total strategy" had sought to convert South Africa's institutions of communication into organs promoting state policy, it had to a large extent succeeded in doing so, but only as far as whites were concerned. Hemmed in by carefully engineered laws and regulations, the media found most unfettered coverage of violent black resistance beyond reach. As a result, whites, who lived apart from most areas of unrest and therefore remained dependent on newspapers, radio, and television for news, were prevented from learning of the scope and intensity of anti-apartheid violence. Only a minority seemed overly resentful of the creeping censorship: polls even indicated continuing white trust in SABC television as an accurate source of information. While some prominent English-language newspapers persisted in printing critical commentary and features, Pretoria could claim to have blocked the most psychologically damaging news from reaching the white community. As a result, it counted on white confidence in the government remaining high.

For most blacks, however, the media's coverage of political resistance directly contradicted what they knew to be true from daily experience in the townships. The more print, radio, and television news veered from reality, the more distrustful blacks became of establishment journalism. Regardless of how anti-apartheid some newspapers professed to be, political activists began to assume that virtually any significant news item appearing in the mainstream press in some way served apartheid's aims. Even when a Soweto paper launched a campaign to free Nelson Mandela from prison, militants questioned whether the veteran ANC leader had in some manner "sold out" to deserve such attention from a white-owned newspaper.

"Total strategy" envisioned state control of communication channels. But in the black community, news regarding the ANC's rebellion reached the public regularly through a vast, informal word-of-mouth network. Censorship laws and regulations could hardly restrict the flow of such information. But by further discrediting the regular media, Pretoria's measures compelled moderate blacks to spurn news appearing in newspapers and on radio and television almost as vociferously as the radicals. Conservatives such as Chief Gatsha Buthelezi, who were quoted regularly and in a generally positive light in the censored media, risked losing support among blacks with each reference. Similarly, Pretoria's periodic "reforms," which were heavily promoted in the press, stood little chance of attracting mainstream black attention or trust. Anything pushed by the media, regardless of merit, had to be suspect.

Another important casualty of Pretoria's total strategy media campaign was that it tended to drive more black communications underground. Unable to count on the independence of the press, the UDF, COSATU, and other organizations turned to informal township networks, or to ANC cells, to pass on information. This meant that the government's own intelligence resources were more hard-pressed than ever to gather material on black resistance.

INTELLIGENCE

Pretoria's "total strategy" granted new power and authority to espionage commands. Information was vital to counterinsurgency. At home, advance warnings of attacks could lead to the capture of Umkhonto units; accurate lists of resistance activists could enable police to paralyze campaigns with mass detentions; tips from township informants could result in the arrest of whole ANC cells. Abroad, inside data on the Congress's headquarters operations could give Pretoria early notice of rebel tactics; details concerning ANC personnel and offices could aid in planning precision military incursions, assassinations, or sabotage attacks. As the SADF's 1977 White Paper on Defense put it, a vital factor in total strategy must be "an outstanding intelligence service . . . to forecast the action of the enemy."[32] Without such information, the government knew it could fall victim to the guerrilla's most potent weapon—surprise.

In the 1950s, the police had successfully planted informants throughout the all-but-open ranks of the ANC and PAC. Spies had eventually provided information leading directly to the arrest of the entire Umkhonto high command in 1963. That one intelligence coup had helped to disable and discourage any significant effort to reignite guerrilla resistance for a decade. Yet the reputation of Pretoria's espionage agencies had suffered in the 1970s from scandals concerning the exotic schemes and reckless practices of BOSS, the Bureau of State Security. P. W. Botha, on coming to power, had shaken up and reorganized the government's entire intelligence establishment.

BOSS disappeared, to be replaced first by a Department of National Security (DONS) and later with the National Intelligence Service (NIS). Botha appointed a conservative academic, Neil Barnard, to head the agency in a move interpreted as underlining the premier's intention to withdraw it from the frontlines of espionage. NIS would become a think tank, much reduced in bureaucratic status, charged with "processing routine information" rather than collecting it in the field.[33] Two other intelligence arms, the police's security branch and the SADF's Directorate of Military Intelligence (DMI), once bitter rivals of BOSS, rose to dominance as Botha's State Security Council reoriented government to carry out "total strategy." With a former fourteen-year defense minister as premier and then state president, military intelligence in particular enjoyed direct access and influence in the council.

Friction between the three departments, believed intense, surfaced in a rare 1983 speech by NIS director Barnard, which included veiled criticisms of the other services and a call to restructure the way Pretoria gathers data on the enemy. "We can no longer afford to be on the losing side of the intelligence battle because of our own actions," he warned.[34] Barnard's pessimistic remarks briefly opened a window into South Africa's most secretive agencies. Little is known about the security branch, and almost nothing at all about the DMI. But circumstantial evidence suggests that each was suffering in the 1980s from serious contractions in the quality and quantity of intelligence it was bringing back to Pretoria.

On the domestic front, which was thought to be primarily the province of the estimated thousand-man security branch, the once large pool of informers available to the police had mostly dried up on account of penalties now exacted by black militants. Improved ANC screening also seemed to keep them out of most rebel cells. In fact, the Rabie Commission confirmed that "information obtained from persons in detention is the most important and, to a large extent, the only weapon of the police for anticipating terroristic and other subversive activities."[35] Gruesome accounts of torture emerging in court cases suggested that information about resistance activities was becoming far more difficult for the police to come by.

A prominent intelligence official boasted in 1986 that if only world public opinion would allow it, the police could round up and shoot all the ANC rebels in South Africa in six weeks.[36] But in reality the security branch seemed to be losing track of the growing numbers of ANC-oriented activists. It often found itself not only failing to learn of attacks in advance, but having to offer cash rewards for information about them.[37] No longer able to count on a network of volunteer informants, the police began paying for spies, or blackmailing youths into collaboration, a tactic which on occasion resulted in embarrassment when the victim confessed to activists instead.[38] Commanders also ordered speculative sweeps through the townships, though arbitrary missions did not necessarily yield useful counterinsurgency information, and risked radicalizing more blacks. In one such action at the end of May 1980, police vans took more than twelve hundred people into detention from the Johannesburg townships.[39] One week later, however, insurgents bombed the Sasol plants and escaped.

The security branch appeared to be particularly strained in identifying the thousands of new, mostly young, activists entering resistance activities each year. In a widespread 1980 student protest against schools, for example, one Cape Town newspaper analysis noted that "even the Security Police, supposedly with their ears close to the ground, have had to raid meetings of the boycott organizers to find out who they are. More than 230 people have been detained since the boycott began but, if anything, it has gathered momentum."[40] The states of emergency in 1985 and 1986 constituted the most dramatic cases of security branch intelligence failures. Despite almost unlimited powers and intense government pressure, the police seemed unable to target for detention all those responsible for radical resistance. Even when such leaders were captured, others—not necessarily known to the authorities—seemed to be taking over protest, if with less skill and impact than their mentors could muster.

At the same time, Umkhonto guerrillas were succeeding in dramatically escalating their attacks on apartheid targets, reaching a record high in 1985. The police continued to report periodic victories in engagements with insurgents, more frequent discoveries of weapons caches, and more arrests of "terrorists."[41] But information was too sparse to conclude whether this was due to improved police vigilance or the fact of greater numbers of guerrillas on the loose.

Even as the security branch was experiencing deteriorating intelligence capabilities, it continued to hone methods of exploiting the byzantine secrecy of insurgent operations with "dirty tricks" designed to disrupt the resistance. One of the most deadly occurred in 1984 when, the ANC later charged, police agents anonymously circulated apparently false rumors that student activist Ben Langa was an undercover government spy responsible for the arrest of Congress activists.[42] Two Umkhonto guerrillas, acting on the rumor, murdered Langa, were arrested, convicted, and sentenced to death. Injecting reports of "sellouts" into the black underground was one of the security branch's easiest and most effective tools.

Another gambit, just as lethal, involved booby-trapping weapons caches identified by informants. In 1985, for example, eight men lost their lives when grenades that they had retrieved from a clandestine arms depot detonated in their hands. Reports suggested that each explosive had been carefully primed by experts to go off as the safety pins were pulled out rather than after the grenade had been thrown.[43]

The security branch was suspected also of regularly engaging in spreading disinformation to distort and upset underground communications. Agents in 1980 intercepted mailed copies of the outlawed journal *Omkeer* and substituted crude facsimiles.[44] On another occasion, a forged signature of UDF leader Henry Fazzie appeared on the first of a series of bogus pamphlets circulated in the eastern Cape. Blacks would have to pay a heavy new tax to the UDF, the piece announced under the slogan "Your sacrifice is our prosperity."[45] Although Fazzie quickly repudiated the sheet and many blacks might automatically have dismissed it as fake, the security police understood that even such simple espionage tactics could cause disruption and distrust in a volatile political atmosphere.

Intelligence gathering that involved other nations was presumed to be largely under the auspices of the DMI as well as the security branch, though additional departments may have been responsible for surveillance of international mail and telecommunications to and from South Africa. But until an investigative article appeared in *The New York Times* in July of 1986, almost nothing had been known about the DMI's capabilities. Writer Seymour Hersh revealed that the directorate, lacking satellite intelligence equipment, had been compelled to request help from Britain and the United States for surveillance information concerning ANC headquarters and the frontline states.[46]

The story came as a surprise to many observers, who had assumed that Pretoria had long possessed independent means to intercept transmissions in the subcontinent. In return for reporting weekly to the Reagan administration and Thatcher government on Soviet activities in southern Africa, the DMI had apparently asked Washington and London to monitor a list of frequencies used by the governments of Zambia, Angola, Mozambique, and Tanzania for intelligence and diplomatic traffic. The directorate had also filed a top priority appeal for information about the ANC. British and American intelligence services were requested to track Congress

President Oliver Tambo's international travel and to alert Pretoria when he was found flying in Cuban and Soviet airlines. Most importantly, DMI asked the two governments to monitor frequencies used by the ANC for military communications. Hersh wrote that a U.S. National Security Agency source considered it clear that the directorate "was unable to independently intercept all of the communications it deemed essential."[47]

Still secret is how much information was passed to Pretoria and how long the barter arrangement lasted. In any case, despite the newly exposed gaps in the SADF's espionage resources, directorate or police agents were assumed to be operating in the sanctuary states and in key foreign capitals such as London. They were suspected of bombing the Congress's British and Swedish offices and assassinating ANC figures such as Joe Gqabi in Harare and Ruth First in Maputo by means of car or letter bombs. Control agents regularly attempted to infiltrate spies into ANC institutions and maintained surveillance of ANC offices in Lusaka and other cities. Congress officials normally assumed that their phones were tapped and their houses watched.

Yet in at least two cases where defense forces had relied on intelligence data in order to perform surgical strikes against neighboring states, the accuracy of information had turned out to be seriously flawed. A 1983 raid on Mozambique, launched in retaliation for the bloody ANC car bombing of Air Force headquarters in Pretoria, aimed to destroy Umkhonto weapons training centers and command posts in Maputo's western suburbs. Instead, the early morning strike by seven war planes hit a jam factory, a crèche, two private homes, one hut, and one ANC residence. Only one of the twenty-five casualties could be linked to the ANC.[48]

Similarly, much publicized multiple strikes on Zambia, Zimbabwe, and Botswana in 1986 appeared to have hit several mistaken targets. Armed with intelligence provided by the security police, South African forces, in their first admitted incursion into Zambia, bombed a bar, a shop, and a U.N. refugee camp never used by the ANC. Zambians and Namibians, but no black South Africans, wound up on the casualty lists. In Botswana, raiders hit a group of homes near Gaborone and killed a ministry of agriculture official. Only in Zimbabwe did the defense forces successfully attack ANC targets—a downtown office and a suburban home—but these had been publicly identified as Congress sites for years. A surprised ANC later described the mission as a "dismal intelligence and military failure."[49]

The conclusion is not that South Africa's foreign espionage was incompetent; SADF raids on Lesotho and Mozambique in the past had struck ANC buildings with brutal accuracy. But Pretoria's knowledge of Congress operations contained far more gaps, errors, and misjudgments than most observers, and the ANC itself, had suspected. The reputation that government intelligence had earned in the 1950s and 1960s for omniscience apparently could not keep pace with the demands of insurgency in the 1980s. Watching some thirteen thousand exiles, who now used more sophisticated codes and communications beyond the range of the government's interception equipment, required a combination of inside informants, Western assistance, and field surveillance. But judging from the rising number of Umkhonto attacks and the uneven record of SADF strikes, the payoff from any vast new "total strategy" intelligence network was falling far short of Pretoria's needs.

Ultimately, thorough, regular, and penetrating intelligence in a guerrilla war is almost always the product of public support. As long as significant parts of the dissident community feel politically loyal to the government and physically secure in reporting to it, information concerning rebels—where they stay, whom they recruit, what they plan—will flow into the counterinsurgency command with little prompting. But if a government suffers a widespread loss of credibility and cannot protect its supporters, volunteer informants are bound to disappear, and paid or blackmailed informants tend to be much less reliable substitutes. The Botha administration, unable to muster constituent backing for the thoroughgoing political reforms necessary to attract black confidence, found itself relinquishing the intelligence high ground to its enemies.

Secrecy surrounding DMI and security branch activities prevents any precise measurement of the slippage. The agencies had clearly retained their skills in misinformation and "dirty tricks," and their surveillance work across the nation had continued to hamper ANC operations. They seemed able to capitalize on the smallest guerrilla errors and could by no means be underestimated. Yet for the most part police and military reconnaissance had been forced to the periphery of the resistance movement, compelled more often to watch for mistakes rather than anticipate attacks. Once all-seeing, Pretoria's espionage bureaus now found themselves working in the dusk against South Africa's rebel underground.

MILITARY AND POLICE FORCES

An axiom of insurgency theory is that the attitude of the government's military forces toward the conflict will in large part determine the victor. As one scholar puts it, "few revolutions succeed as long as the officer corps remains firm in its allegiance to the state. Alternatively, few fail in circumstances where military institutions respond to deep social tensions by defecting from the state or assuming a position of neutrality between the insurgents and the incumbents."[50] On these terms, South Africa would appear to be inhospitable turf for a triumphant insurrection: black militants might seem unlikely ever to maneuver the white military elite toward neutrality, let alone defection. Yet the range of outcomes in the subcontinent is far broader than a choice between apartheid and revolution. In fact, the least likely result may be the total collapse of one side or the other. The ultimate solution may well fall somewhere in between the extremes, with the balance of power determining whether the future South Africa looks more like radical social change or reconstituted minority rule.

Pretoria's military institutions remain a critical factor in such calculations. Healthy armed forces could be expected to ward off the debilitating effects of rebellion with high morale, substantial public support, effective strategy, and appropriate equipment. On the other hand, the symptoms of an infirm military would include draft resistance, public skepticism, and blueprints for warfare that ill address the threat.

Until the Portuguese coup stripped South Africa of two secure white buffer states, and the Soweto rebellion gave rise to "total strategy," Pretoria had taken a relatively relaxed view of military challenges to white rule. "None of . . . [South Africa's] immediate neighbors . . . are likely to launch an attack against South Africa, or even countenance harboring an 'Army of Liberation' within their borders," observed a 1973 article in a defense force publication.[51]

Spending reflected the calm: for years only some 2 percent of GNP, and less than 10 percent of the government's budget, had been devoted to defense.

The sea change in military budgeting came suddenly in the mid-1970s when an alarmed administration boosted defense expenditures to 5.3 percent of GNP. By 1980, nearly one-fifth of state spending had been dedicated to national security. Six years later it was approaching an estimated one-fourth, with the total more than seven times the amount spent on black education.[52] Exact figures were impossible to determine because officials spread defense costs through various departments, especially the police and the homeland budgets. In addition, a 1974 act of parliament established a special secret defense account into which some 60 percent of the SADF budget was placed, thereby allowing the State Security Council new flexibility in appropriations without accountability. A U.N. analysis estimated that real spending on security programs could be up to 35 percent more than the official defense figures revealed.[53]

Budget expenditures marked only one measure of the militarization of white society as total strategy came into force. The change most widely felt was the steady increase in military duties required of white men. By 1980, lengthened conscription service had combined with new militia and reserve demands to make it "virtually impossible for any physically capable white male under the age of 65 to legally avoid some sort of physical commitment to the defense force."[54] At the same time, Pretoria's strategists were trying to boost public enthusiasm for defense through media propaganda campaigns and an extensive new cadet system, which obligated white students in most state secondary schools to participate in weekly military drills. The traditional Afrikaner concept of "the nation at arms" aimed to incorporate almost every white into the defense of the state.

Police

The first trench line against insurgency was the South African Police (SAP), a national force charged with border patrol, underground intelligence, and riot control responsibilities, in addition to the normal anticrime activities assigned to law enforcers. It has been described as essentially "a wing of the SADF with additional training in crime prevention."[55]

Serious manpower shortages and a negative image of the SAP in both the black and white communities constituted the force's most serious problems in coping with its broad military mandate. An official commission investigating white attitudes cited a combination of poor pay and the lack of an "aura of romance" as reason for the low esteem in which the SAP was held.[56] English-speakers in particular shunned the police because of its reputation as a haven for poorly educated Afrikaners. Most blacks disdained the SAP as a symbol of apartheid, and enlistment in the force carried a high risk of peer condemnation as well as ANC intimidation or assassination. As many as 941 homes of policemen, almost all of them black, had been attacked and destroyed by protesters in the thirty-one months prior to August 1986. Therefore, even the obvious attraction of a salaried job seemed a dubious benefit to unemployed blacks.

As a result, the SAP experienced chronic difficulty in maintaining the quality and quantity of its authorized manpower. In the twelve months between July 1978 and July 1979, white force levels were some 13 percent below the official quota of 21,118, and nearly a thousand less than the year before despite a major promotion campaign. Selectivity yielded to an all but open-door policy: nearly 90 percent of all white applicants won places in the SAP. Twenty percent of those could claim no high-school degree.[57]

Success in recruitment among blacks was so limited that the commissioner's 1979 annual report said only that "everything possible was done to fill existing vacancies."[58] Manpower levels were 12 percent below the 17,447 quota for all nonwhites, including coloreds and Indians.[59] Black members therefore totaled about twelve thousand—and that representing a racial group population of nearly twenty million, with overwhelming unemployment. The situation by 1984 had improved, so that half the service—some twenty-one thousand troops—were listed as black. But another problem persisted: the SAP's "exceptionally high resignation figure" among blacks.[60] The service admitted having lost 1,483 black policemen in 1979, more than five times the previous year's figure, and gained only some 1,577 more through recruitment drives.[61] Six years later black resignation had declined, but some 1,113 had still left the force, and more were expected to depart as pressure on them intensified.[62]

To cope with the shortfall, Pretoria was forced to siphon SADF draftees into the SAP, beginning with a group of five hundred in

1975, some one thousand annually after that.[63] Plans were laid, too, in 1980, for full-scale recruitment of women, extension of service obligations, and the establishment of a junior reserve police force for schoolboys. Law and Order Minister Louis Le Grange also ordered in 1986 a new recruitment package to boost the size of the force from 48,000 to 86,000 by 1994. All of these measures were designed to overcome the SAP's deficiencies at a time of escalating guerrilla war, but none promised short-term relief. The number of whites that could be tapped without causing serious damage to the economy was limited. Blacks, who represented an almost bottomless pool of potential workers, showed reluctance to enlist.

Because one SAP responsibility was riot control, police tacticians had helped to design South Africa's townships and hostels to facilitate crowd containment. Blacks were separately housed in migrant labor barracks according to ethnic group in order to discourage coordinated protest. Tall steel fences and barbed wire sealed their compounds off from other areas. Five hundred-foot dirt strips surrounded the barriers, enabling troops and SAP armored vehicles to isolate the men inside.

Townships themselves were made structurally hostage to governmental authority by the placement of water and power facilities away from dwelling areas and under the control of white administrators. Supplies could be cut at any time as a siege tactic against urban uprisings. Tall searchlights loomed above each block, helping roving SAP patrols to spot suspicious activities. Straight avenues, built sufficiently wide to permit tanks to execute U-turns, ensured that troops had easy access to all residences. Housing areas were typically situated in valleys or low-lying areas to facilitate long-distance surveillance from high reconnaissance vantage points. Architects separated dwellings from each other by spaces large enough to allow unimpeded firing and to deprive fugitives of alleyway shelter.[64]

Observers generally credited security considerations as the prime motive behind Pretoria's anxious efforts to eliminate squatter settlements, which tended to be as architecturally inhospitable to armored vehicles as they were helpful to snipers.[65]

Crowd control and counterinsurgency duties merged in urban areas, as the government tacitly admitted in a 1980 plan to construct a three million-dollar SAP complex in Soweto, combining both riot and security police units. But the public was normally given only the merest glimpse of the force's work in combating the ANC. The 1979 annual report, for example, summarized police activity in this area in three terse sentences in the last paragraph in a short section on the next-to-last page.[66]

What was known is that the SAP operated in close coordination with the defense force, in both border regions and urban areas. It had ready access to the military's air and ground support. But in 1980 one of the last legal distinctions between police and defense-force counterinsurgency missions fell away. Amendments passed without objection in parliament in March and April authorized the deployment of both the SAP and the related Railways and Harbour Police in foreign countries to "assist in the defense of South Africa."[67]

Six homeland police services containing up to twenty thousand men trained and in some cases led by white officers constituted another source of SAP strength.[68] Virtually all command ranks in the bantustan forces were filled with graduates of South African police instruction, or with SAP men seconded to them.

The development of the Venda National Force (VNF) was a typical example of Pretoria's efforts to foster black buffer groups between white rule and majority discontent. In 1978 the Venda cabinet voted to establish a single body responsible for police and defense functions. A Venda who had served in the SAP was named to lead the new VNF, and a project committee to plan the force came into being. Headquartered at police offices in South Africa and composed largely of whites representing the SAP, SADF, and South Africa's Prison Service and Department of Cooperation and Development, the committee shaped the Venda National Force in the SAP's image. Vendas then employed in South African security services were ordered transferred into the VNF, though one report indicated that some two-thirds refused the move in protest at the loss of South African citizenship.[69]

Cooperating recruits reported to the SAP's Hammanskraal base for counterinsurgency training. Many of these subsequently joined the Venda force's security branch, launched with the assistance of South African personnel commissioned by Pretoria to wear VNF uniforms and aid VNF officers at command.[70] News of armed engagements with Umkhonto units, arrests made by bantustan police at the behest of the SAP, and of political prisoners turned over by the homelands to Pretoria for trial, underlined the complementary role

played by Venda and the other "independent" black states in counterinsurgency. The SAP had even expanded the buffer program to
black townships in South Africa proper, where authorities gave community councils permission to hire municipal paramilitary forces.

South African Defense Force

Army, air force, and navy all fell under the umbrella of the South
African Defense Force. Its role in "total strategy," like that of the
SAP, was formally determined by the State Security Council. But
defense-force men dominated both the staff and membership of the
council, and the SADF's former chief, now state president, chaired
the body. In practice, the SADF was well placed to claim the lion's
share of influence over national policy.

Nevertheless, no political leadership wanted militarization of society used as a cover for a rising independent locus of power in the
SADF. To help assure loyalty and subservience to the National Party, Broederbond members had been placed in top military posts. In
1978 some 143 senior officers were secret members of the bond,
along with SADF chief, later defense minister, General Magnus
Malan.[71] Because the lower officer ranks tended to be dominated by
verkramptes, Afrikaner reactionaries potentially sympathetic to
rightist parties, NP authority over the upper ranks was considered
vital in guaranteeing the force's fidelity.

Doctrine identified two defense tasks for the SADF: countering
landward and seaward threats. An estimated 80 percent of the
defense budget was allocated to meet the landward threat, which
included conventional invasion as well as insurgency.[72] The bulk of
the SADF was deployed and trained, however, to combat guerrilla
warfare.

Much of the SADF's counterinsurgency strategy overlapped and
coincided with that of the SAP. The defense-force mission, for example, encompassed halting infiltration, annihilation of Umkhonto's
bases and guerrilla units, and defense of sensitive installations. In
these areas, the SADF served as a backup to the police, lending
assistance when needed, taking over operations when they taxed
SAP resources. Beginning in 1984, soldiers even began performing
the regular duty of suppressing black resistance in the townships.

The SADF drew its white manpower from three major sources:

The Permanent Force (PF), National Service (NS), and Citizen Force (CF). At the hub of the defense wheel was the careerist PF, which comprised only 9 percent of SADF's strength in 1979.[73] The figure had risen to 28 percent by the early 1980s, but remained low in comparison with most countries.[74] Pretoria's objective was to finance a small professional body less expensive and more flexible than a larger force. Around it, the government established National Service conscription and the auxiliary Citizen Force.

As of 1983, nearly every white man reaching the age of eighteen, having already trained in school military clubs, could expect to serve a two-year tour of duty in the National Service, followed by another twenty-four months spread out over fourteen years in the Citizen Force, followed in turn by an annual twelve-day term in the Active Citizen Force Reserve for five years, another annual twelve-day service period in the paramilitary Commandos until age fifty-five, and finally a ten-year stretch in the National Reserve. These requirements represented dramatic and often unpopular increases over previous years, and were bound to rise even further. But they were able to put over seventy thousand men under arms at any one time.

Despite the impressive manpower totals, the SADF had difficulty in both recruitment and conscription. The Permanent Force's target strength remained far above actual numbers. In 1977, in fact, the PF was as little as half its assigned size.[75] Recruitment over the following years was hampered by "an onerous brain drain" of attrition amounting to approximately 15 percent annually.[76] Officials blamed higher pay in the private sector for the turnover. But growing political resistance to the idea of enrollment in the PF was a factor. So too was the English-speaking community's perception of the SADF as a haven for unskilled Afrikaners. One SADF officer noted obliquely in 1977 that "the number of good young men who avoid a military career because of current social attitudes cannot be known, but is undoubtedly large."[77] Spokesmen later admitted that only some three percent of Permanent Force careerists were enlisting on a direct voluntary basis.[78] Still more problematic was the "real shortage of the leadership element" caused by annual intake shortfalls.[79] In its 1979 White Paper, the Department of Defense appeared to recognize that a ceiling of white Permanent Force recruitment would soon be reached and hinted that nonwhites would in the future be tapped to fill the gaps. The government ordered conscription for Indians and coloreds to begin in 1982 as a step in this process. The Citizen Force, for its part, boasted adequate manpower levels but suffered from persistent shortages of senior and noncommissioned officers.[80]

The SADF's most serious difficulty, however, lay in the National Service. Morale for many years had been recognized as low; even P. W. Botha had admitted, as defense minister in 1975, that only between 20 and 30 percent of conscripts were highly motivated.[81] But it plummeted further on the heels of Pretoria's 1977 decision to extend minimum service from one year to two. A variety of indicators suddenly began registering white discontent, particularly among English-speakers and political liberals.

Draft evasion rose spectacularly. In 1975, over 3,000 of the total annual January and July intake of 27,000 failed to report for National Service duty. The figure jumped to 3,814 in 1977,[82] and after a lull of several years reached a record high of 7,589 just in the January call-up for 1985.[83] Even in the unlikely event that all other enlistees had reported for duty in the July intake, the figure represented a massive 25 percent evasion rate among eligible conscripts. The final figure for the year would probably have been well over 30 percent. The government, alarmed at the situation, refused to divulge updated draft statistics for 1985 and 1986[84] and soon issued an emergency decree outlawing any drive encouraging resistance to conscription. The ban, coupled with detentions, crippled the two-year-old End Conscription Campaign (ECC), which had gained support in the wake of Pretoria's September 1984 decision to deploy defense forces in the townships. By September 1985, the momentum of discontent on the part of youth had even propelled the opposition Progressive Federal Party to endorse an end to the draft.[85]

Many conscripts had not anticipated taking part in military action against their countrymen, and the mounting casualties accentuated their anxieties. Indeed, most white enlistees had never visited black residential areas and knew little about life in them, even though some townships are located just miles from white suburbs. Pretoria had long advertised the SADF as a body conceived for national defense against external enemies. The experience of tens of thousands of white recruits battling South African blacks sparked a new round of resistance to the demands of total strategy.

Applications for conscientious objection, normally approved only for a tiny minority of conscripts, reached 350 in just the first six months of 1985, compared to the same number for the whole of 1984.[86] The most popular and still available escape route from service proved to be educational deferments. Eligible men could delay entrance into the SADF until after advanced studies, and then leave the country rather than serve. The ECC estimated that up to 4,000 whites had gone into exile between 1979 and 1984 to avoid the draft. But the SADF's entry into the townships may have caused a sharp rise in the exodus. The Committee of South African War Resisters (COSAWR) reported in 1985 "an unprecedented number of conscripts or South African men opposing conscription and seeking help or asylum" through its London headquarters. The organization estimated that some 7,000 conscription evaders were living in Europe alone, while an unknown number of others had sought residency in the United States, Canada, and Australia. "Since last year the trickle has become a steady stream," said a COSAWR spokesperson.[87]

Another symptom of what the ECC termed a "crisis of conscience" was the military's suicide rate. The official tally of suicides among soldiers in 1984 was twenty-five. One year later, however, reports listed at least seventy self-inflicted deaths and some 260 attempted suicides in the SADF.[88] Observers also anticipated an increase in courts-martial stemming from troop dissatisfaction. The number of cases had "veritably exploded" in the first four years after the Soweto uprising, more than quadrupling from 486 in 1976 to 2,146 in 1980, as National Service tours lengthened and involvement in the Namibia insurgency deepened.[89] The impact of township deployment was expected to produce still more numerous disciplinary problems.

Army

The army, the largest component of the SADF, accounted for over 70 percent of full-time manpower and half the budget. To compensate for shortages and inexperience in the junior officer corps, it periodically sought and absorbed foreign troops, particularly Portuguese military refugees from Angola and Mozambique and whites from Zimbabwe.[90] Following the end of the Rhodesian war, members of three elite units—Selous Scouts, Special Air Service, and the Rhodesian Light Infantry regiment—were shuffled into various divisions of the South African army. The logistical backbone of the army was its fleet of over three hundred tanks and sixteen hundred armored cars. The force included eight infantry battalions of National Servicemen, two black infantry battalions, a parachute brigade, and reconnaissance commando. In addition, some one hundred Citizen Force battalions took orders from army command. The development of parachute and reconnaissance groups in the wake of the Soweto uprising significantly expanded the army's counterinsurgency repertoire. A paratroop force provided it with a rapid reaction unit that improved the SADF's ability to respond to and support infantry contacts with ANC guerrillas, thereby cutting Pretoria's 1972 estimate that troops could be ferried to virtually any part of the Republic in ninety minutes.

Special counterinsurgency forces such as the Reconnaissance Commando duplicated Rhodesia's use of the Selous Scouts to perform unconventional military assignments against guerrillas. In Namibia, such tasks had included tracking guerrillas on horseback and motorcycle or posing as SWAPO units outfitted with Soviet weapons and appropriate uniforms.[91] Like the Selous Scouts, disguised groups could be used either to engage authentic insurgent companies or to discredit rebels by performing brutal deeds—such as stealing, raping, or even killing—in their name. The Reconnaissance Commando was revealed in 1979 to have begun extensive recruitment of blacks, giving the "Recces" the ability to launch such special operations in South Africa or abroad by impersonating Umkhonto soldiers.

Counterinsurgency preparations were most visible in frontier areas abutting foreign states and "independent" bantustans. New bases allowed headquarters to station units adjacent to homelands and international boundaries permanently. Armed with a 1979 act of parliament that established six-mile-wide "no-go" strips along all borders and granted the military exclusive jurisdiction over them, SADF engineers launched a massive strategic road-building program. At the same time the government uprooted whole villages judged to be too close to military access thoroughfares: planners feared that rebellious blacks might obstruct strategic routes during emergencies.[92] The new patrol roads stretching along borders and the Transkei coastline were built with thick tar so as to accommodate military vehicles, and many were broadened in key areas to double as emergency airfields. In addition, the army ensured that bridges and strategic routes could be blown up at certain points by the SADF in the event of an enemy invasion.

Defense plans also called for construction of deadly anti-infiltration barriers on the frontiers with Mozambique, Zimbabwe, and Botswana. Eleven 20,000-volt strands atop tall walls and rolls of blade wire were to be "switched on" in mid-1986 along parts of the border.[93] A "living barricade" of sisal plants backed by minefields, tall fences, sand strips to detect footprints, and electronic sensing equipment girded both sides of the new electrified parapet along the Limpopo River. Meanwhile the SADF quietly converted much of the Mozambique–South Africa frontier, occupied by the vast Kruger Park game preserve, into a militarized buffer zone. Engineers reportedly cleared sections of the border strip of vegetation to a depth of as much as one mile and erected lighting and a network of mines to deter and detect guerrilla infiltration.[94]

Matching the flurry of military activity at the Republic's extremities, Pretoria initiated a costly new program to repopulate white agricultural lands adjacent to infiltration-prone frontiers. Using lures such as subsidized home fortification systems and low-interest loans, the government sought to integrate border farmers into the SADF's security systems. Each landowner was expected to participate in local paramilitary commando exercises and maintain round-the-clock communication links with regional defense offices through MARNET, the Military Area Radio Network. But even after five years of strong incentives and urgent appeals, nearly 40 percent of all Transvaal border farms remained unoccupied in 1985.[95]

"Total strategy" envisioned not just military defense against insurgents but political reforms aimed at cultivating a black constituency in support of the government. Even if at a national level the Botha administration was unwilling to introduce changes broad enough to attract significant numbers of blacks, the army's civic action program would attempt to win black trust with parochial aid projects.

Strategists modeled the army's efforts on the long-established program in northern Namibia, where through a combination of economic development and propaganda, the defense force had attempted to "align the people with the aims of their lawfully constituted government" rather than SWAPO. South African "information officers" had been dispatched to villages to help "identify the armed forces with civilian well-being, and protection for the civilian from guer-

rilla depredations and atrocities."[96] Brigadier C. J. Lloyd, architect
of the army's Natal and Transvaal versions of the Namibia civic
action scheme, based his plans on the assumption that the black
population's "loyalty, good will and cooperation will determine the
outcome of the struggle."[97] Lloyd told a Durban conference that the
army was working on development programs coordinated with "indoctrination, propaganda and counter-propaganda" to secure black
support on South Africa's sensitive frontiers.[98] Soldiers skilled in
medicine, agriculture, and manufacturing could improve the standard of living and alleviate "friction points, grievances and dissatisfaction" among the border populace, thus "giving [the villagers]
something worthwhile to defend in this revolutionary war."[99] In
October of 1985, in one example of the civic action plan, a Transvaal
defense-force unit built five sports fields in the black community of
Tembisa and turned them over to the official town council.[100]

Lloyd's plan also provided for modified Vietnam-style "protected hamlets" designed to guard cooperative black civilians from
Umkhonto raids or assassination squads. These stockades would be
defended by regional commando units under the army's control. But
where the SADF's field agents encountered hostility and resistance
among border dwellers in spite of the military's good works, Lloyd
asserted that "we will have to move them out of the critical areas and
resettle them elsewhere."[101]

Another tactic the army turned to as counterinsurgency demands
mounted was recruitment of black troops. Pretoria shunned a draft
for the black population for fear of insubordination and mutiny stemming from anti-apartheid sentiment. But black troops, carefully
screened for political docility, would boast major advantages. They
would ease manpower pressures on the white community, increase
the range of military options, accentuate divisions among blacks,
and bolster the government's image abroad as reformist.

By 1980, the army had succeeded in enlisting and training
enough black soldiers for them to account for up to 25 percent of the
forces actually mobilized for battle at any one time in South Africa
and Namibia.[102] Pretoria energetically exploited black presence in
the SADF for public relations purposes, though many had joined for
the benefits of steady employment rather than out of allegiance to the
state. Yet blacks still formed barely 5 percent of total SADF troop
strength, and despite the recruitment incentives, the actual number

applying for admission to the SADF was reported by the defense minister to have declined between 1981 and 1983.[103] It was clear that Pretoria wished its black soldiers to bear a highly visible and disproportionate share of the frontline combat burden on the borders and in the townships.

Twenty-one Battalion, a black multiethnic unit led by an all-white officer corps, formed the nucleus of black participation in the army. Trained primarily in counterinsurgency at Lenz base, just beyond Soweto, companies of the unit's some four hundred men had fought in Namibia and helped to organize homeland armies. But in 1978 the government moved to reestablish ethnicity instead of race as the guide to black soldiery. Rather than create more multiethnic battalions, Pretoria mandated the formation of eight tribal units to be stationed on frontline borders with Zimbabwe, Swaziland, and Mozambique; the policy was another "total strategy" effort to counter resistance group efforts to deemphasize tribal identity. Four new ethnic brigades were unveiled in May of 1980: 121 Battalion of Zulus, 113 Battalion of Shangaans, 111 Battalion of Swazis, and 112 Battalion of Vendas (separate from the Venda homeland's own army). SADF strategists hoped to organize at least eighteen more similar units.[104]

In addition to these tribal units, the army planned to develop the strength of the small homeland military services in order to shift the growing burden of counterinsurgency combat on to a buffer force of blacks. Pretoria first demanded that each of the four "independent" reservations sign nonaggression pacts, which outlawed transit by guerrillas heading into the Republic proper. Homeland recruits would then be dispatched to SADF training schools, while South African instructors would organize or command the new military establishments. The Bophutatswana National Guard, for example, was formed under the wing of the defense force's North Western Command, and its first minister of defense was seconded to the bantustan from the SADF. Transkei, for its part, was the earliest homeland force to be organized. Between 1974 and 1979, some one thousand Transkeians were trained at SADF facilities.[105] When the territory's army was expanded to 1,100 men in 1981, a controversial new chief took charge: Ronald Reed-Daly, a white Rhodesian who had achieved infamy in black Africa for atrocities he was said to have perpetrated as commander of the Selous Scouts.[106] Reed-

Daly's promise to shape the Transkeian military into an effective combat force against insurgency echoed Chief Matanzima's pledge to his legislative assembly that the homeland army would "stand side-by-side the Republic's."[107]

Though traditionalist black cohorts could complement the white elite's frontline defenses in border areas, the task of battling guerrilla insurrection in the nation's townships fell to the South African army working backup duty for the police. In 1985 some 35,372 members of the SADF were called upon to serve in ninety-six black communities on missions "preventing or suppressing internal disorder."[108] The defense ministry claimed that only six of the 104 soldiers killed during the same year had lost their lives in street combat, while forty-four had been wounded.[109] But army deployment in the townships marked the force's expansion across new frontiers of counterinsurgency warfare. Once portrayed as a nonpartisan body serving in distant terrains against foreign enemies, the army now acted as an occupying power on the outskirts of white suburbs, fighting other South Africans in a bitter and manifestly political conflict.

Aiding the army in its new "total strategy" role was a nationwide civilian network of paramilitary defense units. Under SADF and police supervision, administrators were to install security systems in all public buildings, schools, and hospitals. Meanwhile, in 1977 Pretoria ordered the establishment of civil defense organizations throughout the Republic to maintain essential community services in the event of military emergencies. Plans were circulated secretly to designate petrol stations as ammunition supply dumps. Officials urged that commercial enterprises, schools, and universities establish internal civil defense organizations, and by 1979 a total of 636 such groups had been created around the country.[110]

At the same time, the volunteer Commando system, compared by some to a more militarized U.S. National Guard, claimed to be able to mobilize a hundred thousand men into over three hundred local militia units trained to hold off attacks until army and police forces could arrive on the scene.[111] Commandos practiced guerrilla warfare tactics at Kimberley's Theron Combat School before being assigned either to defensive or offensive sections of regional posts.[112] But enlistment in Commando units was reported to be so sluggish that as many as 37 percent were understaffed, with rural detachments particularly hard-pressed to find volunteers.[113] Alarmed, the SADF channeled draftees into key Commandos but complained that the army could not afford to make up for recruitment failures in both the police and civil defense. "With the present limited numbers in the Commando Force," the defense ministry concluded in 1982, "the Force is under strength and can therefore not fulfill all its obligations, particularly those in the rural areas."[114]

Air Force

The ten thousand-man South African Air Force (SAAF) occupied both primary strike and support positions in counterinsurgency warfare. Manpower problems plagued the SAAF more severely than either the army or navy on account of its almost total reliance on the Permanent Force for experienced and highly trained air crews. National Servicemen, with their comparatively short instruction, filled ground-based service jobs. According to the 1979 White Paper on Defense, high turnover in junior officers and pilots undermined the air force's ability to maintain a state of maximum readiness.[115]

The SAAF's second major headache was the U.N. arms embargo. A disproportionate dependence on sophisticated equipment, in comparison with the labor-intensive army, laid the air force open to cutoffs of imported parts and technology, particularly those needed for helicopters and jet aircraft. Nevertheless, a combination of jury-rigging and covert international arms purchases enabled the SADF to continue its modernization of the air force, if at a higher cost and slower pace than desired. The U.S. Defense Department estimated that the SAAF was equipped with some 160 jet fighters, 5 bombers, 60 transports, and 25 maritime aircraft, making it the most powerful south of the Sahara.[116]

Four commands divided the SAAF into Strike, Transport, Light Aircraft, and Maritime missions. Strike Command, based at five Transvaal facilities, had responsibility for high-altitude reconnaissance, interception, and long-distance ground attack, and was well suited for incursions into frontline states. Some 220 Mirage and Impala aircraft were equipped with air-to-surface missiles, which were most effective against fixed targets such as Umkhonto bases and railway lines in neighboring countries.

The Transport Command operated in conjunction with the army, using its aging fleet of Lockheed C-130s and L-100s and European Transall C-160s to ferry heavy equipment, troops, and supplies. While these aircraft were too lumbering to be of much use in fast-paced counterinsurgency warfare, they could be employed in major strikes against Umkhonto bases abroad. Later model Hawker Siddeley 125s and Merlins could carry lighter loads more quickly in actions against guerrillas.

The SAAF's main arm of counterinsurgency combat was the Light Aircraft Command. Flying Cessna Skywagons, CE-185s, and Italian Bosboks, pilots in the command formed the SADF's reconnaissance vanguard. Aided and often directed by radar and electronic sensor signals channeled to them through SADF communication centers,[117] the aircraft constantly monitored roads and borders. In addition, they could direct ground fire against guerrilla targets.[118] Along with the other commands, the SAAF's Light Aircraft section also boasted helicopter squadrons, which transported army infantry units and operated as gunships to provide air cover, tracking, and medical evacuation work in encounters with guerrillas. These, in turn, could be backed up by some thirteen squadrons of Air Commandos, which were formed by private plane owners and trained by the SAAF to play light support roles in military actions.[119]

Finally, the Maritime Air Command deployed its refurbished Shackletons, Westland Wasp helicopters, Dakotas, and Albatrosses in coastal reconnaissance.[120] Since Umkhonto rebels were not known to infiltrate by sea, these aircraft had seen no counterinsurgency service.

Apart from modernizing and expanding its forces, particularly in those forward-based units such as helicopter, light aircraft, and Air Commando squadrons responsible for counterinsurgency missions, the SAAF had made few fundamental changes in the post-Soweto period. Nevertheless, new conventional and emergency airfields strung along frontier areas had given the force improved ability to project SADF power across the country more rapidly than ever before.

Navy

Weakest of the SADF's three armed services, the 5,500-man South African Navy (SAN), until 1975, had been little more than a colonial spinoff of the Royal Navy. Personnel had consisted predominantly of English-speaking Permanent Force careerists. An influx of Afrikaners and tighter governmental control over navy command reduced the proportion to 50 percent and further extended National Party influence over the service. White turnover remained high, however, as it had throughout the Permanent Force, thereby depopulating the junior officer ranks. Indians and coloreds were recruited in large numbers to make up for shortages at lower-skill levels and by 1979 constituted a record 20 percent of the navy's Permanent Force.[121]

The navy had maintained close links with Britain for procurement of equipment. The nucleus of its fleet had been purchased from Britain between 1946, SAN's founding year, and the mid-1960s. Two destroyers, seven frigates, ten minesweepers, and other ships had been acquired from London until the SADF began to shop elsewhere for modern vessels and a diversity of suppliers. Pretoria had taken delivery of three French Daphne submarines before the U.N. arms embargo blocked the shipment of other frigates and new submarines ordered from Paris in the early 1970s.

Even the SAN's mission reflected Royal Navy influence. British and NATO military interests in the subcontinent had focused primarily on defense of the Cape route, increasingly important as an oil shipping lane between the Persian Gulf and the West. The South African Navy, playing the part of dutiful ally, spent its early tutelage with the Royal Navy deployed to protect Western access to the route. Even after the National Party reined in the force, Pretoria used the SAN's resources as a carrot to attract Western cooperation. A $17 million investment in the Advokat military communications and Decca radar systems based at Silvermine endowed Pretoria with marine surveillance coverage of much of the South Atlantic and Indian oceans, in addition to the South African coastline.[122] The SADF even poured $18 million into a construction project tripling the capacity of the Simonstown naval base, long a British facility and already the largest and best equipped in Africa, so that it could be ready for Western military use.[123]

Pretoria's desire to become indispensable to NATO met with persistent American indifference. A U.S. Defense Department official in 1980, betraying little enthusiasm, said of the South African Navy only that it "does not have much capability to defend the sealines of communication and . . . has limited itself to a coastal defense role."[124] Its military courtship unrequited, the SADF began to review the navy's mission. Beginning in 1975, an impending arms embargo and growing overland insurgency combined to force a redirection of SAN strategy from ocean deployment to coastal defense. For the first time, counterinsurgency became the navy's top priority, as it had in the rest of the defense force. No longer would the navy perform "voluntary duty to care for the security of the Cape route," declared SAN chief J. C. Walters in 1978. Instead, the marine command would "concentrate on our primary task of defending our own coast and harbours . . . " from possible guerrilla infiltration or attack by sea.[125]

The SAN command assembled a domestic military ship-building industry to produce Israeli-designed high-speed patrol boats. Armed with Israeli Gabriel ship-to-ship missiles, these vessels led the navy to its new mission: guarding the Republic's eleven commercial harbors and exercising jurisdiction over virtually all water activities along the coast. The Reinecke Commission, ostensibly charged with revising boating regulations, moved total strategy militarization offshore with blueprints to expand naval control over civilian marine matters.[126] At the same time, the admiralty founded a port defense unit, which it christened the Marine Corps, and ordered the navy's Citizen Force troops to perform wide new harbor security duties.[127]

The SAN's strategic about-turn brought it into line with the entire defense force in preparing against internal conflict rather than foreign invasion, even though no evidence of marine-launched insurgency operations by Umkhonto we Sizwe had yet surfaced.

Hardware and Nuclear Weapons

Following United Nations adoption of a mandatory arms sales embargo on South Africa in 1977, Pretoria faced a new range of problems. To procure conventional weapons for its forces, the SADF command had two choices: to rely on local production or to import covertly, at premium prices as much as twice world-market levels. Armscor, the state weapons manufacturer, had already emerged after only a ten-year lifespan as the tenth largest such company in the world, with revenues of $1.3 billion annually.[128] Through over 5,600 business operations, an estimated 100,000 South Africans held jobs linked to the parastatal.[129] Most of the fundamental equipment required for counterinsurgency, such as rifles, ammunition, grenades, mines, bombs, and mortars, could be provided by Armscor subsidiaries. Heavier antiguerrilla machinery such as Mirage and Impala jet aircraft, armored patrol cars, and missile-fitted coastal vessels were also being manufactured domestically under license or other arrangements. The SADF's most serious equipment deficiencies were in items more important for conventional warfare, such as large naval ships, long-range patrol aircraft, and heavy tanks.

Despite the aggregate figures, however, South Africa remained heavily dependent upon foreign technology, particularly in rocketry, aircraft, and computer engineering. Imports of Western tanks, helicopters, and sophisticated electronics, plus key components in otherwise locally built military hardware, totaled some 25 percent of South Africa's weaponry and were critical to developing the counterinsurgency potential of the SADF. "Long lead times . . . and great expense would be required to develop significant productive capability" within South Africa to substitute for these imports, asserted Chester Crocker, later named U.S. Assistant Secretary of State for African Affairs.[130]

Through circuitous clandestine routes snaking frequently across Italy, Portugal, Spain, and Greece, South Africa continued to import Western armaments.[131] In fact, the SADF claimed in 1980 to have allocated at least 20 percent of its weapons purchase budget to foreign shopping.[132] Sales arrangements through sanctions-busting middlemen were costly, inconvenient, and ponderous but promised to fill many of the SADF's import requirements.

South Africa's trump card in military hardware was its nuclear weaponry. Pretoria denied possessing nuclear devices, and security surrounding the nation's nuclear facilities was tight enough to prevent definitive proof of an atomic arsenal to emerge. But enough circumstantial evidence had surfaced to conclude that the SADF probably stocked an unknown number of atomic bombs. Telemetry from Soviet and American surveillance satellites gave the world the first hint of Pretoria's intentions when the orbiting probes detected preparations for a nuclear explosives test in the Kalahari Desert in July 1977. Bowing to international pressure in the wake of the disclosures, the South African government quietly halted its plans. But officials apparently looked for a way to conduct another test, out of sight of superpower intelligence.

On the night of September 22, 1979, a task force of navy vessels steamed into the South Atlantic to conduct secret exercises. Suddenly instruments on an American Vela satellite passing overhead sensed evidence of a low-yield atmospheric nuclear detonation in the same region. Independent devices elsewhere registered similar signals,[133] and soon high levels of radioactivity were found in Australian sheep.[134] The White House later refused to issue any firm conclusions on the incident, possibly out of concern for repercussions in the Middle East if Israel were discovered to have been involved in a nuclear explosives test. But other agencies, including the U.S. Naval Research Laboratory, reported that an atomic device, approximately four kilotons in yield, had in fact detonated off the Cape coast. The bomb was assumed to have been assembled by South Africans, though Israeli participation remained a possibility. In what may have been more than a coincidence, P. W. Botha surprised experts seven weeks after the blast by promoting to one of the Republic's top intelligence posts Dr. Neil Barnard, known as "the first South African analyst to make a public case for the development and actual resort to nuclear weapons."[135]

Use of a nuclear weapon seemed to make more strategic sense in a conventional international conflict than a domestic insurgency. An atomic device presumably could not be dropped on guerrillas inside South Africa, unless Pretoria were willing to obliterate whole townships and threaten white areas with blast effects and fallout. Nor would its use against Umkhonto base camps in sanctuary states seem militarily sensible, since more precise, less perilous, and comparably destructive operations could be ordered with conventional bomb attacks. The same logic held for assaults on economic infrastructures of hostile neighboring states. A nuclear attack would invite international outrage and risk provoking foreign intervention.

It seems likely, however, that the development of a semi-secret atomic arsenal was meant to serve as a psychological deterrent to insurgency. Transit and sanctuary states recognized that a South African bomb indeed seemed to exist. The implicit message was that neighboring states risked virtual annihilation should they aid the ANC. Host-state policymakers had to consider whether the menace was in fact a bluff or a weapon Pretoria would be likely to use. They even had to calculate the possibility that the mere rumor of an impending nuclear attack could spark political upheaval among their frightened populations.

Whether or not South Africa did intend to employ it, widespread knowledge of the bomb's existence tended to boost the image of Pretoria's invulnerability and steadfastness, and increase the strains on subcontinental governments that assisted Umkhonto. For these same reasons, the National Party government might at some point defy international pressure and decide openly to announce the existence of its nuclear arsenal, perhaps in the most dramatic way, by issuing a communiqué in the wake of a successful test.

*   *   *

Veteran Umkhonto commander Ronnie Kasrils frankly outlined the guerrilla group's approach toward the police and military in an important 1986 interview.

> While we may not expect to convert large numbers of White soldiers, we can succeed in weakening the spirit and morale of a good proportion, and . . . we can win over Black soldiers and police. . . . The SADF is a largely conscript army, subject to all the pressures and tensions of South African society—political, moral and material. . . . Differences between the conscripted "troopies" and the officer corps will be accentuated, as well as the old English-Afrikaans language divisions and the difference between those officers and men following Botha-Malan style reform and those whose allegiances lie with the unpredictable HNP-CP rebels.
>
> Under the conditions of a revolutionary crisis it is quite conceivable that the security forces of the State will not be operating at full strength, will be suffering from desertions and demoralization, from mutiny among Black troops, from indecision and differences at the top, and will not be able to cope with the situation.[136]

The government's counterinsurgency forces were far from disabled by fissures widening under the pressure of rebellion. But neither could the police or the SADF be judged in sound enough shape to crush or contain insurgency. By most measurements, in fact, the security forces were losing the war.

There is no disputing the overwhelming superiority of police and military hardware. Pretoria could boast almost unlimited access to the weapons, ammunition, and equipment most useful in combat

against guerrillas. Aided by new bases, faster aircraft, tripwire
border sensors, wider communications, and better training, commanders could now project military power into even the most remote
corners of South Africa in minutes. And indeed, by expanding military coverage over the country, the government possessed new tools
to defeat any insurgency dependent for survival upon massive
infiltration.

But rather than stopping Umkhonto, Pretoria's enhanced powers
had driven the war deeper into the townships. The ANC would find it
far more dangerous to send soldiers and couriers across frontline
borders into South Africa. Yet rebels inside the country, if they
worked quickly, guarded against informants, and found sanctuary,
could carry out attacks and have a good chance of avoiding detec-
tion. Even if Pretoria could respond to an alarm by rushing its troops
to a target, a lightning ANC raid could well be over or a time-
delayed sabotage bomb detonated with the guerrillas long gone. The
government could launch a manhunt, but where insurgents could
rejoin a work force or escape into a black settlement the chances of
capture would be slim.

A home-rooted rebellion is one against which hardware is of
secondary importance to intelligence information generated by political popularity. Tanks, helicopters, and radio-alert systems could
only partially compensate security commanders for ignorance of Umkhonto targets, underground contacts, espionage networks, and operational plans. The army leadership's civic action program was a
naive effort to cull such intelligence data by winning public trust at
the local level. But black grievances ran far too deep for friendship to
be exchanged for athletic fields or agricultural assistance. Even Brigadier Lloyd's plan to protect the army's black supporters in guarded
stockades could not hope to shield such people from anonymous
Umkhonto snipers or midnight grenade attacks. In the absence of
credible reform initiatives taken by the country's political leaders,
the SAP and SADF were reduced to fighting insurgency with a
military infrastructure that, while powerful, lacked the one critical
armament: regular, accurate intelligence.

Undermining Pretoria's counterinsurgency campaign, too, was
creeping political uncertainty and discontent in the white population.
In Israel, a state that considers itself under siege, a striking reflection
of public trust is the fact that citizens routinely volunteer to inhabit

and defend dangerous border regions, and service in the military has always carried high status. By contrast, more than a third of South Africa's rural frontier lands lay uninhabited by white farmers in spite of incessant cajoling. Also, many whites, particularly English-speakers, considered employment in the SAP or SADF to represent low-status positions in society. Poor morale, recruitment troubles, and record-high draft evasion were additional symptoms of wide-spread disaffection. The white community seemed riven, with a large segment uneasy at the prospect of battle. At the same time, Pretoria's efforts to build a "black buffer" composed of homeland armies, tribal units, and black police were encountering mounting resistance in the form of resignations and periodic declines in enroll-ment applications.

These trends pointed to a progressive weakening of the security forces' will to fight, which was what Kasrils had identified as one of Umkhonto's prime objectives. The Republic's officer corps would be unlikely to defect or declare neutrality in the war, but the coun-terinsurgency effectiveness of both the SAP and SADF stood vulner-able to increasing manpower shortages and sinking morale.

CONCLUSION

"Total strategy" started out on paper as an all-embracing strategic bulwark against insurrection. Every institution of white power from the National Party to the corporate boardroom to the editorial desk to the defense force would be tied into the controls of the State Security Council. While shutting channels of rebellion, Pretoria would open doors to reform. Ultimately, violent resistance would be forced into political irrelevance as blacks realized the advantages of dialogue and the futility of warfare.

A critical flaw made total strategy lame. The ruling elite proved so fractious as to be unable to muster the political strength to initiate reforms substantial enough to deter rebellion. The National Party could not even define accurately for itself the political complexion of South Africa's black population, a determination vital to the task of heading off a guerrilla war. "We can do nothing," warned André Beaufre, "unless we understand the events in which we propose to intervene. . . . The concept of strategic action, therefore, necessarily stems from political analysis."[137] But rather than recognize the burgeoning popularity of anti-apartheid resistance, the government chose to diagnose the problem as a far less fundamental threat.

"It was said in evidence before us that those people in the black community who had pro-ANC feelings constituted a very small minority and that their influence should not be overestimated," concluded the landmark Rabie Commission report, which later became the basis for counterinsurgency tactics.[138] Communist agitators carrying orders from Moscow were behind most of the unrest. This distorted analysis of black politics justified the Botha administration's reluctance to adopt major reforms. They simply would not be necessary. Most blacks apparently could be won over by measures well short of power sharing. Yet these steps were to prove so ill-matched to black grievances as to aid only marginally and temporarily in the government's struggle against rebellion. Beaufre's "thoroughgoing reforms," weapons necessary to "cut the ground from under the feet of the malcontents,"[139] had been disarmed by white leaders unwilling or unable to address the real nature of black discontent.

Total strategy thus evolved into a policy managed by generals rather than politicians. Moreover, the building of a bunker state without meaningful incentives for peaceful change meant that Pretoria would be waging a largely conventional war against a politically driven insurgency. The government's massive military power might allow it to slow the rebellion, but not to stop it.

Militarization even weakened the white power base, since it failed to offer a coherent vision of the national future or hopes for peace. This absence of mobilizing leadership sharpened the impact of Umkhonto attacks designed to wear down the white will to fight. Instead of "rallying 'round the flag," white ethnic splits widened, morale dropped, and draft evasion soared. Emigration, while still low, reached record levels in 1985 and again in 1986, as black political unrest intensified. Professionals such as doctors and lawyers led the way.[140] Grimly, with much to defend but little certainty as to how to defend it, whites kept their fingers close to their triggers and waited for Umkhonto.

6. A Pyrrhic Future

One could argue that the African National Congress is the most quixotic guerrilla organization of modern times. Its leadership endorses violence, but with manifest reluctance and an aversion to terrorist tactics. ANC officials shun overt symbols of war, such as PLO-style camouflage outfits, often preferring to resemble establishment attorneys. Instead of refining its ideology, the ANC acts as a consciously federal coalition with little consensus on basic principles other than nonracialism and the overthrow of minority rule. Its main offices and bases lie as far as a thousand miles north of the South African frontier; yet through its underground the movement seeks to influence daily events inside the Republic.

Among its other strengths, the Congress has emerged as the predominant party of rebellion. The ANC's most notable imprisoned leader, Nelson Mandela, has become recognized both inside and outside South Africa as a nonpartisan kingpin in any serious negotiations in the future. Abroad, the Congress has developed a complex infrastructure of command in sanctuary states, enabling it to train, house, feed, employ, educate, and care for an estimated thirteen thousand exiles. By spreading its diaspora institutions throughout three nations—Zambia, Tanzania, and Angola—the ANC has scraped together more diplomatic freedom of maneuver than was once enjoyed by the Zimbabwean liberation parties, whose policies could be, and often were, dictated by host states. The Congress has also attracted sufficient extracontinental patronage, primarily from Soviet-bloc countries, but also from Scandinavian states and a variety of international institutions and private sources, to sustain an eight-thousand-person military and a sophisticated exile bureaucracy. Lobbying efforts on its behalf in Western capitals helped to generate unprecedented economic sanctions against Pretoria. In January 1987, the Reagan administration joined with the Thatcher government in finally recognizing the organization as a legitimate factor in the struggle over South Africa's future.

At home, the ANC has stirred black politics to militancy, thus opening new fronts of anti-apartheid resistance. Through the UDF and COSATU, its agents increase pressure on the government with strikes, boycotts, and demonstrations. Others prepare havens for guerrilla operations. Umkhonto's ability to keep its underground machinery out of sight from the police has permitted a major escalation of violence, and this in turn has sparked increasing white demoralization.

But the ANC also suffers from serious weaknesses. Its surface unity on overall policy masks deep divisions within its ranks, particularly in the exile community. There, some two-thirds of Congress personnel represent Soweto-era escapees, among whom a large faction continues to press the moderate leadership for more military action with less concern for casualties. Many have shifted from black consciousness to Marxist radicalism and resist the notion of compromise. Veterans at the ANC helm found themselves having to accept a rank-and-file-sponsored resolution at the landmark 1985 consultative conference to "erase the distinction between 'hard' and 'soft' targets."

In addition, the Communist Party, a long-time partner in the Congress Alliance, is far more influential in the ANC exile community than at home. Its members are prominent in the National Executive Committee, and its foreign ties with Moscow have become indispensable to the growth of Umkhonto we Sizwe. However, in free domestic elections, most observers believe that the party would have extremely limited appeal among blacks, even the most militant of whom might be wary of a contender so closely tied to an outside power. But the communists have a revolutionary social agenda that extends far beyond the limited objective of nonracial democracy espoused by current Congress executives, and can be expected—with Soviet support—to lobby their point of view, and to try maneuvering the coalition to the left.

Internally, the ANC's underground is weaker than it needs to be to convert the rhetorical allegiance of a majority of blacks into a disciplined and united opposition. To complicate matters, the Congress faces stiff and often violent competition from Chief Gatsha Buthelezi's Inkatha, vigilante gangs, and black consciousness parties. Though largely shielded from police espionage, the underground is short on weapons and unable to maintain regular command, control, and communication links with exile officers. In short, the ANC now holds the reins of rebellion, can finally guide it in one direction or another, but cannot quite predict with confidence whether it will balk, stumble, or charge at the Congress's order.

FUTURE SCENARIOS

South Africa has rarely been kind to prophecy. One need only recall author Kirkpatrick Sale's 1961 assertion that "Revolution . . . is obviously coming to this country—and will obviously be successful—within the next five years" to sample the record.[1] Nevertheless, a review of four possible scenarios based on current trends can at least suggest the dangers and opportunities of future policy.

A strategy of government *entrenchment*, characteristic of national policy in the mid-1980s, would have Pretoria embracing reforms considered token by the ANC camp while suppressing dissent and promoting anti-Congress blacks. It holds little hope of heading off civil war, or even of preserving white power intact. Nevertheless, the Botha administration has tried to make it work by testing out the notion of forging a coalition of blacks who can be persuaded that they have a stake in peaceful change. These have included rural traditionalists, Inkatha members, homeland elites, and urban middle-class blacks. Taken together, such a coalition could represent up to an estimated 40 percent of the nonwhite community. Structural reforms Pretoria could adopt which could solidify a conservative "any-one-but-the-ANC" alliance might include "KwaNatal"-style experiments, providing the homelands with access to and influence over national decisionmaking, and granting further rights and privileges to moneyed blacks. Each tactic could be fashioned to demonstrate that cooperation pays off. The ultimate objective would be to deny the ANC and its adherents safe haven in the black community as increasing numbers come to believe that confrontation is fruitless. Pretoria's black allies would be made to understand that their own upward mobility depends on their ability to curb the ANC.

Unfortunately for the Botha administration, the day when such an approach could succeed has long passed. The Congress itself is firmly entrenched in South Africa. Its agents have politicized too many black communities, laid too extensive a foundation of resistance, and placed too high a cost on collaboration with Pretoria, to collapse in the face of black competition. The ANC's constituency is unlikely to be successfully raided or eroded by a conservative coalition. Nor is there a chance that resistance to apartheid can be stopped unless the ANC leadership decides to do so. The "anyone-but-the-ANC" conservatives, on the other hand, have seen their numbers shrink. As a result, efforts by the government to ignore the Congress or pursue reform that is seen by most blacks as token will fail to curb the rising tide of violence. On the contrary, each offer of reform—especially those touted as substantial—will likely galvanize the radical opposition as it senses Pretoria's desperation.

A second possible future scenario is *crackdown*. In response to spreading white fears of black violence and resentment at governmental policies of "appeasement," the Nationalists, a coalition of white reactionary parties, or a newly installed military junta might abandon even mild reform and turn to wholesale repression. Pretoria outlaws the UDF, COSATU, and other militant but legal organizations believed to be linked to the Congress and employs security forces more fully than ever before to pacify the townships and crush dissent. The death toll mounts as rapidly as the number of people detained, though strict enforcement of censorship laws dampens news coverage of such developments. SADF troops stage unprecedented attacks on Congress facilities and bases in Angola, Zambia, Tanzania, and other neighboring countries. Meanwhile, the state president warns the world against interference, as he announces the detonation of a test nuclear device.

Presumably, the government would hope that this brutal repression would inflict as shattering a blow on the ANC as the one it delivered to both the Congress and the PAC in 1963. Black protest had, after all, been effectively paralyzed for a decade. Yet several important conditions existed then that endowed Pretoria with unchallengeable force. Intelligence agencies could identify and locate most members of the two insurgent groups, including their commanders. Black surrogates for the government could deny rebels safe haven in the townships, especially as Umkhonto could boast only shallow roots in the communities. Nearby states under colonial rule could be counted on to block attempts by guerrillas to use their territories. Moreover, the black public then seemed convinced of the invincibility of government power.

None of these conditions can be fully met today. First, and perhaps most importantly, the government's intelligence resources, at their peak in the aftermath of the Rivonia arrests, are now in tatters. Regardless of the amount of military hardware available, a counterinsurgency war cannot be waged successfully without the ability to identify the enemy, locate his internal bases, and determine where he plans to hit next. In the last decade, the ANC has implemented a screening and internal watchdog system that has effectively shielded most of its compartmentalized underground from penetration. In addition, it has used coercion to reduce the government's formerly abundant supply of informants. Highly publicized executions of suspected spies, assassinations of state witnesses, and continuous warnings against collaboration throughout the black community have helped blind the police to black underground activities. The ANC is not the only beneficiary: a large new stratum of local political activists involved in allied organizations, such as the UDF, or rival groups, such as AZAPO, has emerged across South Africa. It is safe to say that only a minority are known to police intelligence. Any draconian campaign of detentions and arrests would net the police a large number of innocent victims, thereby helping to inflame the black public without necessarily crippling the underground.

Second, in many of South Africa's townships black surrogate powerholders have been expelled, with de facto control passing to irregular anti-apartheid bodies. The Congress's call to make the townships ungovernable has succeeded in denying Pretoria the ability to purge these zones of its opponents. They may be used, in varying degrees, as internal sanctuaries for rebels. Frequent patrols or random house searches by an overextended military are tactics which can only hope to suppress unrest incompletely and temporarily.

Third, the nearby states that in the 1960s were governed by colonial elites hostile to South African dissidents are now ruled by blacks. While nearly all have adopted public policies that prevent ANC guerrilla activity, key figures are at the same time sympathetic to the Congress. With or without official frontline government knowledge, ANC guerrillas, recruits, couriers, agents, and arms smugglers periodically pass through border-state territories into or out of the Republic. ANC administrative, military, and educational facilities are located in an outer tier of subcontinental states. The ANC's exile-based Radio Freedom broadcasts daily, conveying news, strategic decisions, and encouragement to its constituents inside South Africa. None of these rear bases can be shut down permanently by SADF raids.

Finally, the Congress and its allies have so politicized the black public that in many townships, observers have noted, protesters have "lost their fear of death." They are more confident than ever that their cause will triumph, that government power is no longer invincible, and that the "comrades" are on their side. It would seem likely that more violent repression would result in more militant reaction rather than resignation.

For these reasons, crackdown would be unlikely to achieve the objective of crushing the ANC. Some of the practical aspects of underground operations would doubtless become more risky. But a predictable consequence of repression would be expanded popularity for the Congress. Meanwhile, the major casualties of Pretoria's decision to shun mild reform would inevitably include black moderates, principally Chief Buthelezi, who promote the possibility of peaceful evolution to majority rule. Their positions discredited, these leaders might see many of their followers desert to the ANC. The Congress's policy of armed resistance would appear to have been vindicated, and the political consensus behind rebellion strengthened.

A third scenario, as likely as it is hopeless, is *revolution*. The government's adamant refusal to negotiate with the ANC boosts the position of young Congress radicals, who would wrest leadership from veterans still prepared to restrain violence and negotiate the shape of a post-apartheid future. The militants rule out talks, emphasize class struggle rather than nationalist aspects of the conflict, invite greater Soviet aid, and seek a major escalation of insurgent operations, including attacks on civilians, to achieve a revolutionary victory over apartheid. The prospect of such a generational coup within the exiled Congress leadership grows more plausible the longer Pretoria refuses to engage in dialogue. The older nationalists who dominate the National Executive Committee are thought now to represent an ideological minority of the exile community, devoting significant energy to dampening the angry impatience of the rank and file. Yet a newly militarized ANC would still be unlikely to achieve a revolutionary victory in the foreseeable future.

To have the best chance for a successful revolution, a group needs the support of the mass of aggrieved citizens, who recognize the leadership as heading the legitimate popular party. It also requires an underground with the capacity to direct the various tactics of revolution, significant external patronage, and large-scale defections from the ruling elite's administrative and military apparatuses. A radicalized ANC could count on meeting some, but not all, of these conditions in the near term.

First, the Congress can be said to speak for a conservatively estimated 50 percent of the black public (approximately 40 percent of the population as a whole), thus giving it a dominant but by no means monopolistic position in South African politics.[2] It can be expected to expand further into the more conservative constituency of Inkatha, the homeland elites, and the middle class. But that growth advantage could be stalled should the Congress leadership move overtly to the left, emphasizing class struggle and escalating violence. Even its current basic constituency inside the country might shrink, since only a small minority are thought to be sympathetic to Marxism. Moreover, the besieged conservatives might well react violently, with civil war between pro- and anti-ANC forces as a result. Pretoria would surely encourage and support the Congress's opponents. To the extent that the Congress encounters such invigorated competition within the black community, its prospects for rallying the masses to revolution would be much reduced.

Second, the ANC underground is too sparse to supply the discipline, and too ill-equipped to distribute the weapons, to fuel a successful revolution, at least in the short term. The most it can do today is set out broad strategies for the opposition while exercising direct control in selected areas. Small numbers of weapons are stolen or smuggled in, but the demand for them far exceeds the supply. A radicalized leadership would presumably seek to accelerate the pace at which the ANC cells are multiplying and attempt to infiltrate more arms, explosives, and trained guerrillas. Indeed, over time, the Congress could reasonably be expected to accomplish this goal. On the other hand, militant executives could be tempted to follow a shortcut to upheaval: dropping the ban on terrorism. A decision to license indiscriminate killing could unleash the pent-up frustrations of thousands of blacks and lead to the bloodbath long feared by South Africans. Every civilian aircraft, every white home, every rush-hour shopping crowd, would become a potential target for attack.

Yet a radical ANC pursuing terrorism would short-circuit attempts to achieve other prerequisites for a successful uprising. For example, the Congress would be even more unlikely than it is today to generate large-scale defections from the core pro-apartheid constituency. A centrist ANC could hope to lure at least some of the business class to its side, though not perhaps traditional white Afrikaner supporters of apartheid. A revolutionary ANC, on the other hand, would alienate white liberals and moderates, driving them into firmer alliance with the National Party or conservative blacks. Many whites would certainly leave the country in fear for their own security. But the regime's supply of military personnel could be expected to remain loyal and sufficient to maintain the ruling party in power. White commitment to defense might even grow stronger, since Pretoria could more convincingly portray barbarism as the obvious alternative to minority rule.

Fresh leadership in control of the Congress could set off varying reactions among the group's external patrons. Zambia, the host state whose economy has the most to lose in a South African conflagration, could be expected to try and temper ANC policy. The Soviet Union and its allies, on the other hand, would probably be delighted to consider expanding their assistance to a more faithful client. On balance, a revolutionary Congress could probably anticipate sufficient aid to fund its external and internal operations, though it could experience regional dislocations.

Given the mixed consequences of revolutionary politics, the most the ANC could count on achieving would be a sort of "rebellion of attrition," in which the intensity of both peaceful and violent resistance would grow dramatically, together with militant competition among black groups, but fail to reach a breakthrough to successful revolution. A stalemate characterized by deadly and continuous turmoil would result. The government cannot defeat the ANC, and the ANC, though it forces Pretoria to absorb ever greater costs in maintaining white rule, cannot defeat the government. The only way out must eventually lie in a peace conference.

Finally, a fourth scenario for South Africa's future, *negotiation*, holds the only real prospect of an end to civil war. Pretoria makes clear, through such gestures as releasing Nelson Mandela and other political prisoners, that it is prepared to risk the estrangement of the white right by seriously negotiating a transition to a post-apartheid state.

The National Party's objectives in taking a dramatic action such as freeing Mandela would be to relieve international financial pressure on the country and "demythologize" the ANC leader by forcing him to make pragmatic, human-sized decisions that risk splitting the ANC alliance. In fact, the move would only make political sense to Pretoria in the context of a broad deal to begin peace talks. Without such discussions, any relaxation of world economic pressure following the prison release would be brief, and Mandela, rather than having to make controversial negotiating choices, could simply rally Umkhonto into battle. For as long as he remains alive, Mandela's status will be a key to resolving the country's political crisis. The ANC will not enter talks unless he is freed, and Pretoria will let him go only if it judges him moderate enough to strike a deal. For both sides the question is: what would Nelson do?

Among blacks, Mandela's release would be greeted with euphoria, and he would doubtless be granted an implicit "honeymoon" before criticism, even from the most anti-ANC groups in the black community, surfaced. Currently the ANC does not indicate what precise position he would hold in the organization. Though he once headed the Congress's Transvaal branch and served as founding commander of Umkhonto we Sizwe, Mandela never held the post of president of the party. It is not clear that Oliver Tambo would need to step aside for his old colleague and friend. But in light of his stature, Mandela would likely be designated titular head, sharing power with Tambo.

Mandela would be coming out of prison with three major attributes not now held by any black South African. First, according to polls and observers, Mandela holds the admiration of more blacks than any other single leader. His constituency is nonpartisan, extending beyond those who express allegiance to the ANC. Second, he has long-standing ties with groups that compete with the Congress—principally, Chief Buthelezi's Inkatha and the leadership of the Ciskei and Transkei homelands. Third, he has a proven ability to appeal to the West, and is already well regarded there. Mandela would have the opportunity to use these advantages to broaden the popularity of the ANC both at home and abroad. He would be a highly effective spokesman for the Congress in foreign capitals, he is possibly the only person who could patch up the bitter feud between the ANC and Inkatha, and he might succeed in persuading key bantustans to be more hospitable to ANC organizers.

The longer Mandela is free and taking responsibility for such decisions as talking with the National Party administration or escalating Umkhonto actions, the more likely it is that the veteran leader will shed support. His popularity would likely peak in the honeymoon days after his release and, with or without negotiations, decrease somewhat thereafter. There is no evidence to suggest that in battling the government Mandela would adopt any significantly different line than the ANC leadership has taken in recent years on major issues and tactics, especially after a period of orientation to the current political environment. To the extent that Mandela, like Tambo, seeks to restrain violence, young militants might begin to wonder if he had secretly "sold out" to gain his release. To the extent that he, like the Congress today, advocates disinvestment, black traditionalists might consider him too radical for their tastes. If the war continues, Mandela can be expected to possess sufficient stature to contain any major erosion in ANC solidarity. The only genuine chance of his credibility being undermined would be if negotiations actually take place. But then, the instant that Congress agrees to enter into talks, the power of the alliance as a whole would come under siege.

The National Party would surely be under pressure from its right wing to preserve white domination. But the Congress is perhaps uniquely vulnerable to the stresses generated by negotiations. A loose coalition rather than a cohesive party, the ANC's unity rests almost solely on the notion of fighting to attain a vaguely defined state of majority rule. At the point when this goal is in sight, all the various constituent factions that view the ANC as a vehicle for transforming South Africa into their own visions of society may begin to assert their independence and promote their separate agendas. At the same time, an ANC that has had the liberation stage all but exclusively to itself for more than twenty-five years may be forced to cope head-to-head with negotiating competitors such as Inkatha and the black-consciousness-oriented National Forum.

Compromises would be demanded from the very start of the bargaining process. Mandela and his colleagues would have to decide how to respond to Pretoria's anticipated efforts to reassure white constituents—efforts that might include cross-border military strikes or mass detentions. They would also have to confront government demands to sever ties with the Communist Party and Moscow or acknowledge homeland chief ministers as coequal negotiators. All these decisions involve extreme threats to anti-apartheid unity, and a canny Pretoria could be expected to introduce as many divisive issues as possible to delay progress and disrupt the opposition. The lengthier the process and the more compromises made, the greater the loss of Mandela's ability to keep his constituency together and hold a truce. Pretoria might seek to break the coalition on the right by forging agreement with Buthelezi and others. On the other hand, the Marxist and black-consciousness-oriented left might reject any accord that leaves white power substantially intact. Mandela should have more of a chance than any other leader of finding consensus among blacks, but he would have to use every ounce of political capital derived from twenty-four years in prison to succeed.

For a government seeking to preserve white power, the most promising approach, indeed, would be to appear flexible, accommodating, and low-key, while constantly raising issues or proposals to maximize and manipulate divisions among the opposition. If, however, Pretoria were to act as its record might predict, with blunt heavy-handedness, it would probably persuade the anti-apartheid parties to overcome their differences and work as a bloc. The more the National Party acts as an enlightened and credible partner for moderate-to-conservative black elements—in short, quite differently from the way it has acted in the past—the better chance it has of causing ruptures among blacks and forging a reformist alliance without the Congress that could attract international and domestic applause. Such a coalition would presumably preserve most of the perquisites whites now enjoy. The Congress would be faced with having to reactivate its guerrilla struggle, possibly in the face of greater internal and foreign criticism, or to contest the result through political channels designed by its opponents.

The ANC would run great risks in this scenario. If it turned down negotiations even though the release of political prisoners and other conditions were promised, it could incur the wrath of foreign patrons, not least of which might be the sanctuary states of Zambia, Tanzania, and Angola, together with moderate domestic supporters. Should it enter into an all-parties conference, the least likely outcome would be an agreement that assured its coming to power. In fact, perhaps the most realistic outcome might be a compromise between the National Party and conservative blacks that could attract significant international and domestic support, setting the ANC back years if it were to resume guerrilla warfare. Against the bargaining strength of stubborn competitors, the most it could hope to gain in talks would seem to be a chance at electoral competition in a newly structured South Africa that would constitutionally preserve a great deal of white power, thereby forcing the ANC to risk alienating its left wing.

The only way the Congress would seem to be able to steer talks to an agreement on its own terms would be if it captured the allegiance of many more members of rival constituencies so as to maximize its bargaining position, and was able to strengthen its internal underground so as to preserve fully the option of resuming the war. Its objective would have to be to convince other parties that a satisfied ANC is indispensable to a peaceful solution. The earlier negotiations occur, the weaker the Congress will be. The more time the ANC has to build up its popularity and war resources, the weaker the government will be.

In either case, South Africa's can only be a Pyrrhic future, in which neither side can muscle the other out of contention, yet neither side can willingly give ground without pain. When peace arrives, it will probably not be through conquest. Rather, it will come grudgingly, and after seasons of bloodshed, as a fruit of exhaustion.

Abbreviations

ANC	African National Congress
ASSECA	Association for Educational and Cultural Advancement of Africans
AWB	Afrikaner Weerstandsbeweging
AZAPO	Azanian People's Organization
BAWU	Black Allied Workers Union
BCM	Black Consciousness Movement
BCP	Black Community Programs
BOSS	Bureau of State Security
BPC	Black People's Convention
CF	Citizen Force
COSAS	Congress of South African Students
COSATU	Congress of South African Trade Unions
COSAWR	Committee of South African War Resisters
CP	Conservative Party
CUSA	Confederation of Unions of South Africa
DMI	Directorate of Military Intelligence
DONS	Department of National Security
ECC	End Conscription Campaign
ESCOM	Electricity Supply Commission
FOFATUSA	Federation of Free African Trade Unions of South Africa
FOSATU	Federation of South African Trade Unions

FRELIMO	Frente de Libertação de Moçambique
HNP	Herstigte Nasionale Party
IDAMASA	Inter-Denominational African Ministers Association of South Africa
IUEF	International University Exchange Fund
MARNET	Military Area Radio Network
MK	Umkhonto we Sizwe (Spear of the Nation)
MPLA	Movimento Popular de Libertação de Angola
NEC	National Executive Committee
NIS	National Intelligence Service
NP	National Party
NS	National Service
PAC	Pan Africanist Congress
Pebco	Port Elizabeth Black Civic Organization
PF	Permanent Force
Renamo	Resistência Nacional de Moçambique
SAAF	South African Air Force
SAAN	South African Associated Newspapers
SAAWU	South African Allied Workers' Union
SABC	South African Broadcasting Corporation
SACP	South African Communist Party
SACTU	South African Congress of Trade Unions
SADF	South African Defense Force
SAMRAF	South African Military Refugees Aid Fund
SAN	South African Navy
SANNC	South African Natives National Congress
SAP	South African Police
SASM	South African Students Movement
SASO	South African Students Organization
Sasol	South African Coal, Oil and Gas Corporation
SOMAFCO	Solomon Mahlangu Freedom College
SSC	State Security Council
SSRC	Soweto Students Representative Council
SWAPO	South West African People's Organization
UDF	United Democratic Front
UNHCR	United Nations High Commission for Refugees
UNITA	União Nacional para a Independência Total de Angola
UWUSA	United Workers Union of South Africa
VNF	Venda National Force
ZANU	Zimbabwe African National Union
ZAPU	Zimbabwe African People's Union

Notes

PREFACE

1. Related to the author, Johannesburg, 1980.

CHAPTER ONE

1. For detailed studies of South African history, see, for example, Cornelius W. de Kiewiet, *A History of South Africa: Social and Economic* (London: Oxford University Press, 1941, 1966); T. R. H. Davenport, *South Africa: A Modern History* (Toronto: University of Toronto Press, 1978); Monica Wilson and Leonard Thompson, eds., *The Oxford History of South Africa* (Oxford: Clarendon Press, 1969, 1971); Arthur Keppel-Jones, *South Africa: A Short History* (London: Hutchinson, 1949-1966); J. D. Omer-Cooper, *The Zulu Aftermath: A Nineteenth Century Revolution in Bantu Africa* (London: Longmans, 1966); Sheila Patterson, *The Last Trek: A Study of the Boer People and the Afrikaner Nation* (London: Routledge and Kegan Paul, 1957); Edward Roux, *Time Longer than Rope* (Madison: University of Wisconsin Press, 1966); R. Lacour-Gayet, *A History of South Africa* (London: Cassell and Company, 1977); and John Selby, *A Short History of South Africa* (London: George Allen and Unwin, 1973).

2. Accounts of ANC history may be found, for example, in Thomas Karis and Gwendolen M. Carter, *From Protest to Challenge: A Documentary History of African Politics in South Africa 1882-1964* (Stanford: Hoover Institution Press, 1972-1977; Gail M. Gerhart, *Black Power in South Africa:*

The Evolution of an Ideology (Berkeley: University of California Press, 1978); Peter Walshe, *The Rise of African Nationalism in South Africa* (Berkeley: University of California Press, 1971); Edward Feit, *Urban Revolt in South Africa 1960-1964* (Evanston: Northwestern University Press, 1971); Elena Venturini Dorabji, "South African National Congress: Change from Non-Violence to Sabotage Between 1952 and 1964," (Ph.D. diss. University of California, Berkeley, 1979); Tom Lodge, *Black Politics in South Africa Since 1945* (London: Longmans, 1983).

3. I. B. Tabata, *Imperialist Conspiracy in Africa* (Lusaka: Prometheus Publishing Company, 1974), p. 122.

4. Joe Matthews, interview in Gaborone, Botswana, April 4, 1980.

5. Sheridan Johns, "Obstacles to Guerrilla Warfare—A South African Case Study," *Journal of Modern African Studies* 2, 2, (1973): 285.

6. Donald Woods, *Biko* (New York: Vintage Books, 1979), pp. 52-54.

7. Ibid., p. 158.

8. David Davis, *African Workers and Apartheid* (London: International Defense and Aid Fund, 1978), p. 39.

9. Baruch Hirson, *Year of Fire, Year of Ash* (London: Zed Press, 1979), p. 107.

10. Calculated from trial data in Glenn Moss, *Political Trials—South Africa 1976-1979* (Johannesburg: Development Studies Group, University of the Witwatersrand, 1979).

11. Ibid., pp. 117-119.

12. Ibid., pp. 12, 24.

13. Institute member Horst Kleinschmidt was named in 1980 by the South African security police as an ANC intelligence contact based in Europe. Hirson, *Year of Fire*, p. 197 and "The State versus Renfrew Leslie Christie: Summary of Substantial Facts in Terms of Section 144(3)(a) of Act 51 of 1977," pp. 1-2.

14. John Kane-Berman, *Soweto: Black Revolt, White Reaction* (Johannesburg: Ravan Press, 1978), p. 145.

15. Moss, *Political Trials*, pp. 7, 35, and Kane-Berman, *Soweto*, p. 145.

16. Moss, *Political Trials*, pp. 10-11.

17. Hirson, *Year of Fire*, p. 327.

18. Ibid., p. 200.

19. Accounts of the PAC's mid-1970's revival appear in the Bethal-18 trial records. See Moss, *Political Trials*, pp. 56-90.

20. *Rand Daily Mail*, April 17, 1978; *Star*, April 25, 1978 and May 1, 1978.

21. *Sunday Post*, June 17, 1979.

22. *Star,* August 6, 1978; *Sunday Post,* June 17, 1979; and *Azania News* (PAC) 13, no. 7/8 (July/August 1978): 1, 5, 6.

23. *Rand Daily Mail,* June 13, 1979 and June 20, 1979; *Sunday Post,* July 1, 1979; *Daily Dispatch,* May 19, 1980; *Guardian* (U.S.), June 20, 1979; and *Africa News* 17, no. 2 (July 13, 1981): 8.

24. *Africa Confidential* 22, no. 5 (February 25, 1981).

CHAPTER TWO

1. Lindsey Phillips, "South Africa's Future: 'No Easy Walk to Freedom,'" *Working Papers for a New Society* 6, no. 6 (March/April 1979): 28.

2. *Times of Swaziland,* March 24, 1980.

3. Barbara Brown, "South Africa's Foreign Policy toward Its Black Neighbors" (Ph.D. diss., Boston University, 1979), p. 112.

4. Tom Wicker, "Dependent Democracy," *New York Times,* November 28, 1978. See also *National Development Plan 1976–81* (Gaborone: Government Printer, May 1977) and *Statistical Bulletin* (Botswana) 4, no. 3 (September 1979): 20.

5. *Statistical Bulletin* (Botswana) 4, no. 3 (September 1979): 5–7.

6. L. H. Gann and Peter Duignan, *South Africa: War, Revolution or Peace* (Stanford: Hoover Institution Press, 1978), p. 8.

7. *Boston Globe,* February 4, 1981.

8. *Herald* (Harare), May 22, 1983.

9. Richard Weisfelder, "Human Rights in Botswana, Lesotho, Swaziland and Malawi," *Pula: Botswana Journal of African Studies* 2, no. 1 (February 1980): 13; *Times* (London), November 28, 1979; Timothy Skud, U.S. embassy political officer, interview in Maseru, Lesotho, May 21, 1980.

10. Interview in Cape Town, May 13, 1980.

11. Lawrence Mncina, minister of state for foreign affairs, interview in Mbabane, Swaziland, March 25, 1980.

12. *Sechaba,* October 1984, p. 16.

13. Charles K. Ebinger, "External Intervention in Internal War: The Politics and Diplomacy of the Angolan Civil War," *Orbis* 20, no. 3 (Fall 1976): 697.

14. *Africa Confidential* 21, no. 22 (October 29, 1980); *Wall Street Journal,* December 3, 1980; *Southern Africa* 13, no. 8 (November/December 1980): 2.

15. Bill Moyers, "CBS Reports: The Battle for South Africa" (September 1, 1978; 10:00 P.M.).

16. *Rhodesian Herald,* April 12, 1980; *Focus* (International Defense and Aid Fund), no. 28 (May/June 1980): 9.

17. Interview in Harare, August 17, 1983.

18. U.S. Department of State, "Communist Influence in South Africa," released to U.S. Congress January 2, 1987, p. 7.

19. Thomas Karis, "South African Liberation: The Communist Factor," *Foreign Affairs* (Winter 1986/87), p. 281.

20. U.S. Department of State, "Communist Influence," p. 10.

21. Interview in Lusaka, August 27, 1983.

22. Ibid.

23. *Africa Confidential* 26, no. 14 (July 3, 1985), and *Sechaba,* February 1986, p. 1.

24. Interview in Lusaka, August 29, 1983.

25. Joseph Lelyveld, *Move Your Shadow: South Africa, Black and White* (New York: Times Books, 1985), p. 328.

26. Interview in Dar es Salaam, September 6, 1983.

27. Kane-Berman, *Soweto,* p. 144.

28. Stephen M. Davis, "Season of War: Insurgency in South Africa 1977–80" (Ph.D. diss., Fletcher School of Law and Diplomacy, Tufts University, 1982), p. 212.

29. Interview in Mazimbu, Tanzania, September 9, 1983.

30. Interview in Dar es Salaam, September 6, 1983.

31. Interview in Mazimbu, Tanzania, September 9, 1983.

32. Interview in Mazimbu, Tanzania, September 9, 1983.

33. "Comrade Arthur," interview in Mazimbu, Tanzania, September 9, 1983.

34. Interview in Dar es Salaam, September 6, 1983.

35. *Sechaba,* August 1985, p. 2

36. *Sechaba,* February 1986, p. 7.

37. *Rand Daily Mail,* August 2, 1979, which cites the Pietermaritzburg-12 trial; and *Work in Progress,* no. 12 (April 1980): 44, which offers corroborating information in the State v. Bhekizitha Oliver Nqubelani case.

38. *Sechaba,* October 1984, p. 17.

39. *Work in Progress,* no. 12 (April 1980); *Sunday Post,* April 8, 1979.

40. ANC agricultural expert, interview in Morogoro, Tanzania, September 10, 1983.

41. *Africa Confidential* 26, no. 14, (July 3, 1985): 1.

42. *Rand Daily Mail,* August 2, 1979.

43. U.S. Department of State. Secret. "Cable from US Embassy Monrovia to Secretary of State," 78 Monrovia 7493, October 6, 1978. Declassified under author's Freedom of Information request; also, Paul Kaunda, Zambian foreign ministry director of African affairs, interview in Lusaka, April 10, 1980.

44. *Sunday Times* (Johannesburg), September 10, 1978.

45. Giancarlo Coccia, *The Scorpion Sting: Moçambique* (Johannesburg: Libraria Moderna, 1976), p. 164.

46. *New York Times,* January 31, 1981.

47. High British official involved in implementing the Lancaster House peace accord, interview in Boston, 1981.

48. ANC official, interview in Lusaka, September 1, 1983.

49. Ibid.

50. *Africa Confidential* 26, no. 14 (July 3, 1985): 1.

51. Kane-Berman, *Soweto,* p. 228.

52. *ANC News Briefing* 10, no. 9 (March 2, 1986): 2.

53. *Star,* November 16, 1979.

54. Denis H. R. Archer, ed., *Jane's Infantry Weapons 1976* (London: Jane's Yearbooks, 1976).

55. Based on 2,500 students, 8,000 troops, and 2,700 nonmilitary staff.

56. Thomas G. Karis, "South African Liberation: The Communist Factor," *Foreign Affairs* (Winter 1986/87), p. 284.

57. Kay Moomsamy, interview in Lusaka, August 31, 1983.

CHAPTER THREE

1. *Sechaba,* February 1986, p. 5.

2. Glenn Moss, *Political Trials,* p. 22.

3. Thomas Karis and Gwendolyn M. Carter, *From Protest to Challenge* (Stanford, Calif.: Hoover Institution Press, 1977), 3: 36, 37.

4. Leading ANC official, interview in Dar es Salaam, September 6, 1983.

5. Interview in Lusaka, September 4, 1983.

6. *Sechaba,* February 1986, p. 5.

7. Thabo Mbeki, interview in Lusaka, September 4, 1983.

8. *Southern Africa* 13, no. 6 (July/Aug 1980): 8.

9. *Cape Times,* August 20, 1982; *Citizen,* August 7, 1982.

10. "The State vs. Jan Kenneth Malatji (22) and Kerwin Zwane Chiya (26)," in Moss, *Political Trials,* pp. 155–59.

11. "State vs. Ncimbithi Johnson Lubisi," *Work in Progress,* no. 15 (October 1980), p. 41.

12. *Sunday Times,* May 24, 1980.

13. *Rand Daily Mail,* February 4, 1982.

14. Interview in Cape Town, May 14, 1980.

15. *Weekly Mail,* October 24, 1985.

16. *Summary of World Broadcasts* Part 4 (BBC), September 15, 1986.

17. Tozamile Botha, interview in Maseru, Lesotho, May 21, 1980.

18. *Weekly Mail,* May 15, 1986.

19. *Financial Mail*, February 14, 1986.
20. Ibid.
21. *Daily Dispatch*, March 21, 1986.
22. *Weekly Mail*, March 20, 1986.
23. *Sechaba*, March 1986, p. 25.
24. Ibid., May 1986, p. 8.
25. *Washington Post*, January 9, 1987.
26. *Sechaba*, February 1986, p. 31.
27. *New York Times*, November 14, 1979.
28. *Rand Daily Mail*, May 29, 1980.
29. *Boston Globe*, May 18, 1979.
30. *Rand Daily Mail*, May 30, 1980.
31. "State vs. Guy Berger and Devandira Pillay," *Work in Progress*, no. 16 (February 1981), p. 12.
32. *Rand Daily Mail*, November 8, 1982.
33. *Star*, October 30, 1985.
34. *City Press*, February 23, 1986.
35. *Financial Mail*, October 18, 1985.
36. *Weekly Mail*, October 11–17, 1985.
37. Interview in Johannesburg, May 28, 1980.
38. *Work in Progress*, No. 15 (October 1980), pp. 37–38.
39. See, for example, *Weekly Mail*, June 5, 1986.
40. Gatsha Bethelezi, speech delivered in Soweto, October 21, 1979.
41. Hirson, *Year of Fire*, p. 115.
42. Joe Mathews, interview in Gaborone, Botswana, April 4, 1980.
43. *Saspu National*, no. 2 (1980), p. 5.
44. *Business Day*, October 1, 1985.
45. *City Press*, June 1, 1986.
46. *Daily News*, September 30, 1985.
47. *Daily News*, August 26, 1985.
48. *Sechaba*, May 1986, p. 8.
49. *City Press*, March 9, 1986.
50. *Weekly Mail*, April 10, 1986.

CHAPTER FOUR

1. South African Press Association, March 17, 1986.
2. *Sechaba*, April 1985, p. 25.
3. *Sechaba*, February 1986, p. 5.
4. *Sechaba*, August 1986, p. 29.
5. *Summary of World Broadcasts*, part 4 (BBC), September 16, 1986.

6. "State vs. Mosima Sexwale et al.," in Glenn Moss, *Political Trials,* pp. 50–51.

7. *ANC News Briefing* 9, no. 41 (October 13, 1985).

8. *Washington Post,* December 14, 1986.

9. SAP General Michael Geldenhuys, interview in Cape Town, May 14, 1980.

10. *Rand Daily Mail,* June 21, 1978; *Star,* August 13, 1985; *Washington Post,* December 14, 1986.

11. *Citizen,* May 16, 1986.

12. *The Apartheid War Machine* (London: International Defense and Aid Fund for Southern Africa, 1980), pp. 40, 69.

13. *Sunday Express,* March 16, 1980.

14. *To the Point,* November 10, 1978.

15. *Sunday Express,* March 16, 1980.

16. Ibid.

17. *Focus* (International Defense and Aid Fund), no. 25 (November/December 1979), p. 15.

18. *Sunday Express,* March 16, 1978.

19. *Sechaba,* October 1984, p. 12.

20. U.S. political/economic officer James Moriarty, interview in Mbabane, Swaziland, March 25, 1980; Professor Richard Weisfelder, interview in Gaborone, April 2, 1980; Professor Beth Rosen-Prinz, interview in Manzini, Swaziland, March 24, 1980.

21. *Citizen,* October 17, 1985.

22. *Sechaba,* April 1986, pp. 28–29.

23. Ibid., p. 29.

24. *Sechaba,* November 1984, p. 30.

25. *Summary of World Broadcasts,* part 4 (BBC), September 16, 1986.

26. *Summary of World Broadcasts,* part 4 (BBC), October 12, 1985.

27. *Sechaba,* April 1985, p. 30.

28. *Washington Post,* December 14, 1986.

29. South African Press Association, October 19, 1985.

30. *Citizen,* October 15, 1985.

31. *Weekly Mail,* October 25, 1985.

32. Glenn Moss, *Political Trials,* pp. 194–98.

33. *Rand Daily Mail,* June 2, 1978.

34. *Star,* May 14, 1986.

35. *Sechaba,* May 1986, p. 4.

36. *House of Assembly Debates,* no. 8, 24–28 March 1980, col. 540.

37. *Sechaba,* April 1985, p. 25.

38. *Summary of World Broadcasts,* part 4 (BBC), October 12, 1985.

39. *Star*, August 16, 1985.
40. *Sowetan*, March 11, 1986.
41. *Star*, June 21, 1986.
42. *Sechaba*, April 1985.
43. *Guardian* (U.S.), June 13, 1979.
44. *Sunday Times* (Johannesburg), May 24, 1980.
45. Ibid.
46. *Sowetan*, October 21, 1985; *Citizen*, October 23, 1985.
47. *Weekly Mail*, July 11, 1985.
48. Interview in Lusaka, September 4, 1983.
49. *Work in Progress*, no. 15 (October 1980), p. 41.
50. *Rand Daily Mail*, October 25, 1978, and October 28, 1978.
51. *Rand Daily Mail*, May 22, 1979.
52. *New York Times*, June 3, 1980; *Southern Africa* 13, no. 6 (July/
August 1980): 21.
53. *New York Times*, August 20, 1981.
54. "The State vs. Renfrew Leslie Christie: Summary of Substantial
Facts in Terms of Section 144 (3)(a) of Act 51 of 1977," pp. 2–3.
55. *Christian Science Monitor*, July 23, 1981; *New York Times*, July
22, 1981.
56. *Sunday Express*, July 15, 1984.
57. *Post*, March 23, 1979.
58. Interview in 1980.
59. *Azania Today* (PAC) 1, no. 2, (March/April 1980): 23.
60. *Times* (London), January 2, 1980.
61. *Southern Africa* 13, no. 6 (July/August 1980), 8.
62. Interviews in Johannesburg, 1980.
63. *Rand Daily Mail*, May 5, 1978; Claire Sterling, *The Terror Network* (New York: Holt, Rinehart and Winston, 1981), pp. 49–69.
64. *Le Mercenaire* (Aurora, Illinois), May 1979, p. 1.
65. *Sunday Tribune*, January 30, 1983.
66. *Rand Daily Mail*, September 6, 1983; *Star*, September 6, 1983.
67. U.S. Department of State. Limited Official Use. "Cable from U.S.
Embassy Pretoria to Secretary of State," 78 Pretoria 2874, May 18, 1978.
Declassified under author's Freedom of Information Act request.
68. *Talking with the ANC* (Pretoria: Bureau for Information, 1986), p.
25; *Washington Post*, July 8, 1986.
69. *Summary of World Broadcasts*, part 4 (BBC), September 15, 1986.
70. *Talking with the ANC*, p. 22.
71. See, for example, *Resister* (Committee of South African War Resisters), no. 6 (January/February 1980); *Star*, October 17, 1979.
72. *Citizen*, October 17, 1985.

73. *Weekly Mail,* October 8, 1986.

74. *Summary of World Broadcasts,* part 4 (BBC), September 15, 1986.

75. *Talking with the ANC,* p. 22.

76. *Rand Daily Mail,* December 21, 1982.

77. *Rand Daily Mail,* May 14, 1984; *Daily News,* May 15, 1984.

78. Phillips, "South Africa's Future," p. 32.

79. Kenneth Propp and Desaix Myers III, *The Motor Industry in South Africa* (Washington, D.C.: Investor Responsibility Research Center Inc., February 1979), pp. 4–5.

80. *Summary of World Broadcasts,* part 4 (BBC), September 16, 1986.

81. *New York Times,* November 14, 1979.

82. U.N. Economic Commission for Africa. Limited distribution. "Trade Promotion Amongst the Countries of Eastern and Southern Africa," part Four, ECA/MULPOC/LUSAKA/53, September 27, 1977, p. 11.

83. Phillips, "South Africa's Future," p. 32.

84. *1980 Information Digest* (Johannesburg: South Africa Foundation, 1980), pp. 9–12.

85. Based on the police average of five attacks per week, with an estimated 37 percent directed against economic targets, and half of these being challenge rather than linkage strikes.

86. Based on the police average of five attacks per week, with an estimated 37 percent directed against economic targets, and half of these being linked to above-ground protest.

87. *City Press,* July 20, 1986.

88. *Daily News,* April 19, 1985.

89. *Star,* April 30, 1985.

90. *Rand Daily Mail,* August 17, 1984.

91. *Citizen,* March 5, 1986.

92. *Sowetan,* October 28, 1981; *Rand Daily Mail,* October 28, 1981.

93. *Sechaba,* December 1983, p. 8.

94. *Citizen,* April 7, 1984.

95. *Citizen,* April 18, 1986.

96. *Washington Post,* July 31, 1986.

97. *Guardian* (Manchester), December 22, 1983.

98. *Weekly Mail,* July 3, 1986.

99. *Observer* (London), August 3, 1986; *Washington Post,* July 31, 1986.

100. Basil Davidson, *The People's Cause: A History of Guerrillas in Africa* (Essex, U. K.: Longman Group Ltd., 1981), p. 117.

101. *Summary of World Broadcasts,* part 4 (BBC), September 15, 1986.

102. *Washington Post,* December 14, 1986.

CHAPTER FIVE

1. *Sunday Star,* July 7, 1985.

2. Philip H. Frankel, *Pretoria's Praetorians* (Cambridge: Cambridge University Press, 1984), p. 46.

3. *New York Times,* October 12, 1986.

4. *Rand Daily Mail,* May 10, 1984.

5. *Race Relations News,* vol. 42, no. 6, June 1980, p. 3.

6. Frankel, *Pretoria's Praetorians,* p. 33.

7. *White Paper on Defense and Armaments Supply 1979* (Pretoria: Government Printer, 1979), p. 2.

8. *Economist,* June 21, 1980.

9. *Washington Post,* December 26, 1986.

10. *White Paper on the Rationalization of the Public Service and Related Institutions* (Pretoria: Government Printer, 1980), p. 7.

11. Frankel, *Pretoria's Praetorians,* p. 141.

12. Ibid., p. 142.

13. Alex Hepple, *Press under Apartheid* (London: International Defence and Aid Fund for Southern Africa, 1974), p. 8.

14. F. R. Metrowich, ed., *African Freedom Annual 1978* (Sandton, So. Afr.: South African Freedom Foundation, 1978), p. 49. See also Elaine Potter, *The Press as Opposition* (Totowa, N. J.: Rowman and Littlefield, 1975), p. 115.

15. Hepple, *Press under Apartheid,* p. 49.

16. Ibid., p. 23.

17. See Benjamin Pogrund, "The Practice of Journalism," *Nieman Reports,* Autumn/Winter 1975, p. 14.

18. Hepple, *Press under Apartheid,* p. 56.

19. Interview in the United States, 1979. See also Pogrund, "The Practice of Journalism," p. 15.

20. Potter, *The Press as Opposition,* p. 49.

21. Ivor Wilkins and Hans Strydom, *The Broederbond* (New York: Paddington Press, 1979), p. 11.

22. *House of Assembly Debates,* no. 11, April 28 to May 2, 1980, col. 5159.

23. Interview in Cape Town, May 7, 1980.

24. U.S. Department of State, "Cable from U.S. Embassy Pretoria to Secretary of State," May 18, 1978, p. 2.

25. Interview in Johannesburg, March 1980.

26. Wilkins and Strydom, *The Broederbond,* p. 286.

27. Ibid.

28. Ibid., p. 287.

29. Brigadier C. J. Lloyd, "The Importance of Rural Development in

the Defense Strategy of South Africa and the Need for Private Sector Involvement," paper presented at the Urban Foundation workshop on "The Urbanization Process in Natal and KwaZulu: The Need for a Total Development Strategy," Durban, August 10, 1979, pp. 5–10.

30. *Report of the Commission of Inquiry into Reporting of Security Matters Regarding the South African Defense Force and the South African Police Force* (Pretoria: Government Printer, 1980), p. 61.

31. *Rand Daily Mail,* May 28, 1980.

32. Frankel, *Pretoria's Praetorians,* p. 68.

33. Ibid., p. 107; *Sunday Express,* January 8, 1984.

34. *Sunday Times* (Johannesburg), September 4, 1983.

35. *Rand Daily Mail,* February 4, 1982.

36. *Star,* June 6, 1986.

37. *Weekly Mail,* July 11, 1985.

38. *Sowetan,* April 19, 1982.

39. *Guardian* (U.S.), June 11, 1980.

40. *Argus,* June 11, 1980.

41. *Weekly Mail,* October 8, 1986.

42. *Sechaba,* May 1985, pp. 26–27.

43. *Weekly Mail,* July 25, 1985.

44. *Southern Africa* 13, no. 6, July/August 1980, p. 8.

45. *Weekly Mail,* July 3, 1986.

46. *New York Times,* July 23, 1986.

47. Ibid.

48. *Guardian* (Manchester), May 24, 1983; *Times* (London), May 25, 1983.

49. *City Press,* May 25, 1986.

50. Frankel, *Pretoria's Praetorians,* p. xiii.

51. *The Apartheid War Machine,* p. 3.

52. *1980 Information Digest,* p. 67; Robert S. Jaster, "South Africa's Narrowing Security Options," *Adelphi Papers,* no. 159, Spring 1980, p. 28; *White Paper on Defense and Armaments Supply 1979,* pp. 12–14; Gann and Duignan, *South Africa,* p. 27; Frankel, *Pretoria's Praetorians,* pp. 72–73; *Weekly Mail,* March 27, 1986; *Citizen,* March 18, 1986.

53. *Weekly Mail,* March 27, 1986.

54. Frankel, *Pretoria's Praetorians,* p. 90.

55. *The Apartheid War Machine,* p. 47.

56. *Report of the Commission of Inquiry into Reporting of Security Matters,* p. 29.

57. *Annual Report of the Commissioner of the South African Police for the Period 1 July 1978 to 30 June 1979* (Pretoria: Government Printer, 1979), p. 2.

58. Ibid.

59. Ibid.

60. Ibid., p. 1.

61. *House of Assembly Debates*, no. 8, March 24–28, 1980, questions columns 435–36; Lorraine Gordon, ed., *Survey of Race Relations in South Africa 1979* (Johannesburg: Institute of Race Relations, 1980), p. 106.

62. *Citizen*, April 10, 1986.

63. *The Apartheid War Machine*, p. 46.

64. Hirson, *Year of Fire*, pp. 183–84; Gerry Maré, *African Population Relocation in South Africa* (Johannesburg: Institute of Race Relations, 1980), p. 28.

65. Maré, *African Population*, p. 28.

66. *Annual Report of the Commissioner*, p. 8.

67. *House of Assembly Debates*, no. 8, March 24–28, 1980, col. 3824–31.

68. *Weekly Mail*, October 2, 1986.

69. Kenneth W.Grundy, "A Black Foreign Legion in South Africa?" *African Affairs* 80, no. 318 (January 1981): 105.

70. *Paratus* (South African Defense Force), October 1979, p. 28.

71. Wilkins and Strydom, *The Broederbond*, p. 11.

72. Geoffrey Kemp, "South Africa's Defense Programme," *Survival*, July/August 1972, pp. 158–61.

73. *White Paper on Defense and Armaments Supply 1979*, p. 3.

74. Frankel, *Pretoria's Praetorians*, p. 12.

75. *White Paper on Defense and Armaments Supply 1979*, p. 3.

76. Ibid.; Jaster, "South Africa's Narrowing Security Options," p. 29.

77. Jaster, "South Africa's Narrowing Security Options," p. 30.

78. Frankel, *Pretoria's Praetorians*, p. 135.

79. *White Paper on Defense and Armaments Supply 1979*, p. 5.

80. Ibid.; William Gutteridge, "South Africa's Defense Posture," *The World Today*, January 1980, p. 29.

81. Frankel, *Pretoria's Praetorians*, p. 135.

82. *Boston Globe*, March 18, 1979; *Christian Science Monitor*, September 4, 1980.

83. *Weekly Mail*, August 29, 1985.

84. *Weekly Mail*, September 18, 1986.

85. *Star*, September 6, 1985.

86. *Weekly Mail*, August 29, 1985.

87. *Business Day*, September 12, 1985.

88. *Daily Dispatch*, March 7, 1986; *New York Times*, June 15, 1986.

89. Frankel, *Pretoria's Praetorians*, p. 135.

90. U.S. Defense Attaché Colonel Donald Clark, interview in Pretoria, May 27, 1980.

91. *Paratus* (South African Defense Force), July 1979, p. 6; *Resister* (Committee of South African War Resisters), no. 10 (September/October 1980), p. 11.

92. *Sash* (Black Sash), February 1980, p. 15.

93. *Sunday Express*, February 24, 1985.

94. Gann and Duignan, *South Africa*, p. 53.

95. *Star*, February 27, 1985.

96. *Paratus* (South African Defense Force), June 1979, pp. 16–17.

97. Lloyd, "The Importance of Rural Development," p. 11.

98. Ibid., pp. 5–6.

99. Ibid., p. 7.

100. *Summary of World Broadcasts*, part 4 (BBC), October 21, 1985.

101. Lloyd, "The Importance of Rural Development," p. 12.

102. *House of Assembly Debates*, no. 11, April 28–May 2, 1980, col. 5276; *Resister* (Committee of South African War Resisters), no. 9 (July/August 1980), p. 11.

103. *Rand Daily Mail*, June 23, 1984.

104. *Rand Daily Mail*, May 26, 1980; *Sunday Express*, May 25, 1980; Grundy, "A Black Foreign Legion," p. 104.

105. *The Apartheid War Machine*, p. 40; *New York Times*, September 16, 1979.

106. *New York Times*, August 11, 1981.

107. John De St. Jorre, *A House Divided: South Africa's Uncertain Future* (Washington, D.C.: Carnegie Endowment for International Peace, 1977), p. 44.

108. *Daily Dispatch*, May 9, 1986.

109. *Weekly Mail*, September 18, 1986.

110. *White Paper on Defense and Armaments Supply 1979*, p. 15.

111. *The Apartheid War Machine*, p. 23; Colonel Norman L. Dodd, "The South African Defense Force," *RUSI* 125, no. 1 (March 1980): 41–42.

112. *Citizen*, January 10, 1978.

113. Frankel, *Pretoria's Praetorians*, p. 136.

114. Ibid., p. 135.

115. *White Paper on Defense and Armaments Supply 1979*, p. 5.

116. U.S. Congress, House, Committee on Foreign Affairs, *U.S. Policy toward South Africa, Hearings before the Subcommittees on International Economic Policy and Trade, on Africa, and on International Organizations of the House Committee on Foreign Affairs*, 96th Cong., 2d sess., 1980, pp. 8–9.

117. *White Paper on Defense and Armaments Supply 1979*, pp. 18–19.

118. Michael T. Klare and Eric Prokosch, "Evading the Embargo: How

the U.S. Arms South Africa and Rhodesia," *Notes and Documents* (U.N. Centre Against Apartheid), no. 34/78, October 1978, pp. 4-5.

119. Ibid., pp. 2, 7.

120. *Paratus* (South African Defense Force), October 1979, p. 12.

121. *White Paper on Defense and Armaments Supply 1979*, p. 6.

122. Anthony R. Wilkinson, "Insurgency in Rhodesia 1957-1973: An Account and Assessment," *Adelphi Papers*, no. 100, Autumn 1973, p. 36; Gann and Duignan, *South Africa*, p. 22.

123. Gann and Duignan, *South Africa*, p. 22.

124. U.S. Congress, House, *U.S. Policy toward South Africa*, p. 8.

125. *Rand Daily Mail*, April 22, 1978.

126. *Cape Times*, May 13, 1980.

127. *Paratus* (South African Defense Force), June 1979, p. 38; *White Paper on Defense and Armaments Supply 1979*, p. 6.

128. *Boston Globe*, September 28, 1980.

129. Frankel, *Pretoria's Praetorians*, pp. 84, 87.

130. Richard Bissell and Chester A. Crocker, eds., *South Africa into the 1980's* (Boulder, Colo.: Westview Press, 1979), pp. 99-100.

131. Jaster, "South Africa's Narrowing Security Options," p. 16.

132. *Resister* (Committee of South African War Resisters), no. 10 (September/October 1980), p. 16.

133. CBS Evening News, March 6, 1980; *Boston Globe*, January 18, 1980; *Cape Times*, May 13, 1980.

134. *Guardian* (Manchester), May 22, 1985.

135. U.S. Congress, House, *U.S. Policy toward South Africa*, p. 48.

136. *Sechaba*, May 1986, p. 10.

137. Frankel, *Pretoria's Praetorians*, p. 52.

138. *Rand Daily Mail*, February 4, 1982.

139. Frankel, *Pretoria's Praetorians*, p. 52.

140. *Washington Post*, July 22, 1986.

CHAPTER SIX

1. Dispatch from South Africa to the *Chicago Tribune*, cited in Christopher Cerf and Victor Navasky, *The Experts Speak* (New York: Pantheon Books, 1984), p. 273.

2. While Heribert Adam estimates 50 percent, Thomas Karis suggests that in free elections the ANC could win 75 percent of the black vote. Thomas Karis, "South African Liberation: The Communist Factor," *Foreign Affairs* (Winter 1986/87), p. 267.

Index

"AK–47 Song," 116
ANC in Combat, 82
ANC Weekly News Briefing, 53
"Acts of Terror" index, 146
Adam, Heribert, 112
"African Claims" platform, 5
African National Congress (ANC), xii–
  xiii, 1, 13, 24; nonviolent years of,
  3–8; rivals of, 8–12, 106–12, 114–
  15; regrouping years, 21–23;
  response of to Soweto, 26–31; in
  exile, 36–37, 56–60; headquarters
  of, 46–47; administration of rebellion by, 49–55; domestic organization, 58, 78, 124, 129; attitude of
  toward casualties, 60–61, 121–22,
  123–34, 156; exile camps, 61–65;
  UDF and, 88–89, 96; homelands
  and, 111–13, 131; Umkhonto and,
  118, 119; guidelines of, 119–20,
  203; intelligence tactics of, 139–42,
  143–45; weaknesses of, 204–05. *See
  also* Congress Youth League;
  National Executive Committee
  (NEC) of ANC; Targets for anti-
  apartheid attacks; Umkhonto we
  Sizwe
Africanism, 10, 13, 25. *See also* Black
  Consciousness Movement; Pan
  Africanist Congress
Afrikaner Volkswag (Counterbond),
  161
Afrikaner Weerstandsbeweging (AWB),
  161

Afrikaners, 2, 3, 5, 6, 181, 210; organ-
  ization of, 160–61
Air Commandos, 194
Air Force, South African (SAAF),
  193–94
Alexandra, 89–90, 91
Algerian civil war, 152
"Amandla" cultural troupe, 73
Angola, 24, 37, 203; as host country,
  43–44, 45, 46, 119
Apartheid: seeds of, 4, 5
"Appeasement," 206
Aquino, Cory, xiii
Arms, 30, 70–71, 135–38, 196–201.
  See also Umkhonto we Sizwe
Armscor, 196
Army, South African, 187–89, 192–
  93; blacks in, 188, 190–91
Arts and culture bureau (ANC), 52–53,
  54, 73
Assassinations, 139, 145, 154, 177,
  207
Austria, 73
Azania People's Liberation Army, 32
Azanian People's Organization
  (AZAPO), 106, 112–13

Bannings, 6, 11, 93
Bantu Administration Act, 167
Bantu Administration Department, 26
"Bantu education," 92
Bantu Education Act, 8
Bantustans. *See* Homelands, tribal
Baran, Paul, 83

Barayi, Elijah, 103
Barnard, Neil, 173, 174, 198
Basotho Congress Party, 42
Beaufre, André, 159, 162, 201, 202
Berger, Guy, 101
Bethal-18 trial, 32
Biko, Steve, 27, 31
Binda, Sipho, 101
Black Allied Workers Union (BAWU),
    25–26
Black consciousness, 110, 112, 204,
    205
Black Consciousness Movement
    (BCM), 24–26, 34
Black Local Authorities Act (*1983*), 89
"Black-on-black" conflict, 115
Black Parents Association, 29
Black People's Convention, 24–25, 27
Black Sash, 96
Blackmail, 174, 178
Boer War, 3, 161
Boers, 2
Boesak, Allan, 87
Bombings, 42, 122, 145, 147, 164
Bombs, 53, 77, 83–84, 117, 177
Bophutatswana, 110–11, 126, 154;
    National Guard, 191
Border security, 124, 135, 180, 188–89
Botha, P.W., 99, 103, 160, 162, 163,
    173, 198. *See also* South African
    government; Total strategy
Botha, Tozamile, 86, 88–89
Botswana, 39, 42, 46; as corridor for
    ANC, 29, 125–26
Boycotts, 91–92, 103, 109, 112, 113,
    151
British in Africa, 2, 3, 44, 160–61
Broederbond (Brotherhood), 160, 161,
    169, 184
Broedertwis, 161, 162
Bulgaria, 71
Bureau of State Security (BOSS), 143,
    173, 174
Business, 122, 164, 165, 166–67
Buthelezi, Gatsha, 78, 95, 104, 130–
    31, 154, 208; as ANC rival, 106–
    10. *See also* Inkatha movement

CIA, 51
"Cagney and Lacey," 74
Carter, Gwendolen, xiii
Carter, Jimmy, 60
Casualties, civilian, 60–61, 81, 121–
    22, 123–24, 156

Censorship, xii, 76, 95, 122, 172
"Challenge" attacks, 121–22
China, 15, 32, 34
Chissano, Joaquim, 129
Chiya, Kerwin, 83
Christian Institute, 29
Christie, Renfrew Leslie, 141–42
Ciskei, 99, 110, 154
Citizen, The, 169
Citizen Force (CF), 185, 196
Civic Action program, 189
Codes, 83
Coetzee, Johan, 84, 139
Collaborators, 84–85, 147, 207
Color bars, 4
Coloreds, 5, 10, 14, 108, 163, 181,
    186. *See also* Multiracialism
Commando system, 185, 192
Committee of South African War
    Resisters (COSAWR), 187
Communications: in ANC, 21, 23, 55,
    81–82, 83, 136. *See also* South
    African government
Communism, 7, 11, 164, 202
Communist Party, xii, 9, 10, 13, 15,
    213; ANC and, 22, 24, 204. *See
    also* South African Communist Party
Community organizations against apart-
    heid, 86, 87, 88–89, 90–91, 132–33
"Concerned Citizens," 97
Confederation of Unions of South
    Africa (CUSA), 100
Congress Alliance, 7, 10, 85
Congress of Democrats, 7, 9
Congress of South African Students
    (COSAS), 92, 93
Congress of South African Trade
    Unions (COSATU), 94, 102–03,
    113, 114, 172–73, 206; ANC and,
    104–05, 165–66, 204
Congress of the People (*1955*), 7–8,
    10–11
Congress People, 110
Congress Youth League, 6, 7, 9, 10,
    12
Conscientious objection, 186–87
Conscription, 3, 185–86, 187
Conservative Party (CP), 161
"Counterbond," 161
Counterinsurgency doctrine. *See* South
    African government; Total strategy
Courier service, 135, 136, 156
Courts martial, 187
Criminal Law Amendment Act, 167

Criminal Procedure Act (*1955*), 167
Crocker, Chester, 197
"Crowdcure Method," 158
Cuba, 45
Curiel, Henri, 144
Customs Union, 39
Czechoslovakia, 74

Davidson, Basil, 155
Davidson, Peter, 107, 109
Defense Act, 167
Defiance Campaign (*1952*), 6, 7, 10
Democracy, 14
Demonstrations, 4, 76–77
Denmark, 73
Department of Cooperation and Development, 183
Department of National Security (DONS), 173
Depopulation, 126
Detainees' Parents Support Committee, 96
Detentions, 11, 173
Dhlomo, Sibongiseni Maxwell, 151
Diamonds, 2, 39, 43
Dinizulu, King, 106
Directorate of Military Intelligence (DMI), 173, 174, 176, 177, 178
Discipline in ANC, 14, 119–20, 122, 132, 209
Disinformation, 175, 176. *See also* South African government
Disinvestment, 106, 165, 212
Dlamini, Steve, 51, 52
Draft evasion, 186, 201
Duff, Tom, 169
Dumisa, Robert, 134–35
Dutch tradesmen, 1
DuToit, Elizabeth, 144

East Germany, 45, 59, 66, 71, 73, 74
"Economic emancipation," 103
Economic recession, 4
Economy. *See* Targets for anti-apartheid attacks; Total strategy
Education, 8, 25, 52–53; in exile camps, 61–65; military, for townships, 133–34
Educational deferments, 187
Electricity Supply Commission (ESCOM), 39, 150
"Elementary Handbook on Explosives," 134
Embargo, arms, 193, 196

Emergency, state of, 163, 171
Emigration, 79, 187, 202
End Conscription Campaign (ECC), 97, 186, 187
Erwin, Alec, 99, 102
Espionage, 53, 138. *See also* South African government; Umkhonto we Sizwe
Ethiopia, 32, 66
"Ethnic bridge," 126, 128, 130, 131

FRELIMO, 41, 67, 129
Farms: white desertion of, 126, 127, 189
Fazzie, Henry Mutile, 88, 176
Federation of Free African Trade Unions of South Africa (FOFATUSA), 11
Federation of South African Trade Unions (FOSATU), 100, 101, 102
Fine, Alan, 101
First, Ruth, 177
Foreign companies, 12
Forgery, 83, 135, 136, 176
Fort Hare University, 8
Freedom Charter (*1955*), 7–8, 11, 59, 81, 87
Funerals, 90, 109, 116–17

Gangs, 94, 132, 205
Gas for riot control, 158
Geldenhuys, Michael, 84
General Law Amendment Act, 168
General Workers Unions, 15
Generation gap in ANC, 58–59, 60
Geneva Convention, 121
Gerhardt, Dieter, 144–45
Gerhart, Gail, xiii
Germany: Nazi Germany, 5; in Africa, 44. *See also* East Germany
Ghana, 11
Ginwala, Frene, 141
Gold, 2, 4, 149, 151, 164
Goldreich, Arthur, 16
Gqabi, Joe, 177
Greece, 197
Grenades, 70–71, 136
Group Areas Act, 6
Guerrilla warfare, 37–38, 116–17, 155–57
Guguletu township, 116
Gumede, Archie, 88

Hanekom, Derek and Patricia, 142
Hani, Chris, 70, 69, 120, 133, 149

Harbour Police, 183
Heerden, Neil van, 42
Helicopters, 193, 197, 200
Hersh, Seymour, 176, 177
Herstigte Nasionale Party (HNP), 161
High schools, 64, 65
Hodgson, Rica, 65
Hogan, Barbara, 83
Homelands, tribal, 8, 78, 142–43, 212,
    213; anti-apartheid activities in, 110–
    11, 131, 154, 191
Host states, 37, 55, 72–73
Housing, multiracial, 163
Huguenot refugees, 2
Hungary, 71
Hunter, Roland, 142

Identity cards, 4, 163
India, 73
Indians, 5, 9, 10, 14, 108, 163, 181,
    185–86. See also Multiracialism
Industrial Conciliation Amendment Act,
    99, 165
Infiltration, 69, 84, 85
"Influx control" laws, 4
Informants, 6, 17, 77, 80, 95, 121,
    173, 174
Information Department, 169
Inkatha movement, 78, 95, 104, 205;
    present role, 106–10; future role,
    208, 209, 212, 213
Institute of Race Relations, 162
Intelligence, 18, 34, 64, 117. See also
    individual organizations
Intermarriage, 163
Internal Security Act, 167
International University Exchange Fund
    (IUEF), 141
Intimidation, 139, 168
Irgun, 79
Israel, 198, 200; arms from, 70, 196
Italy, 197

Johannesburg Democratic Action Com-
    mittee, 96
Jonathan, Lebua, 39–40, 42
Journalists, 168, 170

Kabwe convention, 50
KaNgwane, 111, 131
Karis, Thomas, xiii, 51
Kasrils, Ronnie, 96, 111, 137, 199,
    201
Kaunda, Kenneth, 46

Kennedy, Edward, 112
Klaas, Jeffrey, 140
Kleinschmidt, Horst, 141
Koka, Drake, 26
Koyana, D. S., 142
Kruger, Jimmy, 57
"KwaNatal" experiment, 108, 205
KwaNdebele, 154–55
KwaZulu party, 107, 108, 154. See
    also Inkatha movement

Labor issues, 11, 15–16, 24, 25–26,
    30, 103; organizations, 98–101;
    assembling united front, 101–04
Langa, Ben, 175
Langa, Paul, 27, 30
Le Grange, Louis, 171, 182
Leballo, Potlako, 19, 32, 33
Lebowa, 110
Lelyveld, Joseph, 55
Lembede, Anton, 10
Lesotho, 38, 39–40, 42, 43, 46
Lesotho Liberation Army, 42
"Liberated" zones, 131, 134
Libya, 32
Light Aircraft Command of SAAF, 194
Lilliesleaf farm, 17, 18, 21
Limpet mines, 136, 151, 153
"Linkage" attacks, 121, 150–51
Lloyd, C. J., 170, 190, 200
Lodge, Tom, xiii, 147
London: as ANC headquarters, 37
London Observer, 143
Lusaka, Zambia, 63, 95, 111; as ANC
    headquarters, 47, 49, 61, 78, 81–82,
    114–15
Luthuli, Albert, 15, 20
Luyt, Louis, 169

M-Plan, 6–7, 13, 18, 49, 80
MARNET, 189
MK. See Umkhonto we Sizwe
MPLA, 45
Mabuza, Enos, 111–12, 131
McGiven, Arthur, 143
Machel, Samora, 41, 67, 129
Maharaj, Mac, 52
Makatini, Johnny, 52
Make, Vusumzi, 33
Malan, D. F., 167
Malan, Magnus, 184
Malatji, Jan, 83
Management, business, 98–99, 100,
    166

Mandela, Nelson, 13, 16, 18, 20, 88, 108, 172; importance of, 6–7, 49–50, 203, 211–12, 213
Mapinduzi, Chama Cha, 45
Marine Corps, 196
Maritime Air Command, 194
Marxist theory, xii, 59, 63, 204, 209
Masekela, Barbara, 52–53, 54
Masekela, Hugh, 53
Maseko, Tim, 58
Masinga, Elias, 30
"Mass combat units," 133
Mass Funeral Coordinating Committee, 90
"Masterplan for a White Country: The Strategy," 170. *See also* Broederbond
Mathews, Joe, 18
Mazimbu exile camp, 61–65, 69
Mbeki, Govan, 18, 20, 52, 88
Mbeki, Thabo, 52, 53–54, 72, 81, 83, 140
Meli, Francis, 53
Migrant workers, 38, 39, 45
Minority rule, 87, 114, 129, 203
Missionaries, 3
Mlambo, Johnson, 33
Modise, Joe, 52, 54, 68
Modise, Thandi Ruth, 140
Moisi, David, 141
Molefe, Petrus, 135–36
Molope, Makanye, 154
Moomsamy, Kay, 74
Morale, 120, 151–52, 186, 201, 202
Morris, Michael, 110, 134
Mothopeng, Zephania, 31–32
Motlana, Nthatho, 84–85
Mozambique, 24, 37, 41, 46, 67, 191; as host state, 39, 128–29
Mpetha, Oscar, 88
Mphephu, Patrick, 110, 154
Mugabe, Robert, 41–42, 67, 68, 127
Multiracialism, 7, 10, 13, 23, 25, 28, 75
Muzorewa, Abel, 42
Mxenge, Victoria, 109

NATO, 195
Namibia, 34, 38
Natal, 2, 3, 108
National Cultural Liberation Movement. *See* Inkatha movement
National Education Crisis Committee, 92

National Executive Committee (NEC) of ANC, 23–24, 37, 50, 51, 79, 204, 209; new generation in, 60–61
National Forum committee, 112
National Intelligence Service (NIS), 173, 174
National Key Points Act, 171
National Party (NP), 5, 6, 8, 114, 160, 161, 195, 210; future role, 211, 212, 213, 214
National Reserve, 185
National Security Agency, 177
National Security Management System, 162–63
National Service (NS), 185, 186, 193
National Supplies Procurement Act, 166
National Union of Mineworkers, 102, 151
National Union of South African Students, 96
Native Laws Amendment Act, 8
Navy, South African (SAN), 144–45, 194–96
"Necklace" killings, 85, 139
Nel, Louis, 146
Netherlands, 73
New York Times, 176
News, xii, 76, 169, 175, 176
Nidal, Abu, xiii
Nigeria, 32
Njokweni, Chief, 99
Nkadimeng, John, 52
Nkobi, Thomas, 52, 72, 73
Nkomati Accord (*1984*), 41, 67, 128–29, 135, 145–46
Nkomo, Joshua, 22, 38, 125
Nkrumah, Kwame, 11
No Easy Walk to Freedom, 49
Nonracialism, 4, 87, 203
Nonviolence, 21, 25, 88, 117
Norway, 73
Ntuli, Piet, 155
Nuclear targets, 139, 143, 150
Nuclear weaponry, 197–99
Nyerere, Julius, 44
Nzo, Alfred, 50

Official Secrets Act, 167
Okhela, 143
Omkeer journal, 143
"Operation Root Out Thugs," 91
Orange Free State, 2, 3, 147
Organization of African Unity, 73
Oxfam, 73

Pahad, Aziz, 52
Pan-African Freedom Movement con-
    ference, 16
Pan Africanist Congress (PAC), 8, 10–
    12, 13, 45; failure of, 19, 20, 22;
    response to Soweto, 31–33
Pass laws, 4, 5, 12, 103, 163
Passive negotiation, 5
"People's courts," 77
"People's institutions," 90
"People's war," 119
Permanent Force (PF), 185, 193
Petersen, Hector, 26
Pityana, Barney, 25
Platinum, 164
Pokela, John Nyati, 33
Poland, 71
Poqo, 20
Port Elizabeth Black Civic Organization
    (Pebco), 86, 88
Portuguese in Africa, 23, 24, 129, 179,
    197
Post Office Act, 168
Pretoria. See South African government
Primary school (ANC), 62
Prison Service, 183
Prisons Act (1959), 167–68
Progressive Federal Party, 161, 186
Propaganda, 31, 53, 60, 170
Psychological resources, 25, 159, 167,
    170
Public-service rationalization, 162, 163
Publications Act (1974), 168

Quail Commission, 110

Rabie Commission, 174, 202
Radio Freedom, 53–54, 60, 69; func-
    tions of, 83, 101, 113–14, 208
Radio Moscow, 65
Radioactivity, 198
Railways, 44, 147, 149–50
Railways Police, 183
Ramokgadi, Martin Mafefo, 28, 29
Rand Daily Mail, 99, 169
"Re-education," 91
Reagan administration, 59, 60, 204
Reed-Daly, Ronald, 191–92
Refineries, 139, 141, 171
Reforms, 163, 165–66, 201, 202
Regional Political Committee, 64
Reibeeck, Jan van, 1
Reinecke Commission, 196

Relly, Gavin, 97
Renegade fighters, 119, 120
Residents Joint Committee, 90
Resistência Nacional de Moçambique
    (Renamo), 41, 129
"Retaliation" attacks, 121
Revolutionary Council, 23
Revolutionary People's Committee,
    132, 133
Rhodesia. See Zimbabwe
Rhodesian Light Infantry regiment, 187
Richer, Peter, 101
Riotous Assemblies Act, 168
Riots, 77–78, 132, 158, 180, 182
Rivonia, 21, 117
Rotberg, Robert, xiii
Rumania, 71

Sasol facilities, 141, 150, 171
SWAPO guerrillas, 46, 49, 188, 189
Sabotage, 14–15, 20, 21, 34, 146
Sabotage Act, 168
Sale, Kirkpatrick, 205
Sanctions, 164, 165
"Sanctuary states," 46, 124
Savimbi, Jonas, 45
Seathlolo, Khotso, 30
Sechaba magazine, 53, 59, 60
Second Police Amendment Act, 171
Segregation, residential, 6
Self-sufficiency of exile camps, 53,
    62–63, 72–73
Selous Scouts, 187, 188, 191
Seme, Pixley, 4
September, Reg, 52
Shabalala, Thomas, 109
Shaka (Zulu monarch), 2
Shangaans, Battalion of, 191
Sharpeville, 12–14, 26, 27
Shope, Gertrude, 52
Shortages, 63, 164
Sibasa raid, 153–54
Sibeko, David, 33
Siege economy, 165
Sisulu, Walter, 18, 20, 88
Sithole, Mdudzi, 151
Slabbert, Frederick van Zyl, 161
Slovo, Joe, 50, 59, 68–69
Smuggling, 134, 135, 156
Smuts, Jan, 5
Sobukwe, Robert, 11, 12, 19, 20
Socialism,. 7, 112
Sokoine, Edward, 45
South Africa, Republic of, 45–46, 165;

creation of, 3; other countries' dependence on, 38–39, 41–43, 44; government entrenchment, 205–06; future crackdown, 206–07; revolution scenario, 208–10; negotiation, 211–14

South African Allied Workers' Union (SAAWU), 100, 101

South African Associated Newspapers (SAAN), 169

South African Brain Research Institute, 158, 159

South African Broadcasting Corporation (SABC), 76, 169, 170, 172

South African Colored People's Organization, 7

South African Communist Party (SACP), 8–10, 16, 34, 50–51, 52; as intelligence source, 143–44

South African Congress of Trade Unions (SACTU), 7, 9, 15, 30, 52, 100–01, 103, 104

South African Defense Force (SADF), 41, 46; efficacy of, 67, 78, 177, 178; espionage and, 142–43; attacks against, 152, 153, 154, 155; secrecy in, 170–71; organization of, 184–87; problems in, 200–01

South African Freedom Organization, 27

South African government, 23, 158, 207; Soweto and, 33–34; coercive tactics of, 41–44, 45, 95; response to ANC, 47, 114–15, 118, 125; communism and, 59, 60, 170; disinformation, 82, 122–23; townships and, 88–90, 131–32, 135; unionism, 98–100, 165–66; espionage, 139–40, 173–78; dependence of on domestic resources, 149–50, 165; political components of, 160–63; media and, 167–72. *See also* Total strategy

South African Indian Congress, 7, 10

South African Military Refugees Aid Fund (SAMRAF), 143

South African Natives National Congress (SANNC), 3

South African Police (SAP), 28, 32, 93, 152, 154, 168, 179; response to uprisings, 12, 26, 27; press and, 169–70; secrecy and, 170–71; duties of, 180–83

South African Students Organization (SASO), 27

Solomon Mahlangu Freedom College (SOMAFCO), 62, 63, 64–65, 69

Soviet Union, 15, 34, 35, 117; aid to ANC from, 22, 24, 28, 59, 66, 73, 74, 204, 208–09; as intelligence source, 143–45

Sowetan, 138

Soweto African Students Organization (SASO), 27

Soweto rebellion, 1, 26–31

Soweto Students Representative Council (SSRC), 27, 29–30

Spain, 197

Sparg, Marion, 152

Special Air Service, 187

Stalinist doctrines, 8

Star, 138

State Security Council (SSC), 162–63, 180, 201

State witnesses, 17, 121, 147, 207

Steyn Commission, 171

Strike Command of SAAF, 193

Strikes (labor), 4, 25, 30, 100, 117, 166

Students, 27, 31, 56, 57–58, 92

Suicide rate in military, 187

Suicide Squad, 27, 30

Suppression of Communism Act (*1950*), 6, 9, 167

Swaziland, 38, 42, 46, 191; as corridor, 29, 125, 128, 129–30, 131

Swazis, Battalion of, 191

Sweden, 73

Tabata, I. B., 18

Tambo, Oliver, 7, 16, 66, 74, 75, 79, 129; as leader, 20, 21, 22, 23, 28, 37, 38; tactics of, 46, 72, 121, 122; reelection of, 49, 50; whites and, 97–98; Buthelezi and, 108, 109; future role of, 211, 212

Tanks, 197, 200

Tanzania, 37, 43, 44, 45, 46, 63, 203

Targets for anti-apartheid attacks, 139, 141–43, 147; economic, 148–51; governmental, 152–55

Taxes, 4, 109

Television, 76, 172

Terrorism, xii, 121, 210

Terrorism Act, 168

Terrorism Research, Institute of, 110

Thatcher government, 176, 204

Third Consultative Congress (*1969*), 23

Thompson, Leonard, xiii

Tikly, Mohammed, 63, 64
Tloome, Dan, 51
Torture, 27, 55, 58, 84, 154
Total strategy, 160, 161; defined, 159–63; economic issues in, 164–67; communications, 167–72; intelligence, 173–78; flaw in, 201–02
Townships, 12, 117, 131, 172–73, 207–08; government control of, 89, 90, 91, 182–83; as sanctuaries, 132–35
Trade unions, 9, 87, 93–94, 163, 165–66
Transkei, 142–43, 154, 191
Transport Command of SAAF, 193–94
"Transit states," 46
Transvaal, 2, 3, 147
Transvaal Agricultural Union, 126
Treason Trial, 11
Trials, 6, 8, 17, 18, 21, 32, 139
Tsiki, Naledi, 30, 122–23
Tswana people, 126
Tutu, Desmond, 74

UNITA guerrillas, 45
Ulundi, battle at, 2, 3
Umkhonto we Sizwe (MK), 28, 30, 58, 109; development of, 15–16, 34–35, 204–05; early impact of, 17–21, 22; organization of, 23, 29, 38, 68–69; goals of, 37–38, 75, 120–24; training camps, 47, 66–67; secrecy of, 50, 54; arms for, 70–71; funding for, 72–73; new power of, 117–19; infiltration tactics, 124–31; sanctuary bases for, 131–35; domestic training, 133–34
Underground network of ANC, 14, 27, 34, 79–85, 118, 119; reconstruction of, 23–24; problems in, 113–14
Unemployment, 98–99
Unionization, 6. See also Trade unions and individual organizations
United Democratic Front (UDF), 132, 172–73, 204; founding and purpose of, 86–90; objectives and problems of, 91–95; appeal to whites, 96–97; COSATU and, 104, 105, 113, 114; Inkatha and, 106, 107
United Nations, 33
United Nations arms embargo, 193, 196
United Nations High Commission for Refugees (UNHCR), 73
United States Defense Department, 193, 195–96

United States National Guard, 192
United States Naval Research Laboratory, 198
United Workers Union of South Africa (UWUSA), 104
Unity Movement, 18
Unlawful Organizations Act, 12, 168

Valli, Mohammed, 93
Venda, 110, 128, 153–54
Venda National Force (VNF), 183–84
Vendas, Battalion of, 191
Verwoerd, Hendrik, 8, 12
Vorster, John, 46

Walters, J. C., 196
War statistics, 145–47
Warsaw Pact, 71
Weihahn Commission, 99
White Paper on Defense, 173, 185, 193
Whites, 7, 9, 10, 184–85, 204; in anti-apartheid movements, 87, 96–98, 108, 121, 143
Whites-only referendum, 87
Williamson, Craig, 142
Women's groups, 4, 52, 53, 87, 92, 182
Work-within-the-system approach, 24–25, 27, 75
World Council of Churches, 73
World newspaper, 57

Xhosa, 2
Xuma, Alfred Bitini, 5

Young African Christian Movement, 32
Youth leagues, 20–30, 53, 87, 92; militancy of, 55–56, 75, 93, 94
Yugoslavia, 71

Zambia, 23, 119, 203; as host state, 37, 38, 46, 210; South Africa and, 44, 45–46
Zimbabwe, 34, 37, 67–68, 191, 203–04; South Africa and, 38, 39, 41, 42; as host state, 44–45, 127
Zimbabwe African National Union (ZANU), 42, 67–68, 127
Zimbabwe African People's Union (ZAPU), 22–23, 38, 42, 66, 67, 125
Zondo, Andrew, 119–20
Zulu wars, 2, 3
Zulus, Battalion of, 191
Zvobgo, Eddison, 47, 125